THE CALL OF THE KIMBERLEYS

a life well loved

R. Jocelyn Doran

Published by Boolarong Biographies
an imprint of Boolarong Press
38/1631 Wynnum Road
Tingalpa Qld 4173
Australia.
www.boolarongpress.com.au

First published 2021

A catalogue record for this book is available from the National Library of Australia

ISBN: 9781922643056 (paperback)

Typeset in Amiri 12pt by Boolarong Press

Cover design by Boolarong Press

Printed and bound by Watson Ferguson & Company, Tingalpa, Australia

CONTENTS

PART 2

PROLOGUE

The De Haviland Dove circled the red dirt airstrip of Inverway Station in the East Kimberley. Below was a man dressed in a blue stockman shirt with the sleeves cut off, standing nonchalantly beside a bough shed. The year was 1965.

PART 1

MY LIFE BEGINS

December 24th 1941 was a memorable day for my mother and me, mainly because we both nearly died on that day, and also because it was the day I was born.

Only recently did I find out that I had been an emergency Caesarean, which had terrified my mother and resulted in my being six weeks premature. My sister June remembers Mum standing in a pool of blood before she was whisked off in an ambulance to hospital for the operation. This method of arriving in the world didn't exactly endear me to my mother as she didn't want any more children (I was the fourth), and if it was necessary to have another baby, she would have much preferred a boy. I didn't fit either of these descriptions, so I started off behind the eight ball in our relationship which, to say the least, totally lacked any motherly love.

Despite this early setback, I remember her now with admiration for the way she coped with a life that was quite often fairly traumatic. As I grew older, my feelings towards her changed to sympathy and compassion for the muddled marriage she was trapped in and her inability to cope with having four children in five years. June was born in 1936, Mollie in 1939, Roger in 1940, and then I brought up the rear in 1941, a very rapid expansion of the family.

I was lucky, though, to have a loving aunt and a doting father, so I look back on my childhood as being a happy one, aided by an enduring love of horses and dogs. Mum had plenty of help from two of her sisters who were living with us at the time and this should have been able to alleviate the situation, but owing to the conflict between them and Dad, I think they were more of a hindrance than a help.

Mum had a lady who did the washing and ironing, and at least two of the maids who were employed to help were named Hazel! They also had a lovely lady, Mrs Gray, who lived in self-contained quarters down the back of our place, and who was employed to cook the evening meal. She eventually left us as she said she was getting too attached to the children, and I don't think she was replaced. I remember feeling very sad at the prospect of her departure.

One incident that occurred with Mrs Gray — we were coming home about dinnertime from a family outing, and as we drove down the drive, there was a loud explosion. We walked into the kitchen to find our dinner of peas, pumpkin, cabbage and potato splattered all over the ceiling! Mrs Gray had omitted to put the pressure cooker lid on securely and it had literally blown its top. Needless to say, dinner was boiled eggs that night.

Dad went out of his way to give us four children a wonderful life, but owing to the fact that two of Mum's sisters were sharing our home in the lovely North Shore suburb of Gordon, there was always conflict. Despite the fact that Mum and Dad both shared a love of travelling and outdoor life, they argued over the rearing of the children, and of course, the aunts always took their sister's side whether she was right or wrong, so it was a very conflicted time for Dad. Fortunately, he often prevailed, so instead of our being wrapped in cotton wool as the female members of the family would have had it, we had a free and exciting childhood. For this, I am forever grateful to Dad.

Though my childhood was a happy one, the memories of constant fights between my parents will stay with me forever. They really were totally incompatible and should never have married, but Mum was a product of a wartime shortage of men and probably didn't want to be "left on the shelf" as her sisters were. Dad had worshipped Mum from an early age — they were childhood sweethearts, having met at Chatswood Primary School.

As far as I know, neither of them ever went out with anyone else. They finally married in 1932, but I don't think there was ever a great deal of happiness — Dad's happiness emanated from his children, all of whom he loved very much. Poor Mum, I don't think she really had much happiness until later in her life. It is interesting that, though they married in 1932, the first child, June, was not born until 1936, followed my siblings Mollie and Roger until I managed to bring the process to an end!

MY FAMILY

My father was born in 1906, and he never got over the loss of his father from bowel cancer when Dad was eighteen. The family had followed the Christian Science manifesto, with the result that the necessary medical intervention that might have saved his life was not allowed. Dad never followed the faith again, and continued to visit his father's grave on the anniversary of his death until well into his eighties, when geography prevented him from doing so.

His family had been prominent in Sydney at the time. My great grandfather was a stock and station agent and sharebroker, his brother a civil engineer in the Water Conservation Commission, another was a solicitor, and Dad's maternal grandfather was editor of the Sydney *Daily Telegraph*, a very prestigious paper at the time. He was the fastest shorthand writer in Sydney at 212 words per minute! Dad's cousin was a dentist–chemist in Holbrook NSW, and his aunt had been a missionary in India for three years. An uncle was a housemaster at Geelong Grammar School.

Dad's father was a well- known Sydney singer and pianist, a musical talent that has been passed on to subsequent generations of my family. June became a very good pianist and would play and sing at nursing homes in Sydney, while her son Adrian won prestigious singing competitions in Sydney in 1985 and is currently an opera singer in France. Her three other children are still involved in the music world, and daughter Julie had the lead female role in a school production of *Jesus Christ Superstar*.

Mollie went to the Conservatorium of Music in Sydney, and though she didn't continue her career professionally, she has sung at many public functions. Her daughter Sonia studied at The University of Queensland and obtained a Bachelor of Music and a Diploma of Secondary Education, majoring in music. After completing her degree, she obtained a job teaching music at the Canberra School of Music, ANU. She had planned to pursue further study in Budapest,

Hungary, but her plans were thwarted after she met a certain young gentleman!

Roger followed an academic career, gaining his master's degree in civil engineering, and I can't remember him having any musical talents – if he did, he didn't display them. He then went on to Hawkesbury Agricultural College outside Sydney, where he obtained a Diploma of Agriculture before finally settling on his chosen career, that of Health Director for the Natural Health Society of Australia, a position in which he excelled and which he still holds today.

I was occasionally asked to sing at functions, though my standard was well below that of my siblings. My main memory is singing in the Cathedral Chamber at Jenolan Caves during a geology excursion to that beautiful attraction in the Blue Mountains. Owing to the chamber's perfect acoustics, many prominent singers have been requested to perform there, and it is also a popular venue for weddings. My choice of "One Fine Day" from the *Madame Butterfly* opera was a bit ambitious, but I got through it all right, helped greatly by the fantastic acoustics.

My other public singing was at the Beecroft Community Hall during a pony club annual general meeting. At the age of fifteen, I stood up on the stage and sang "Annie Laurie", an old favourite from our family singalongs around the piano. Sadly, can hardly sing a note now!

Dad, it seems, was very brainy. He went to North Sydney Boys High, which was a select school for talented boys. Then he went on to win a scholarship from the Colonial Sugar Refining Company, where he spent his entire working career. He studied mechanical engineering and became a CSR apprentice, before rising in the company to be Inspecting Engineer of the Refineries, very close to the top job. Towards the end of his career with CSR, he was sent overseas to do research into atomic energy. But his main love was farming.

He was bit of a daredevil, and when his mother was having bridge parties, Dad would pinch one of the players' cars and take it for a joy ride up the Pacific Highway! One day he was not back in time, and arrived at their home to find a very angry mother and car owner waiting at the front gate. I think this was his last joy riding episode.

Mum was born in the same year as Dad, but the only thing I know is that she had three sisters and a "brother who died at birth", despite there being a photo in the family album in which he looked to be about six months old. The poor little fellow was wrapped in so many swaddling clothes I used to think it was no wonder he died!

There was a nine-year gap between Mum and her next oldest sister, and I believe Mum was very spoilt by her siblings. Mum's father was a coachbuilder, a very necessary profession at the time as that was the main means of transport, apart from riding a bicycle or a horse. He died of pancreatic cancer at a very early age, so I never knew either of my grandfathers, and I barely knew my maternal grandmother, remembering her as a shadowy figure who was dressed from head to toe in black.

Of Mum's three sisters, the oldest was Alice, who was finally married in her fifties to Ted, a Scottish gentlemen. They lived in Wau, a lovely village in the New Guinea Highlands. When the Japanese were preparing to invade New Guinea, they were evacuated to Australia. All their possessions were stacked on the wharf in Port Moresby, which was subsequently bombed, resulting in their losing everything.

They also lost their home in Wau because the government had a scorched earth policy, so that all the dwellings were burnt down. After the war, they returned to New Guinea and rebuilt their home, but once again they were thwarted when fate intervened and their house was again destroyed by fire.

We loved Uncle Ted's visits to our family in Sydney, as he always came laden with delicious treats for us children, such as apple pie and ice cream — rare luxuries such as puddings were never on our normal menu. Alice was one of the aunts who subsequently lived with us and constantly criticised Dad, though I remember her with fondness as I was too young to understand the ramifications of her behaviour.

The marriage to Ted could not have been an outstanding one as, sometime during the seventies, he disappeared completely from all our lives with no farewell nor forwarding address. Many years later, June and I read a death notice in the *Sydney Morning Herald* that seemed to refer to Uncle Ted. All very sad as I remembered him with much fondness, and actually shared his flat at Potts Point later in my life.

Mum's second sister was Gertrude, always known as Truda, a kind and generous lady who sent us lovely gifts from America at Christmas and on birthdays. She spent almost her entire working life in America, where she was secretary for a couple who established Dairy Queen Ice Cream in America and Australia. They finally moved to Australia, bringing Truda with them. She never married and ended up in a dementia unit in Turramurra, where she sadly died. In her previous abode, a retirement village, she had started to turn on all the gas ovens at night, and had to be moved on to more secure accommodation.

The third sister was Lilian, usually just called Auntie, and she was my motherly love and saviour. I loved her dearly, and had many memorable holidays at her various properties. She had worked for Dempsters Jewellers in Sydney and always had lovely homes in fashionable suburbs. I think it was a measure of her unhappiness that she was constantly on the move, a loving lady who should have found contentment in marriage, but it seemed to elude her. I am told that a potential suitor came to the family doorstep one time wearing working clothes and was discouraged from visiting forthwith, but I don't know if this is true. If so it would help to explain why she never married.

She must have been ahead of her time, as I can clearly remember her 1928 Dodge sedan, which she drove very capably. This was in an era when women didn't even drive cars, let alone own them. Even as late as 1958 when I finished my schooling, women were discouraged from doing academic subjects at university such as medicine and engineering.

Her various homes were in Wallacia near the Blue Mountains, Bowral in the Southern Highlands, West Pennant Hills where she had a ten-acre (four-hectare) farm, West Pymble, and finally Dural, where she owned a forty-acre (sixteen-hectare) farm that was a constant delight to our family. On it was a friendly draught horse named Dick, who pulled a sled and sometimes allowed small children such as me to sit astride him.

We children loved to play with some of the local kids. Mum said they were "common" and we weren't supposed to play with them, which advice, of course, we ignored. I shudder now at the thought of such snobbishness, but that is how things were with Mum. She was always proud of the fact that one of her ancestors was aide-de-camp to Governor Macquarie.

Auntie's death in 1971 when I was thousands of miles away was a terrible shock. My only contact with the outside world then was through Outpost Radio, so I received this devastating news by letter some time after she had died. Had I even known that she was sick I would have left no stone unturned to fly to Sydney to be with her during her last moments. She was my PRECIOUS AUNTIE.

Dad had only one sister, Auntie Betty, who married a handsome ex-serviceman, Uncle Allan. They had a small farm at Riverstone west of Sydney where they raised poultry, but they were unable to have any children. Auntie Betty was a great cat lover but didn't believe in having them desexed. The most I remember her having on the farm at one time was twenty-eight! These were fed a mixture of egg and bread every morning, but despite this limited diet, they seemed to be able to reproduce rather too successfully. I used to love my visits there as I could have scrambled eggs on white bread toast, another luxury in our family.

As none of our aunts had children, we kids were deprived of any cousins, for which I feel quite sad. It would have been nice to have those extra members of the family. My future husband also had no cousins, so we were both deprived of this special relationship.

As Mum was quite snobbish, she maintained very high standards in the household and in the upbringing of the children. She was very conscious of what other people thought — another trigger for discord between my parents, as Dad couldn't care less as long as we were happy. However, Mum was very hardworking and economised to feed a large family with lots of fruit and vegetables by buying "bruised fruit" from the local greengrocer.

Another source of discord between my parents was the fact that Mum never liked the home Dad had bought in Gordon from his Uncle Fred. In fact, she hated it mainly because the dining room had been taken over by Dad for his study, so meals had to be taken in the breakfast–family room.

This did not suit Mum's high ideals when having dinner parties, as it was also the room the tradesmen would have to use! It was a credit to Dad that he was able to purchase the house and send his four children to private schools with no help from anyone and only one income, but also to his detriment that he persisted in purchasing a house that was total anathema to his wife.

The next-door neighbour used to ring Dad every night for a chat, and prattle on endlessly to the extent that Dad would put the phone down, go down the back to shut the chooks up, return to the phone to find Stan still talking!

One time for her bridge party, Mum made salmon sandwiches and put the empty tin at the back door for the cat to lick. Sadly, the cat had been run over and a kindly neighbour had put the body at the back door also. When Mum came out and discovered the dead cat she went into a panic, thinking she had poisoned her guests with her salmon sandwiches, so they all had the content of their stomachs diagnosed! I don't recall whether the truth of the matter was ever revealed to the other bridge players, but the neighbour eventually enlightened Mum.

My parents lived through two World Wars and the Great Depression, but I am not aware that we ever suffered any great hardship thanks to Dad's reliable job with CSR.

During the Second World War, the company made him general manager of the Munitions Annexe, which was established to manufacture eighteen-pound shells for the war effort. Thus he was in an essential service and could not be called up, even though he was thirty-three at the time.

He believed in being prepared and consequently built an underground air raid shelter in our backyard (that of our previous rented home, also in Gordon), which of course was never used. It consisted of a corrugated iron tank dug into the ground, with a roof covered with sand, a trapdoor and a ladder for descending. I do remember that during and after the war we had ration coupons. I think it was mainly for staples such as petrol, tea, sugar, butter, meat and clothing.

GROWING UP

Our large backyard contained a sandpit, a little cottage Dad had built for my sister Mollie and me, a model train shed, a tennis practice board, a set of parallel bars and five chooks runs. I think it must have been at this time in life I developed a penchant for records and bookkeeping, as Dad gave me a fowl run of my own, eight laying hens and a book to record daily egg tallies, food consumed and any other detail of the venture. I just loved being a productive member of the household, and used to follow my father round on my tricycle. We were great mates.

Our home in Gordon was the social hub for all the local kids, who would congregate at our place after school and pursue various activities such as hopscotch, marbles, knuckles, building sandcastles, roller-skating on the footpath and, later on, horse- and bike-riding.

Dad built a model train set in a shed in the backyard, and this was a great attraction. He also had a workshop in the garage containing a large and substantial set of tools, and it was a great source of annoyance that my brother Roger's friends would borrow tools and either put them back in the wrong place or not put them back at all!

We four kids all had terrible teeth (probably inherited from our parents, who both had false teeth at a very early age). Memories of hours spent in Dr Moxham's chair in Macquarie Street, Sydney, are still easy for me to recall. There was no high-speed drill in those days, and the low-speed one would seem to grind on interminably, removing the copious amounts of decay. Since we never ate sugar (in fact, we didn't even keep it in the house), this awful phenomenon can only be put down to genetics.

My oldest sister June acquired a horse, Kim, which she kept in a vacant allotment (of which there were many in Gordon at that time), and sometimes in our backyard. June had many adventurous trips on Kim, including riding out to Auntie's farm at Dural, a fair ride for a teenager carrying all her gear on her back and on the horse. Eventually Kim dropped dead from a heart attack, which devastated June and was very distressing for all of us, also a lesson in life and death.

I had my first rides on Kim, which commenced my love affair with horses. This was augmented by my daily association with the patient baker's horse, whose owner delivered our daily bread. These wonderful animals would stand patiently while bread was delivered to each house, then move on as the baker progressed. These placid old draught horses were stabled in a dungeon-like establishment on the Pacific Highway in the Gordon Shopping precinct — now replaced with the humdrum of city traffic and fancy shops. An ice chest was another commodity often found in houses then, and ice was also delivered as required, even though we had a refrigerator.

We all attended Gordon Public School, whose lovely buildings were carved out of the abundant Hawkesbury sandstone. It was there that I established a lifelong friendship with Jenny, who lived a few streets away from us in Gordon. We attended the same secondary school and remained best friends until Jenny's untimely death in 2013 after a two-year battle with a brain tumour. We shared much of our lives together — adventures, husbands and children — and she will be forever in my heart.

In my pursuit of horse-riding, I persuaded Mum and Dad to let me attend a riding school at Lane Cove, where I was given a very quiet horse and proceeded down to the Lane Cove River with two girls I had teamed up with, both of whom were older than me and could ride. While riding along the riverbank, we spotted a man wearing nothing but a hat and carrying a stock whip!

Naturally my newly found friends turned for home and took off at a very fast pace. I had no choice but to follow suit as this was the preference of my mount. I clung on for dear life while the horse propelled itself and its rider at high speed back to the riding school, where I miraculously arrived in one piece!

BOGLE AND CHANDLER MYSTERY

It is interesting to note that Lane Cove was the area of the Bogle and Chandler mystery, which fascinated Sydneysiders in the sixties. Sydney socialites and both married (not to each other!), they had attended a party at Chatswood on New Year's Eve 1963, left at four o'clock in the morning and drove to a section on the Lane Cove River, which was known as Lovers Lane. Several hours later, their bodies were found. Both were in a state of semi undress, and it was established many years later that they had died of some sort of poisoning.

Many theories were put forward as to the cause of death and the strange state of their clothing. The episode remained a source of constant theorising by Sydneysiders. It wasn't until 2006 that it was concluded the most likely cause of death was from hydrogen sulphide poisoning from a factory that had pumped gas into the river since the 1890s. So glad I didn't fall off my bolting horse into the gas-poisoned river round about the same time.

Our primary school years were filled with many adventures provided by an enterprising father who took us on bike rides round Middle Harbour, camping trips all over New South Wales, rowing outings from Bobbin Head and motoring all round Pittwater in hired Halverson cabin cruisers. These were six-berth vessels towing dinghies and a great source of joy to all of us by way of fishing, driving the boat and heading off in the dinghy.

In 1941, Dad bought our first car, a 1934 Studebaker, for 100 pounds ($200). It was a very spacious car with a running board, boot (back box in those days), luggage rack, and two prominent headlights mounted on the front wheel guards. Later, when driving on bush roads, Dad let us ride on the outside of the car, two on the running boards and two straddling the headlights, a source of great joy to us children, but probably a source of terrible anxiety to our mother!

It was a very sophisticated car for its time. It had a free-wheeling facility, which consisted of a knob on the dash that, when released, enabled the vehicle to coast while still in gear — a very dangerous operation I would have thought, and now illegal of course.

Camping trips were undertaken without the modern luxuries of portable fridges and toilets, eskies, gas stoves, blow up mattresses and sophisticated folding chairs and tables. There was just a tent with a centre ridge pole, lots of guy ropes to trip over in the night, and non-waterproof sides. How we all fitted into this space and did all the sleeping and eating necessary to sustain life on holidays, I have no recollection of. I do remember it was all lots of fun, though probably not so much for Mum, who got the raw end of the pineapple catering for such a large family in primitive conditions.

Places visited included Tumut River, from which we climbed to the top of Mount Kosciusko and froze in the icy waters of the river, Jenolan Caves, Lake Burrill, Sussex Inlet and Wee Jasper, the three latter on the south coast of New South Wales and all delightful places for families to enjoy.

One day while travelling to Wollongong, we were descending Bulli Pass, a very steep incline, when Dad encountered a coal truck in front of us, blocking our forward descent, doing barely five miles an hour. Coming up the other way was a horse and sulky rendering any possibility of overtaking the coal truck non-existent.

At this crucial moment, the Studebaker's brakes were unable to hold the weight being put on them and it looked as though a collision would be unavoidable. Dad, being a very competent driver, was able to wrench the gearstick into bottom gear, thus averting a catastrophe.

Given that car gearboxes had three forward gears and were not equipped with synchromesh, enabling an easy switch from a higher to a lower gear, this was no mean feat, but a disaster was averted. I can still remember the occasion very clearly, also the fact that I let out a blood-curdling scream, mimicking the brakes that were also screaming, as we appeared to be hurtling into the back of a heavily laden coal truck.

When June was old enough to obtain her licence, Dad bought a second car, an Austin A40, so travelling with two cars then became quite luxurious.

Evenings at home in Gordon were filled with family singalongs round the piano, which my father played very expertly by ear. Mum was also a very good pianist and I think she could play the third movement of Beethoven's "Moonlight Sonata", quite a complicated piece.

I also learnt music for five years and I was very attached to my piano teacher, but I realise looking back that she must have had endless patience as sight-reading was never my forte, making me a slow learner. However, I did manage to play the first movement of the "Moonlight Sonata" at her concert, where musical scores were not permitted. June also learnt the piano and still plays at retirement villages, accompanying it with her sweet singing voice.

Card games were also popular night-time activities, and meals were always partaken with the whole family sitting round the dining table and discussing the day's events.

JAPANESE SUBMARINES ENTER SYDNEY HARBOUR

On the night of 31 May 1942, three Japanese midget submarines, each with a two-member crew, entered Sydney Harbour — avoiding the partially constructed anti-submarine boom net — and attempted to sink Allied warships. Two of the midget submarines were detected and attacked before they could successfully engage any Allied vessels and inflict any damage in Sydney Harbour.

The crews scuttled the submarines and committed suicide. The vessels were raised from the harbour the next day. The third submarine attempted to torpedo the heavy cruiser USS *Chicago*, but instead sank the converted ferry HMAS *Kuttabul*, which was anchored at Garden Island, killing twenty-one naval rankings.

This submarine's fate was unknown until 2006 when amateur scuba divers discovered the wreck off Sydney's northern beaches. June remembers being frightened of the searchlights and the sound of the air raid sirens going off the night of the raid. This episode was a wake-up call to Australians, and to our family in particular.

Darwin, Adelaide River, Broome, Derby, Wyndham, Port Hedland, Townsville and Cairns were also attacked by the Japanese over many months. The Prime Minister of the time, John Curtin, underplayed the severity of the destruction and death, and it was many years before many Australians even heard of the Japanese assaults and the dire threat to Australia at the time.

WE DISCOVER YERRANDERIE

Our wake-up call prompted Dad to take a trip to the far reaches of the Blue Mountains west of Sydney, thus Yerranderie came into our lives in 1942. This spectacular and once thriving silver and lead mining town was situated at the end of the road through the Burragorang Valley (now flooded to form Warragamba Dam, Sydney's main water supply), and was fairly inaccessible to all but the very determined.

It was the perfect escape if the Japs did further their attempts to gain a foothold in Sydney, and I believe the Burragorang locals had plans to blow up the only road into the valley if this were to happen. For our family it provided, apart from a safe haven, a wonderful relief from city life, and a never to be imagined number of unique bush experiences over the coming fifteen years, including a honeymoon!

In Sydney during the war, blackouts were imposed that required all windows and doors to be covered at night with suitable material such as heavy curtains, cardboard or paint. Car lights were also deflected and subdued and petrol was rationed. Some people resorted to using gas producers and charcoal burners, but these were cumbersome devices, difficult to operate and regulate. As Dad could travel to work via Shank's Pony and the train, he was able to save all his petrol coupons for our Yerranderie trips during the war.

To travel to Yerranderie, which was eighty miles (120 kilometres) west of Sydney, we drove in our 1934 Studebaker with trailer in tow through the town of Camden, thence to "The Bluff", a precipitous road winding down the spectacular sandstone cliffs so common in the Blue Mountains. This road was also used by coal trucks transporting that commodity from the bottom of the pass, and an encounter with one of these monsters was not an appealing prospect.

They had been known to go over the side, but this didn't happen in our time. There were many sharp hairpin bends, with mirrors in the really bad spots, but the views over Burragorang Valley while descending were breathtaking. The first bullock team that descended that earliest road at one stage had to be unhitched and the dray dismantled and lowered over the side with ropes, then reconnected with the team lower down.

At the bottom we crossed the Nattai River, a lovely sandy expanse with gently flowing water, which in pre-bridge times had bogged a few horse teams in the quicksand. We kids then changed our form of seating to running boards and headlight straddling as previously mentioned! Quite a highlight for us kids, but a different story for poor Mum, who totally disapproved.

Then on to the Wollondilly River, where we had a swim and lunch, then resumed our original seating inside the car before proceeding along another sixteen kilometres of very rough road to Basin Creek. Here the road became very steep, and Roger recalls one time when the Studebaker became so hot that it started to boil. June had the unenviable task of sitting on the mudguard and feeding fuel into the carburettor, enabling us to complete our journey. Upon arriving at the old courthouse and police station, we diverted on to our private road, which led us past a small dam to the most beautiful location in Yerranderie — our new residence.

This was some distance from the main town and was reached by traversing lovely paperbark-lined creeks and gentle rises, passing the site of the old school, which still had desks and blackboards in situ, also times tables and rules for etiquette!

Our cottage nestled on a gentle rise, giving us 360 degree views over a large amphitheatre, and through Byrnes Gap to the far hills of Scott's Main Range and the Kowmung River valley in the blue distance. The amphitheatre was hemmed in by beautiful mountains topped off with Mount Colong, a well-known landmark.

The cottage was a very dilapidated old miner's shack, for which Dad paid thirteen pounds ($26) and a rent of sixpence (five cents) a week to the mining company that owned the land. The walls were lined with layer upon layer of old, rat-infested newspapers; it was very dark. The floors were bare earth and the outer walls were timber slabs filled with wattle and daub. My sister June recalls that her initial comment on entering was:

"This is the nastiest house I have ever been in!"

It certainly was creepy, but it did have its charms, which included a cute little front verandah festooned with multi-coloured geraniums, the whole of which was enclosed with a timber slab fence like a little playing-card house. I didn't know at the time but this little verandah, shared with my brother Roger, would be our future bedroom during holidays to Yerranderie, fairly Spartan in the winter to say the least.

Lighting was supplied by hurricane lamps and water from a rainwater tank, and cooking was done over a large fuel stove or "black bitch", which also doubled as a water heater for our baths taken in a big tub on the kitchen floor. There was actually a bathroom that contained an enamel bath, but no plumbing of any kind so I wasn't really sure of its purpose.

The huge kitchen also served as the dining room, a very congenial area where many happy family gatherings took place, and where we welcomed the numerous visitors who liked to spend adventurous days with us. The lounge room was very cosy (once restored) and contained a welcoming fireplace, and off this room was the "master bedroom", which led to another smaller bedroom that my sisters shared.

On the outside, but attached to the house, was a room made of stones held together with daub, and this, I believe, was the maid's quarters. The outhouse was just that — a double-holed affair about twenty yards from the back fence. Having two exits to the large pit at the bottom, it was a very sociable part of the establishment!

The cottage eventually became a very comfortable residence and we now had our very first holiday home.

Dad and his uncle quickly set about making the cottage liveable. They ripped out all the paper lining and replaced it with filter-cloth, a heavy canvas made by CSR. They installed skylights and timber floors and, with a roaring log fire in winter, it became a cosy little haven for family holidays during our childhood and teen years — and June's honeymoon!

Our days there were spent in a kids' paradise. We loved exploring the many abandoned mines that covered the countryside and fossicking on the mullock heaps for all sorts of interesting rocks and minerals. Visiting the old miners and hearing their tales around the kitchen fuel stove was a novel experience for us city folk.

There was delicious fruit to be found in abandoned orchards, derelict buildings to explore and rabbit shooting excursions to be had with Mum and Dad (rabbits were plentiful and supplemented our diet). Visits to Mrs Burke, a miner's widow living in the township, were also popular as she always provided us with delicious home-made pumpkin scones.

The country offered superb bushwalks, including a rough track down to the Tonali River where there was a spectacular rock hole. This track eventually found its way through Byrnes Gap and out to the distant Kowmung River, a track which I encountered years later during an adventurous and rather nail-biting excursion with a friend.

One of our weekday highlights was trekking the mile or so cross country to meet the big black mail car from Camden, driven by a very dashing gentlemen (so June thought) by the name of Ritchie Jeffrey, who brought the daily perishables and mail and papers. Non-perishable items could still be purchased at the quaint old general store, which sported the sign: "Herald — 1 Penny".

Beside this store was a dance hall where many miners strutted their stuff. I was too young, but Mollie later found herself attracted to a handsome young miner named Mick, much to Mum's disapproval. Fortunately owing to geography, nothing came of the relationship.

Return trips from Yerranderie were eagerly looked forward to by us all as that was when we had a really special treat — a mixed grill that Dad bought at the Greek café, The Capitol, in Camden, and for which he paid the princely sum of ten shillings (one dollar). These protein-packed meals consisted of sausage, steak, chop, chips, tomato, fried onion and gravy. Not bad value for six people! We still remember this café as this is where we also bought another family favourite, pink lolly pigs, which I don't think I have seen anywhere else (in the world?).

Life at Gordon resumed as normal. Saturday mornings were a highlight as in those days there was a forty-four hour week. Dad would take us to his office in O'Connell Street in the mornings, after which we would catch a ferry to Manly for lunch. We loved sailing past The Heads as it was always a bit rougher there and we seemed to have inherited pretty good sea stomachs.

Every holiday was spent at Yerranderie — long weekends, short weekends, Easter, and some of Dad's annual leave. All food had to be taken in the trailer, so it was tinned this and that, all fairly basic, and the only form of cooling was a Coolgardie safe. I don't think we ever went there without taking friends of one or other of the children or of our parents. The old Wollondilly mine was not far from our house and there were no restrictions on where we could explore — sometimes descending well into old mine shafts or up the ramps to the poppet heads. It was a good lesson in self-preservation and we hoped it taught us to be responsible citizens.

FURTHERING OUR EDUCATION

We were grateful that our parents had been able to further our secondary education at Presbyterian Ladies' College Pymble (now Pymble Ladies' College) — one of Sydney's most prestigious schools, established in 1916 — and for Roger, Barker College at Waitara. Pymble's grounds encompassed fifty acres (twenty hectares) of pastureland dotted with spreading eucalypts and running a few cows, guaranteed to make the many boarders feel at home.

The main two-storeyed classroom block sported an impressive colonnade running the entire length of the building, one end of which housed the headmistress's office. This very well-known and respected lady, Miss Dorothy Knox, usually affectionately referred to as Knocky, steered Pymble along an outstanding path for thirty-one years. Under her guidance the school greatly expanded. She drove everywhere in a little brown Austin A40, always accompanied by her diminutive Australian terrier Mulga. A meeting with Knocky if we had been misbehaving struck fear into the most intrepid heart.

House marks were awarded for both good and bad behaviour, and three bad house marks earned one the dubious distinction of having to sit outside Knocky's office and knit six-inch squares for Service Corps, an organisation set up to assist returned soldiers' families.

Despite this, she commanded enormous respect and admiration from the thousands of students who came under her tutelage. Amazingly, she was able to remember the names of every girl in the school, which I think numbered about one thousand at that time (present enrolment 2100).

The spacious grounds contained three boarding houses, numerous classrooms, a swimming pool, tennis courts, gymnasium, playing fields, science building, music rooms, library and later a chapel.

Secondary school was five years of three terms, and at the end of each term we were given our report for the period. These reports were contained in a folder tied with a blue ribbon, and contained the reports for our entire time at the school. They were addressed to our fathers and were not supposed to be opened by anyone but those gentlemen, but most of us did have a peek. Mine was addressed to: "R. O. French, Esquire". This form of address seems to have been largely abandoned these days, but it was evidently a title used for anyone who did not have a grander title!

I will never forget the day that Knocky announced in assembly that a chapel would be built forthwith and that every girl would be permitted to carry a brick on to the site. The entire gathering of one thousand girls erupted into laughter, which annoyed Miss Knox to the extent that she marched out of the hall in disgust. The occasion was never referred to again although we did contribute to the building of the chapel by carting our bricks.

Lifesaving was taught and certificates for the various grades awarded beginning at Elementary, progressing to Advanced, Resuscitation and Instructor's Certificate. The certificates were awarded "For the practical knowledge of rescue, releasing oneself from the clutch of the drowning and for the ability to render aid in resuscitating the apparently drowned". One of the exercises involved diving into the pool fully clothed to retrieve a brick from the bottom.

We were supposed to put our names on a list whenever we used the pool (after school) and cross ourselves off when we exited. One day I forgot to remove my name, and when I arrived home from school that afternoon I received the shock of my life to find that Miss Knox was on the phone! I had forgotten to strike my name off the list and my punishment was to be banned from the pool for the rest of the term. This was particularly sad for me as I had qualified to swim in the breaststroke in the upcoming school carnival and, not being an outstanding swimmer, I had been keen to participate.

My sister Mollie was once expelled for a day for playing tennis in bare feet — Knocky's standards were of the highest order. We were not permitted to appear in public without our gloves and Panama hats, and a jumper could not be worn in winter unless covered by the school blazer. The school motto *All Ultimo Lavoro* translated as "Strive for the Highest", and that's what most pupils endeavoured to do.

The college has been greatly expanded and the new swimming complex is used by Olympic swimmers for diving training, as it is one of the few pools that contains a high diving board. This new pool is a far cry from the one we used during the fifties to retrieve our bricks for lifesaving!

One day I needed to take my horse to the farrier in preparation for a gymkhana during the weekend, and somehow I had to get there during a school day. Some of the kids in the class were in on my scheme. I had them pull my ear to make it red then complained to the teacher that I had earache.

This somehow worked and I was sent to the school sister, who kindly rang my mother and asked her to collect me and take me home. This she duly did and I was able to have the horse shod, all the time petrified that Knocky would drive past in her little brown car and my ruse would be sprung and I would probably be expelled! However, all went well and Mum didn't even admonish me for my deceitfulness, something that came as quite a surprise to me. I think secretly she must have admired my ingenuity!

I will always remember with great fondness our French teacher, Mrs Ladd, who most appropriately drove a Citroën. Though quite Australian by birth, she lived and breathed the French language and customs and was able to put many of us on a successful French learning path.

I loved my days at school and made many friends, many of whom I still have contact with today. It was at this time in my life that I became very much aware of that other species of human being – BOYS!

I NOTICE BOYS

One of the highlights of those days was travelling to school by train, as most of the passengers were school students. The majority were boys going to Knox Grammar, Shore and Barker College, so it was always fun to look for any boy that happened to catch one's eye.

As I matured, Saturday night dates were common, either to the pictures or to parties put on by school friends. These parties were elaborate affairs with scrumptious suppers and dancing. Later in the evening sometimes the lights were dimmed, which was a bugger if you happened to be dancing with a boy you didn't like. The parties were either formal or informal. Beautiful dresses and ballerinas were the order of the night if formal, and just plainer clothes if informal, but always very smart — no jeans and thongs!

If you didn't have a date on a Saturday night, you felt as though you were a wallflower. Mostly dates were to the pictures or one of these parties — it was so much easier to meet a future boyfriend or husband in those social days of the fifties.

During the Intermediate year, most of the students attended Miss Kaye's dancing classes at Killara, where we learnt such perennials as the Barn Dance, Canadian Three Step, Pride of Erin and the Waltz — dances that are still handy to know even today. The girls would sit on one side of the hall and the boys on the other. When Miss Kaye said, "Select your partners for the -------", there would be a wall of boys skidding across the floor to choose their partner — it was great fun.

One time I was lucky enough to have a really good partner in a competition and we won the Pride of Erin. I felt quite chuffed going on to the stage with Pete to get our box of chocolates, even though I knew it was his expertise that had made it possible.

He was also a very good surfer and taught me how to catch a wave. Most weekends saw "the mob" sunbaking and surfing at Newport or Bilgola, where no one wore any sunscreen, only zinc cream on the nose. I never heard of anyone having skin cancer, so I often wonder about the present method of smothering the skin with an alien substance and having to take vitamin D tablets in lieu of sunshine.

My very good school friend, Rob, a boarder whose family had a property at Baerami in the Hunter Valley, often asked me to accompany her family to spend a week at their holiday house at The Entrance, north of Sydney. I accepted these holiday invitations with alacrity, and Rob and I had marvellous times with the handsome surfers who used to frequent that part of the world.

Rob and I used to partake in midnight rides round the back streets of Gordon on occasions when Rob spent a free weekend at our place. We would make peanut butter and honey sandwiches in advance and leave a note under the pillow in case our parents discovered our absence. They never did.

On one occasion, we were midnight riding in East Killara at Coolah Park when we were pulled up by two policemen who told us to go home as it was not safe to be out riding at that hour. Needless to say it was a bit scary to be pulled up by a police car. Disappointed but considerably sobered, we reluctantly made our way home. It didn't deter us, however, from future midnight riding, and we still have a giggle at the mention of peanut butter and honey sandwiches.

I also spent many enjoyable holidays at their family property in the Hunter Valley where, as you can imagine, horse riding occupied a lot of our time.

OUR RIDE TO THE KOWMUNG RIVER

Fiona, another school friend, accompanied the family during one of our many trips to Yerranderie. Both mad on horses, we were able at times to borrow horses from the then postmaster of Yerranderie, Mr Jack Martin. As well as being the postmaster, he was also the unofficial mayor, but more to our interest, he had horses and ran a few cattle out in the Kowmung River valley, quite a long way from Yerranderie.

One day he told us that he was riding out to check his cattle and asked if Fiona and I would like to accompany him. Would we?! My mount was a mare in foal and Fiona was mounted on a draught horse. We set off after lunch with Mr Martin and a helper.

Down the Tonali River Valley and through Byrnes Gap we rode, then through rugged and beautiful mountainous country till we reached the Kowmung River, where Mr Martin gave us a tin of fruit to share to sustain us on the return trip. We parted company with the men at about four o'clock. There was no particular track to follow, but one of the important instructions Mr Martin gave us was to "Turn right at that overhanging stringybark tree".

There had been the remains of bushfires still smouldering in the trees, but before we started on the return track, a small storm had largely extinguished the fires and shrouded the country in fairly thick smoke, making our track look a bit different and difficult to find. However, we pressed on regardless, and when we came to what I thought was THE TREE, Fiona didn't agree.

Much discussion followed, after all, we were in a very isolated and rugged part of the Blue Mountains and a wrong path now would see us spending a night in the bush, a prospect that had little appeal to either of us. Not to mention the fact that my parents would be sick with worry.

Anyhow, after much verbal to-ing and fro-ing, I won the round and we turned right at THAT TREE! Thank goodness it was the right one, and eight o'clock that night found us riding up the Tonali Valley, singing at the tops of our voices to keep warm and to let anyone who could hear us know that we were coming. And my parents did hear us.

They had been terribly concerned when darkness fell and we were still out bush. I can imagine their relief when they finally heard our happy voices in the distance. What a welcome we received! I will always be grateful to Mum and Dad for giving us a pretty free rein in our childhood, enabling us to do things that many children were deprived of and hopefully teaching us to be self-reliant and responsible for our own actions.

Years later after I had left school, Mollie and I decided to go bushwalking. We drove in her VW Beetle to Kanangra Walls, a spectacular area of Hawkesbury sandstone encompassing the well-known sheer rock faces of the Blue Mountains. Here we parked the VW under an overhang and set off to walk to the Kowmung River, this time via a totally different route. How ill-prepared we were!

With totally inadequate maps for such an arduous walk in wild, beautiful, uninhabited country, we set off with gay abandon, taking our dog Flicka. We had backpacks and had planned to spend a night by the river then return, but obviously the return trip would be a lot more demanding as it was mainly uphill.

We made the Kowmung all right, but got slightly lost on the way back. All this was not helped by the fact that Mollie started to feel unwell and I was forced to push her up some of the hills, of which there were plenty. Every time we breasted a crest thinking that would be the last, another would loom in front of us.

Owing to our inadequate maps (they had no contour lines, as most sensible bushwalking maps have), we were no longer travelling through the bush on any sort of visible track. We were starting to get extremely worried and wondering if we would ever see the VW again. Just on dusk, however, we breasted the last rise and miraculously we had come out at the right spot! Exhausted, we flopped into the car and sat for a while to regain our composure and energy.

GOLDEN DARRAN

During my Intermediate year, 1956, I had managed to save enough pocket money to buy my special horse Golden Darran, which was owned by friends living a few blocks away. My dreams had been realised. I now had a horse I could take to gymkhanas and shows. He had been well educated and was a beautiful showy horse, with a golden coat and a golden mane and tail.

Thence every weekend was taken up with long rides to pony club or any horsy event that was within riding distance. These often occurred on a Sunday, which prompted the minister of the church our family usually attended once a week to comment that: "I worshipped an idol in the form of my horse instead of God." Naturally, this did not endear me to this form of Sunday occupation, and I ceased to go to church forthwith.

My friend Fiona and I used to ride huge distances to pony club meetings at North Rocks. This involved riding up the Pacific Highway to Wahroonga, then down Pennant Hills Road to Beecroft, then further on to North Rocks — a marathon for the horses, as they had gymkhana events as well as the long rides there and back.

One time we rode to Newport Beach and back, but looking at that road now, I don't know how we ever managed it. There was always a lot of traffic even then, and the road hugs the cliff in places. However, we survived somehow.

The annual pony club camps held at Castle Hill Showgrounds were a highlight of the year. Lots of horses, instructors, parents and, of course, BOYS. Flirting with members of the opposite sex was popular, and Fiona and I were no exceptions. We had to help with the cooking and cleaning up, so it was also a lesson in community endeavours.

One of our instructors was one Sergeant Collum, a likeable ex-Army man who put us through army drill, namely working in pairs and fours, doing figure of eights and all sorts of manoeuvres.

SYDNEY ROYAL

This must have stood me in good stead as, four years later when I was competing in the Sydney Royal Show with my school friend Rob and two other girls, we won the Team of Four Lightweight Hacks.

The main object was to keep exact distance from each other, four inches from knee to knee, while executing various passages including a figure of eight! Our horses also were beautifully matched, four bays with black points. My horse was a borrowed one. Slick was her name, and I rode her in several events at that show, also having success in one of the riding classes. She was a lovely mare to ride and beautifully trained, enabling me to concentrate fully on riding correctly. Doing the victory ride round the arena, in front of hundreds of people clapping in the stands after the ribbon presentations, was an exhilarating and rewarding event for all of us.

During that time, horse owners camped in special quarters above the stables. Our particular area was not far from one of the sideshows, whose beckoning call echoed through the stable area from dawn till midnight. I still remember one of the sideshow men's repeated announcement — "Step right up, only two shillings, a little bit naughty but oh! so nice, the girl in the goldfish bowl!"

At that time, in 1961, Sydney Royal was held in the showgrounds at Moore Park, directly opposite Centennial Park. This would have to be one of the most beautiful parks in the world, and exercising our horses every day in these glorious surrounds was a most exhilarating experience. We were so lucky.

On one occasion, I was chatting with two of the ring stewards in their little cubicle when I became aware of a couple of people standing outside for a while. They soon revealed themselves to be two policemen who had been listening to our conversation (harmless) for some time and were concerned for my safety.

To that end, they rang my parents, who were obliged to come to the venue to collect me and take me home. I hadn't been doing anything wrong so was not chastised — maybe the police thought my parents had been a bit lax in their care for me. I guess the police figured that I was at a vulnerable age, uneducated in the ways of older men.

During this period, 1961, Rob and her mother were renting a flat in Macleay Street at Potts Point, and at one stage I lived with them. It is interesting to note that Rob and I could quite safely walk in the streets of Kings Cross, along Darlinghurst Road and down Macleay Street, quite unmolested, and with no male chaperone. Doing that today one is just as likely to be king hit!

Somehow I was introduced to Tom, a handsome officer off the USS *Enterprise*, an American aircraft carrier that was anchored at Garden Island in Sydney Harbour.

We went on a date in Kings Cross, after which he walked me home. We sat outside the flat chatting, and he was the perfect gentleman. Next day I was lucky enough to have a tour of the *Enterprise*, and though I received a letter from Tom weeks later, our contact fizzled. Somehow, years later, I gained information that made me suspect that he was married, but he was definitely a gentleman.

A SAD TIME

Sadness, however, was just round the corner.

Mum and Dad's friends, the Spencers, had invited all our family to go sailing with them on Sydney Harbour, an invitation not to be refused. It was a magic day out, but when we arrived back to our home in Gordon, I found that my precious, beautiful Golden Darran had eaten a large quantity of wheat.

I often left him in the backyard over the weekend, but in this yard was the feed shed where the chooks' wheat was stored in a two hundred litre drum. He had obviously pushed the door open and gorged to his heart's content. My heart sank, as I knew that wheat was lethal to horses, swelling up inside their intestines and eventually blocking the bowel.

Two days of sheer, terrible pain followed, dosing him with paraffin, walking him and trying to comfort him. Colic is a dreadful condition for a horse, and though common, it is still sometimes a death sentence. It was a holiday weekend and my normal vet, Mr Monk, was away. Every other vet I contacted just said to "walk him for a while" or "give him some barley water" or "give him more paraffin oil". Through this terrible ordeal, my friend Jenny stayed with me the whole time, both of us sleeping on the back lawn to be with Darran.

On 27 January 1958, my beautiful horse drew his last breath. He died in agony in our backyard. I loved this horse dearly and I'm sure I was special to him too.

The aftermath of this tragedy is still a blur in my mind, but I was able to go to Jenny's place for a while to get over the initial shock.

It was the Leaving year for me and school was due to start. Concentrating on study was difficult, but I had terrific support from my classmates, to the extent that Gail, who was in my class, offered to give me a horse, Pasha. This was a lifesaver, which helped to keep me occupied and take my mind of those dreadful events. Gail, I am forever grateful to you.

Pasha was a taffy-coloured horse with a silver mane and tail. He was well educated in the show ring, but he never filled the hole in my heart that was left by Darran's loss.

WE MOVE FROM GORDON

The next disruption in my life came a couple of months later when Dad retired from the CSR, sold the Gordon home and bought a ten-acre (four-hectare) farm in the outer western suburb of Quakers Hill. Dad was in his element, he had always loved the outdoors (which he passed on to all his kids) and was able to establish a successful poultry farm, as well as dabble in a few poddy calves. I became a boarder at Pymble, and as I had always been friendly with quite a few of the boarders owing to my friendship with Rob, I settled in to that life fairly easily.

It was a considerable disruption, however, to my social life, as only the most ardent suitor was prepared to drive the twenty-four kilometres from the North Shore to Quakers Hill during my holidays from school. It was about this time that I met my first serious boyfriend, Eryl. His father also worked for the CSR and our families had been friends. He went to Barker College and was in the same year as my brother Roger.

Our first contact was at family tennis days at their home in Carlingford and our relationship gradually blossomed. We would go on a date and have a cuddle in the back seat of the car, but as this was his mother's car and about the tiniest car made, an Austin A30, Eryl would have his feet dangling out the window — he was six foot four inches (193 centimetres!)

I SIT FOR THE LEAVING EXAMS

The last exams, then called Leaving, were approaching and study was foremost. We were given a week off school, called Stu Vac, to concentrate on cramming as much into our brains as was possible without them bursting. I had taken on a couple of Honours subjects, French and geology, as well as maths 1 and 2, English and biology.

I would have preferred to do three Honours subjects, but Knocky didn't approve of girls doing three Honours courses. I think she thought they were too academic for girls, so instead of doing general maths and biology Honours, I opted for the more difficult maths 1 and 2, with which I struggled and only scored Bs in the Leaving. However, we were told that schooling teaches one how to use one's brain, so hopefully this had the right effect if nothing else.

I still appreciate geology, as this can be used in lots of situations when travelling, but of coordinate geometry, calculus, algebra, trigonometry, and permutations and combinations I have little memory!

I also did Alliance Française, for which I had to travel to the city once a week, but I loved the French accent and thoroughly enjoyed the interaction with this beautiful language. It is interesting that, despite having studied French for five years, sixty-two years later I can only remember a few verbs and nouns, and can barely understand a phrase when attempting to converse with someone who speaks fluent French (as my nephew does — they are so VITE!).

In fact, June's son, Adie, sings and speaks in five languages in his role as opera singer in France, where he lives with his beautiful wife Martine.

I was staying at The Entrance with Rob when our Leaving results were published in the *Sydney Morning Herald*, so it was up at daylight to be at the newsagent when they opened at six in the morning. I had achieved two honours, an A and three Bs, sufficient to give me a Commonwealth Scholarship, which enabled me to go to university free.

These were awarded to about thirty per cent of students each year and were a very satisfactory way of encouraging students who wished for a university degree to work hard. However, this system all came to an end with the election of Prime Minister Gough Whitlam, the first Labor government for twenty-three years. In January 1974, he abolished university fees, and along with the introduction of Medibank, this took a huge toll on the federal budget.

It also had the side effect that most young people chose to go to university, as this was, and still is, a great social life. Sometimes they would do two or three degrees, with the result that education in trades suffered, and we are still feeling this result today with a desperate shortage of tradespeople.

By the mid-1980s, however, there was consensus between both major parties that the concept of "free" tertiary education in Australia was untenable due to the ever-increasing participation rate.

Thus the HECS (Higher Education Contribution Scheme) was introduced in 1989, and has now become an integral part of the Australian education system. In 2020, there are now approximately 2.7 million Australians with debts from their tertiary study. This debt is required to be paid back once your income reaches approximately $46,000 per annum. The HECS debt to the Australian Taxation Office is now billions of dollars and climbing.

Later Malcolm Fraser abolished Medibank, but there was such an outcry that he had to reinstate it as Medicare, which is still our very successful healthcare system today, even though a very costly one.

END OF SCHOOL LIFE

Being an outdoors/horsy type, I opted not to go to university, instead doing a night-time secretarial course at Sydney's Metropolitan Business College, studying shorthand and typing, doing shorthand at 120 words a minute (all forgotten now) and typing at eighty words a minute. The latter has been handy all my life and very convenient when writing a book!

My father got me a job during the day with his sharebroker, Wolff Dunlop & Company, in Hunter Street, Sydney. I became the "bitch at the switch", or the telephonist/receptionist/typist. I loved my job so much that I always looked forward to Mondays, as opposed to the more common "Mondayitis".

The only drawback with this arrangement was travelling home to the farm at Quakers Hill, where I was currently residing. This involved travelling by electric train to Blacktown, then changing to a steam train (our family had always been in love with trains and still is) for the short ride to Maryong, where a family member would collect me.

Imagine a young girl travelling alone at night in the western suburbs of Sydney? I wouldn't do it now, but never felt threatened in those days (1959). The only thing was that most of the inhabitants of the area were European farmers who had come to Australia to work on the Snowy Mountains Scheme, and their main obsession was eating garlic. I think it must have been with every meal! They would fall asleep on the train and their head would sometimes loll on to my shoulder, with the overpowering garlic smell crawling up my nostrils. A gentle nudge worked for a while, then the whole episode was repeated.

Eryl and I were still pretty keen on each other, though it was a long-distance romance as he had gone to University of New England in Armidale to study veterinary science. We would catch up during his holidays, but once I had the opportunity to travel to Armidale to visit him.

My sister Mollie had bought herself a Messerschmidt, a fascinating little bubble on three wheels that had four forward gears and four reverse. Imagine going backwards in fourth gear! Quite exciting! It only had two seats, one behind the other, and as Mollie had very long hair at the time, almost the entire cab would be taken up with her hair. She was very pretty and attracted a lot of wolf whistles, also a lot of date offers.

One of her most memorable date offers occurred on the Sydney Harbour Bridge, where she had somehow come in contact with a double-decker bus. The policeman who handled the affair was more interested in getting her phone number so he could ask her for a date.

So Mollie and I set off for Armidale in her "Mess o' Shit", but when we got halfway up the Moonbi Range, the little vehicle decided that was too steep and refused to go any further, no matter what gear we engaged. So we had to turn around and descend this steep hill back to Tamworth. Not to be deterred, Eryl came to Tamworth and we had a lovely weekend with him (note I had a chaperone!).

WE GO TO GUNNEDAH

One day an old school friend, usually called Crick, which was her surname, rang me and said: "There is an ad in the paper for two girls to groom polo ponies in Gunnedah. What do you think about applying for the job?"

"That sounds great. What do we do?"

"We have to ring Gunnedah 186 and ask for Mr Thomson."

So we got together and rang Mr Thomson. "Sorry but the job has been taken," was his response.

We were crestfallen. Not for long though. A week later, Mr Thomson rang and said, "If you would like to travel to Gunnedah, I will give you a trial. The two girls I employed didn't even know how to rug a horse, so you are welcome to come as soon as possible."

We wasted no time. I resigned from Wolff Dunlop and Crick gave up her job and we purchased train tickets for Gunnedah. We were so excited we could hardly wait – going to the bush to spend our lives riding horses, we couldn't believe our luck. Crick was just as horse mad as I was, and we were pretty good mates so the job was perfect.

We travelled to Gunnedah on the mail train as far as Werris Creek, where we had to change to a rail motor to complete the trip. The boss's son, Tony, met us at the station, and Crick and I shared the back seat for our trip to Ruvigne, the beautiful property that was to be our destination. Tony could hardly keep his eyes on the road. The previous groom had been middle-aged and male, so to find himself in the company of two teenage girls was quite a shock. We were fascinated with Tony – he wasn't so bad looking himself.

Mr and Mrs Thomson showed us to our quarters, a charming three-bedroom weatherboard cottage with front and back verandahs, a fuel stove and a tin roof. Next door was a similar cottage where "Snow" resided. He was a Timor Islander, and was the cowboy/ gardener for the establishment. Snow was easy-going and fun to talk to, and had no hang-ups about living in an all-white society, completely separate from his own people.

We would get our rations from the "Big House" and cook for ourselves. And big it was. It was a huge federation-style mansion with vast verandahs, six bedrooms off a wide central hallway, a study with an open fire, and a vast ballroom that occupied the entire middle of the house. Perfect for having polo carnival parties for wives, players and also GROOMS (we were to find out to our great pleasure).

The property itself was 2600 hectares of top-quality black soil running sheep and cattle and growing wheat. The Mooki River ran through the middle, so it was paradise personified. We couldn't believe our luck, riding horses all day, living in this paradise AND being paid for it! The princely sum of sixteen dollars a week and keep, but with nothing to spend it on, we considered it a fortune. My very first purchase was a radio, which we kept in the stables and kept up with the doings in the world while we were grooming and feeding.

We had twelve polo horses to care for as Mr Thompson, spelt with a p, had his team stabled there too, also a few young horses coming on. This involved getting up at half past six, running the horses in from their 160-hectare paddock, giving them breakfast (one large prune tin size of oats and one of chaff), going back to our cottage and having our own breakfast of rolled oats, brown sugar and milk (yummy on a frosty morning), then returning to the stables.

The two teams in work, eight in all, had to have sixteen kilometres a day at a pretty reasonable pace, mainly a fast trot. Before saddling up, they would all be groomed to the "nth" degree. At the beginning of the season, each horse had to be clipped trace high, that is all over the body as low as the elbows and above the hocks. After this process, they were all double rugged, as winter nights were fairly severe in western New South Wales.

We rode one horse and led three, one on the near side and two on the off side. This could be a fairly demanding exercise at times, as the horses were full of feed and became very fit with the substantial exercise routine.

We would have to negotiate four gates to the polo grounds before proceeding through a second gate to the Oxley Highway, where we could have an uninterrupted fast ride beside the road (which led to Tamworth).

Once we got proficient at leading the horses, we would jump logs when going through the paddocks to the polo grounds – endless fun.

My favourite riding horse was Cloud, a black mare with lots of go. If I could hold her to a trot she was controllable, but once in a canter she was right on the bit, so I found it better to keep her down to a trot while leading the other three horses.

Saturdays were great fun as this was the day when all the Gunnedah players met at the polo grounds for the weekly practice. For this the horses had to have their tails plaited, all their legs bandaged and bell boots put on their hooves to protect them from flying mallets.

Tails were plaited to prevent entanglement with the tools of play, so there was a fair bit of preparation before the fun started. I became fairly quick at plaiting tails, so would sometimes swap with Crick, who would bandage my legs (my horses' of course) in exchange for me plaiting her tails. On a frosty morning, both jobs were fairly onerous when fingers would be reluctant to thaw out!

At the end of each chukka (there were six altogether, with a two-minute break in between), the next horse had to be ready and waiting for the player to quickly dismount and remount for another fast gallop chasing a ball round the field with the other three members of the team.

After the practice, there was a lavish afternoon tea with yummy slices and biscuits, all made by the wives. Women did not play polo in those days. One time, Mrs Thomson had made a decorative slice for the Saturday practice and stored it in the pantry cupboard.

During the night I felt hungry, so I raided the pantry in the dark, selecting whatever my fingers landed on first. It just happened to be the meringue decorating the beautiful lemon tart!

Next day Mrs Thomson said to me, "Do you know, Joce, there are even rats that can lift lids off biscuit tins!"

I had been well and truly sprung, but Mrs T was really nice about it all the same, she was a lovely lady.

They were very social occasions, and we grooms were privileged to be included in all the social life which, after all, was what polo was all about, apart from an hour of fun on a horse. After a few practices, we noticed that one of the players was shouting us drinks and being very attentive. We were not sure who he had his eye on (whether Crick or me), but it soon became obvious when he asked me to accompany him to the polo ball on the Saturday night.

I gradually got to know Brian over the coming weeks at polo functions and on dates, and we became pretty keen on each other.

We often went to the pictures on Saturday nights along with his brother G, sister-in-law B, and a couple of other members of the team and their girlfriends.

One time, the Gunnedah team went to Narromine in southern New South Wales, but for some reason Brian was not playing this time — maybe he had a problem with his horses or just could not get away for the four days.

I was terribly disappointed that he would not be there, but got such a thrill when he turned up for the Saturday's play. He had driven 310 kilometres from Gunnedah. It was terribly romantic just to turn up without telling me, and he gave me a hand preparing the horses for the match.

Later on in the season, Mr Thomson broke his collarbone in a fall from a horse so was unable to play anymore. Weren't they being considerate when they asked me to go to Scone with Brian and groom his horses? How very thoughtful of them, as it was a lovely opportunity to get to know Brian a lot more.

END OF A ROMANCE

I have done some silly things in my life, and I was about to perform one of the silliest. It still embarrasses me today to think of it. Eryl had come to Gunnedah for the weekend and was staying in a pub not far from the Regal Hotel. I don't think I had told him about Brian. While having our usual after pictures drinks, I said to Brian that I was going to the toilet.

Crick accompanied me and we ran down to the pub where Eryl was staying to say a quick hello. Unfortunately, Eryl offered to walk us back to the other hotel. By the time we got back, Brian and the mob had come to the door wondering where we were.

I will never forget the look on his face and Margie's, one of the other girls who was with us that night, comment: "Who is Tarzan, Joce?"

I wished the ground could just swallow me up. Anyhow, the obvious outcome was that Brian didn't want to have anything to do with me ever again (and rightly so, too).

How could I have been so stupid? But I still had to be in his company at the forthcoming practice matches and polo carnivals, so it was a very difficult time, not to mention the fact that I was nursing a broken heart. I was vaguely aware that Brian already had a steady girlfriend, so we had both been two-timing.

Later in the year, Mr Thomson had to take his truck to Sydney, and he very kindly brought our horses back to Ruvigne for us. Now instead of having our Sundays off, just for a change we rode our own horses! I guess it was relaxing not having to lead three other horses.

I had a nasty accident while riding at Ruvigne. I rode a young horse, Puff Puff, bareback out to a back paddock to catch my horse and lead him back to the stables. Unfortunately, my horse broke his lead rope, so I removed one of the reins and rode home with one rein and leading my horse.

When we reached the lane going to the stables, Puff Puff bolted and I had no control at all. At the end of the lane there was a right-angle bend, and I knew Puff Puff wouldn't be able to negotiate this in the muddy ground. I screamed, as I knew the outcome wouldn't be good. He crashed into the fence and rolled over. I landed heavily on a heap of old fencing material.

Fortunately, the horse was not injured, but I had bruises all over, a black eye and a broken cheekbone. This along with my sadness over Brian made it a very unpleasant time in my life.

Obviously I broke it off with Eryl, though we remained friends. I was sure he had a girlfriend at uni anyhow, and he later married Verna, a lovely girl. My brother happened to say to me just recently, "Did you know that Eryl died nine years ago?" I was shocked as I didn't know. I always had fond memories of him, even though our paths rarely crossed again. So I Googled "Eryl ......, veterinarian", and there it was. All his notable achievements in his field and his death from cancer in 2011.

A NEW JOB

The polo season came to an end, but Crick and I were reluctant to return to the city after such a wonderful time in the bush. We were able to secure a job at Tambar Springs, west of Gunnedah, looking after three young children while their parents, true Aussie battlers, had a well-earned break in Tasmania for six weeks, for which they had managed to save enough money. The youngest child was eighteen months and the oldest about eight, so it was quite a responsibility.

We knew plenty about horses and not a thing about children, but we thought since there were two of us we could bluff our way around the situation. We agreed to share the pay, and at least we were in the bush for a while longer.

Amazingly, we had no dramas except for one incident when Richard, the eldest, got my lipstick and proceeded to paint one of the bedroom walls! We were grateful that nothing drastic happened on our watch, as it did soon afterwards.

We got to know the boys next door who taught us how to play canasta, so many evenings were spent playing this entertaining and challenging game. In fact, I think we came to enjoy it too much, as one night we were still playing at six o'clock the next morning. When Richard got up, he rubbed his eyes in amazement at finding us still sitting at the table where we had been when he went to bed the night before.

Sadly, the following year, tragedy struck both these families we had been involved with that first year. Little Jasmine, Richard's sister, drowned with her head in a bucket, and the next-door neighbour's five-year-old son was electrocuted while playing underneath their home. The parents were so rocked by these disasters that they moved away.

Crick and I eventually made our way back to Sydney, and I was lucky enough to be able to resume my job with the stock and sharebroker, so it wasn't too bad.

BACK TO GUNNEDAH

Mr Thomson asked me to return to Ruvigne for the next year's polo season, and I was excited at the prospect of returning to the horses and a job I loved. Crick had groomed the horses that belonged to the father of the electrocuted child. He was no longer playing polo, but another Gunnedah player, Bill Maslin, asked Crick to live with him and his wife Sibbie and groom for them.

Naturally Crick accepted immediately, so we were both Gunnedah bound once again for another exciting season of polo matches, practices and never-ending social life. Bill also used to cart the Gunnedah team to matches throughout New South Wales as he had a forty-foot semi, which nicely accommodated the sixteen horses of the team. We would lead them on to the truck, then remove their headstalls so they would travel like a mob of unbroken horses instead of the valuable, well-bred animals that they were. There was never any drama transporting them this way.

I will always remember during matches that were being contested by the Gunnedah team, we grooms, wives and hangers-on would all barrack madly from the sidelines yelling: "Come on Gunnedah, come on Father!" We all called Mr Thomson "Father" as he was the oldest in the team, and also the captain and the president of the club.

Mr T surprised me one day when he suddenly came up with, "Do you know what HESTIA stands for?" (Hestia, the ladies' underwear manufacturer and retailer.)

"No, what is it?"

"Holds every size tit in Australia," was his reply. I was quite stunned but amused, as this was totally out of keeping with Mr Thomson's normal conversation!

I moved into the "Big House" and lived with the family, which consisted of three sons and a daughter, Gai, who happened to be attending PLC Pymble at the time. I had lovely times riding with Gai when she was home on holidays, but for the rest of the time I missed my previous mate on the job. Winter nights spent around the log fire in the study at Ruvigne were very congenial times, and I felt just like a member of the family.

One time I went to a picnic race meeting in Gunnedah with Reg, one of the players with whom I was friendly. On the second night he got rather full and asked a girl if he could drive her home. Turns out she was staying at Currabubula, sixty kilometres away — sixty kilometres of stock route road over the Breeza Plain. Reg really didn't know what he was doing so he asked me to drive.

After getting quite lost a few times, Reg being sick, nearly getting bogged and driving at about eighty kilometres an hour over the most dreadful road, we finally arrived at Currabubula at quarter to six in the morning, only to discover my handbag was missing. We had a coffee then set off again, taking all the wrong turns we had taken earlier to locate my handbag. We finally found it where Reg had been sick — it had obviously fallen out of the car.

We set off again, only to run out of petrol in the middle of the plain, so I sent Reg off to the nearest house, about a kilometre away. He returned, still walking, about forty-five minutes later. He had climbed through a bedroom window, couldn't wake the people, so had helped himself to four litres of fuel!

I finally arrived back home to be confronted by a fairly livid Mr Thomson. I had to get straight back to work at eight o'clock. I was feeling very self-conscious about my bare, dirty feet and sloppy appearance, but eventually someone told Mr Thomson what had happened and he was very sympathetic.

Once again, the season came to an end and I moved back to Sydney and the share broking job. How lucky I was to be able to juggle the two jobs that I loved, including going back to Gunnedah for a third year of polo grooming. This time, there were young horses coming along and I also had to give them a bit of training — lungeing and dressage work. Crick was still working for the Maslins, but tragedy struck once again when Bill, a tall and terribly handsome man, blew himself up in a freak on property accident. The whole district was rocked as Bill was a larger than life character and a pillar of the district.

So Crick left and our paths didn't cross much again until years later when we were both married and living in the bush.

A NEW ROMANCE

During that third year at Gunnedah, I found that Tony, the oldest son, and I were becoming attracted to each other. Thus followed an exciting time of parties and pictures until Tony left to take up a jackarooing job at Talyalyea. This lovely property was on the outskirts of the very isolated town of Hungerford on the Queensland–New South Wales border. Mr Thomson thought that it was a good idea for sons to get experience working on other people's properties or at an agricultural college to vary their knowledge and experience.

I will always remember Tony's homecoming — I think he brought half the red soil of the desert country with him. He was covered in red dust and so was his tool of trade, his swag. It was great to have him back again, and we picked up where we had left off.

His father, Mr T, was becoming increasingly concerned about Tony's and my relationship, as I think he thought that I was a "gold digger", in other words, I was after their very beautiful property, as Tony was the oldest son. The tradition then was that properties almost automatically passed on to this member of the family. To this end, Mr Thomson cornered me one day and informed me that Tony would not be inheriting!

I was flabbergasted, as this had never been even remotely in the back of my mind. I had always thought it would be much more satisfying to set up one's own life rather than acquire one where all the hard work had been done. This interesting revelation, however, did not affect our relationship, and we went on as we had done before Tony's Hungerford venture.

I had bought my first car, a funny little Morris Minor utility, about all I could afford. However, I was very proud that I could now be independent. When I left Ruvigne at the end of the polo season, I decided to give my parents a surprise, so didn't tell them I was coming home. This was pretty stupid really, as I was driving most of the night on a lonely, narrow winding road, most of it dirt — the well-known Putty Road, which goes from Singleton to Windsor. Anyhow I made it, but it was a very risky thing to do I now realise looking back, foolhardy as I was then.

After working the young horses again, it was back to Sydney for me and a complete career change. When I was thirteen, Dad had taken me on a DC3 flight from Sydney to Brisbane, and I absolutely loved it. So I applied to Ansett ANA for a job as an air hostess early in 1964. (This company became Ansett Airlines of Australia in 1968.)

A NEW CAREER

The main airlines flying in Australia at the time were TAA (the government-owned airline), Ansett and Qantas (Queensland and Northern Territory Aerial Services, founded in Queensland's outback town of Winton in 1920 and originally only servicing outback Queensland). In 1935, Qantas commenced its first overseas flight from Brisbane to Singapore, thus Australia's first international airline was established. It has gone on to become the famed and successful operation that it is today.

In those days, the criteria for being accepted into the prestigious position of air hostess were very strict. One had to be single, female, between five feet two (1.575 metres) and five feet six (1.676 metres), and weigh no more than eight and a half stone (fifty-four kilograms)! Marriage or attaining the age of thirty-five would result in immediate dismissal. Some girls secretly married during their flying career, but wore their rings around their necks.

Nervously, I approached the first of two or three interviews, and after having been accepted, I was flown to Essendon Airport (the main Melbourne airport at the time) for three weeks theory and on-the-job training. How exciting it all was. There were about twenty girls in the class and we were all billeted in crew accommodation at the airport.

Aircraft in service at the time included: DC3, DC4, DC6B, Fokker Friendship, Super Viscount, Deluxe Viscount and Lockheed Electra (now known as the Orion and used by the Air Force as a surveillance aircraft). Apart from the DCs, they were all prop jets, in other words, jet engines with propellers. During 1964, the first pure jet was introduced to Ansett, the Boeing 727, so a new training program was necessary. DC9s also came into service at this time.

We had to learn all the details and locations of fire extinguishers and fire axes, first aid kits, emergency exits, ropes, emergency lights, oxygen and torches on every aircraft, as well as how to open toilet doors from the outside, how to operate and use emergency evacuation chutes and ditching ropes, about pressurisation and time zones, air pockets and air conditioning.

It was three weeks of cramming in a huge amount of information in a very short time, but all so very exciting, especially experimenting with using an evacuation chute. We were sent to a June Dalley-Watkins school and taught about etiquette, grooming and deportment, and finally we were given exams on all the subjects we had studied.

On completion, we were sent to our allotted port for commencement of operations. It was company policy not to send girls to their home port, but for some reason still unknown to me I was sent back to Sydney. This was all very embarrassing, as there had been a few farewell parties before I left Sydney and there I was back again to stay.

Early morning flights found me on a western suburbs train at about half past five, surrounded by mainly working men, all staring at me as they didn't often have an air hostess travelling with them! We were supplied with a very smart uniform for both summer and winter, but I never liked subsequent uniforms as much as the first one with its navy blue winged cap and very pale grey dress, also navy jacket in winter.

The pay was encouraging too — I think about forty-eight dollars a week with three weeks leave every nine months. I guess it was realised that hard work, pressurisation and stress would take a fair toll on the girls so we needed a holiday more often than the average worker.

My first day on the job was two Fokker Friendship flights to Canberra and return. I felt so excited I couldn't stop smiling the whole time which, of course, is what hostesses are meant to do anyhow.

Other days were "four legs on the Electra", that is, Sydney to Melbourne and back twice — a fairly tiring day, as I think the flight time was about one and three quarter hours each way. Sydney to Adelaide, Brisbane, Coolangatta and Alice Springs, it was all great fun, but we worked hard. There were no trolleys, each meal or light snack was delivered individually on large or small trays, depending on whether first class or tourist.

Service was very comprehensive. When seated, passengers were offered a magazine, then after the no smoking sign went off, we were able to commence cabin service. On a meal flight, first class passengers were first offered a drink from the bar, followed by a three-course meal, then coffee and liqueurs.

Tourist passengers had a light snack and tea or coffee. If meals were left over from these flights, we would pile them into sick bags and take them home for consumption. This could also be topped off with unfinished liqueurs, which were served in small, one-serve sized flasks. Life was pretty good!

I recently travelled on a flight and happened to be sitting next to a hostess who was going on leave, so we had a good old chat. She informed me that they could no longer load unused meals into sick bags for home consumption as this was considered stealing. This was not the case in 1963 and "stealing meals" was quite legal.

On most flights, someone would request a visit to the flight compartment, usually kids, but sometimes adults. They would be goggle-eyed at the complexity of lights, gauges and controls that confronted them. Occasionally, we hostesses would go "up front" for landing if there was a spare seat. This was great fun — "flaps thirty degrees, wheels down, reverse thrust," the instructions reeled off.

Flying into and out of Sydney, arguably the most beautiful city in the world, was always an experience to look forward to. I never tired of the fantastic view from the air. At night, cabin lights would be dimmed to reveal a nature's wonderland of harbour, bridge, headlands and house lights twinkling in all directions.

I was also able to keep up my relationship with Tony whenever he came to Sydney. Unfortunately, he was in a car accident and ended up with a broken neck, which resulted in a rather longer stay in hospital in Sydney, but I was able to visit him every day. Great for me, but not so good for him in his uncomfortable-looking neck brace.

PARTIES WITH THE RAAF PILOT OFFICERS

During this time, we somehow became associated with a group of pilot officers from the Richmond Air Base, thus another round of parties ensued, once again with plenty of alcohol. Mum and Dad were very tolerant as we were not exactly quiet in our partying. They must have been fairly sleep deprived but they never complained.

One morning after one of these parties, Mum said to me, "What's that on the lawn, Joce?", pointing to a strange-looking collection of red lumpy things. Turns out that Arch, one of the pilots, had consumed too much rum and saveloys and the mixture didn't agree with him, so it was neatly deposited just outside the back door. Naturally, I feigned ignorance with Mum, who was a teetotaller.

We were all keen bushwalkers, and as we were very close to the Blue Mountains, we planned a walk with three of the pilots along with Mollie, my friend Jenny and me. The plan was to drive to Batsch Camp via Oberon and Shooter's Hill, then walk to Colong Caves, a fairly arduous undertaking.

Since Arch was a navigator with the Air Force, he just set a compass course for the caves and off we went! Not the easiest way to negotiate that rugged country, as it involved steep hills and never-ending creek-bestowed valleys, all of us carrying our packs.

True Air Force style, when we arrived at the caves the boys set up their parachute — that was our tent for the night! We were all just good friends, so it was a nice platonic relationship.

I soon found travelling from the western suburbs to Mascot very tiring, especially when I had an early morning flight. I teamed up with a couple of Gunnedah friends, twins Mary and Louie, and we rented a flat in Rose Bay — a much nicer location with easier access to the airport. Our social life became pretty hectic too, with lots of parties, as between the three of us we had plenty of acquaintances.

Towards the end of my first year of flying, I was transferred to Adelaide. They must have woken up that I had been originally sent to my home port. I was pretty excited about this as it meant a whole new life and different flying routes, including Perth flights in the noisy, lumbering, vibrating, slow but incredibly reliable DC6B. Also Alice Springs, Tennant Creek, Katherine and Darwin, where we would overnight.

The hostess superintendent in Adelaide, Miss Nan Witcombe, teamed me up with two other girls, Bev and Pat, to share a flat at Glenelg, a lovely seaside suburb and an easy tram ride to the airport. We got along like we had been friends from childhood, and it was a very happy time except that it meant that I would rarely see Tony unless I made the trek to Gunnedah myself.

The company also found us a house to rent, a large, imposing two-storey house, "Chevron", in Saltram Road, with plenty of room for the three of us in the downstairs flat. Rents were very cheap in Adelaide at the time, about half as much as we had been paying in Sydney. It was only about half a kilometre from the pier at Glenelg, a very popular holiday resort on Holdfast Bay in St Vincent's Gulf.

PARTIES WITH RAF PILOTS

We soon got into the partying routine as Miss Witcombe organised for RAF (British) Vulcan bomber pilots to join other hostesses at our flat for some R & R when they were doing exercises from the Edinburgh base. The other hostesses included some TAA girls, one of whom was Adrienne Colville, with whom I am still friendly today, fifty-five years later. All good platonic fun helped along with generous servings of alcohol, which was the normal adjunct to social life at the time.

Another TAA hostess who shared our partying evenings was a pretty girl with the rather unusual name of Katherine Mary Magdalene McKenzie McHarg! She was more of a friend to Adie, but because of her unusual name, I have not forgotten her.

Obviously when spending one's time in the air, there are always incidents of a minor or major nature. One time on a Perth flight in an Electra, I was carrying a tray loaded with all sorts of goodies down the aisle to a first-class passenger. On a long flight, first-class meals were just that — first-class — so my tray contained entrée, roast dinner complete with all the trimmings, dessert, and cheese and biscuits.

One lady had stashed her handbag in the aisle, and the heel of my shoe caught in the handle, sending me flying. It took me about five rows to eventually come to an ignominious rest on the floor, leaving a trail of peas, carrots, gravy, roast beef, roast potatoes and pumpkin, and everything else that was on that tray scattered over four or so rows of the aisle.

Embarrassed, I somehow got to my feet and continued on towards the flight compartment, where I took refuge until I had regained my composure with the sympathetic ear of the three pilots. The chief hostess meanwhile was left to clean up the mess and deal with the errant lady who had left her handbag in such a stupid place.

Another time I was flying to Coolangatta (the airport for the Gold Coast) as a supernumerary, in other words, travelling as a passenger in order to crew a returning flight. The aircraft in those days could be terribly rough in turbulence, not like the sleek jets of today, and on that occasion it was a VERY ROUGH flight, so much so that the girls crewing the aircraft could not keep up with retrieving used sick bags and cleaning up the passengers. So I was pressed into service to give a hand! There were a few surprised (and very green looking) passengers when I, dressed in civilian clothes, relieved them of their burden. Fortunately, air sickness has never been a problem for me.

A major incident during my time with Ansett occurred when an engine became dislodged from the wing of a DC6B in flight and was just hanging suspended underneath. The captain, Keith Hants, did an incredible job of landing that plane intact by carefully manoeuvring it so that the engine stayed in position so as not to cause any more damage. How he landed it was an amazing feat of airmanship, but land it he did, and no one was injured. He was an overnight hero.

Australia is one of safest countries in the world for flight owing to its moderate climate, lack of high mountain ranges and lack of heavy aircraft traffic.

MORE ROMANCE

One of the features of my lifestyle to date was that I had lived a fairly nomadic life, therefore had had the opportunity to meet a variety of people, including handsome young men! It was at a hostess party one time that I met Marty, a tall, good-looking lieutenant in the Australian Regular Army, 4RAR, based at Woodside in the Adelaide Hills.

Many dates followed, including visits to the exclusive Officers' Mess, drives in the Adelaide Hills in his FJ Holden (and didn't he know how to navigate those curves?), trips to Victor Harbour and visiting friends round the area. It was a very romantic time.

September 1964 I was due for holidays. My very best friend, Rob, had married Graham, and they had gone to the Kimberley to manage Kirkimbie Station on the Northern Territory–Western Australia border. This property, along with about twenty-six other stations scattered throughout the Kimberley, the Northern Territory and Queensland, was owned by the prominent English family, the Vesteys.

I thought it would be great to see the real outback, so I booked a flight to Wyndham via Alice Springs and Darwin for a long-dreamed of holiday with my school friend Rob on this remote cattle station.

In those days, holiday pay was handed out in cash in small envelopes. On arriving back at the flat, I left my pay on my bedside table a couple of days before I was due to fly.

The hostess superintendent had sent another girl to share our flat, Kay, but the harmony that had existed between Bev, Pat and myself was immediately thrown into disarray, as Kay just didn't fit in.

My holiday pay disappeared! Kay was immediately suspected, and we contacted the police in Glenelg to investigate the matter. You wouldn't believe the number of detectives who suddenly found it necessary to look into this relatively minor offence. We seemed to be entertaining detectives daily. Hard as they tried, the money remained missing.

I VISIT A KIMBERLEY CATTLE STATION

Rob and her husband Graham picked me up in Wyndham and we set off on the long route to Kirkimbie via the Duncan Highway. It has now been renamed more appropriately the Duncan Road, owing to the fact that it is barely maintained anymore and the population in the area considerably lessened.

Through what is now Kununurra, on to Argyle Station (now mostly under the water of Lake Argyle), Rosewood, Mistake Creek, Spring Creek and Ord River Stations (the latter subsequently resumed by the Western Australian Government), Nicholson Station and finally on to Kirkimbie, five hundred kilometres of bone-shattering roads in a hot and uncomfortable four-cylinder Land Rover.

However, I was spellbound by the spectacular Kimberley country as we passed close to the Bungles, which at that stage had not been discovered by the general public. There were numerous fast-flowing creeks and rivers, surrounded by red basalt-topped, spinifex-covered hills. We also passed through the Rosewood Wall, a perpendicular limestone outcrop going for hundreds of kilometres through the Territory and Western Australia.

I was amazed when, after travelling for hours, we saw lights in the distance and Rob and Graham announced, "That will be Cec Watts."

In all that isolation, they knew who would be in the Land Rover, and sure enough Cec, the manager of Ord River Station, pulled up for a yarn, and the billy was boiled in the middle of the road. I was being educated about the true meaning of Outback Australia.

We arrived at the homestead too tired for any refreshment and flopped gratefully into bed. The homestead had a large kitchen–dining room area and two large bedrooms, the whole of which was surrounded by a fly-wired verandah, which was where most of the living was done owing to the fierce temperatures nature could bestow on that area. There was no form of cooling, the only concession to this was a six-inch gap between the walls and the floor to allow for some form of "air conditioning"!

I MEET TIM

Next morning, I was introduced to Tim, the head stockman. The attraction was instant. He was the typical bushman, the strong, silent type, with his easy-going manner and manly build, a man of few words, but every word worth listening to. Tall and good-looking, I thought he was gorgeous, and I felt I could happily spend more time with this man.

Luckily that was in the plan of the manager, Graham. Tim was to go out with the stock camp a few days later to muster round Mount Panton. This would be a token gesture to remove the last of the cattle from country that had been resumed by the government in the Argyle Dam catchment area.

I was thrilled when they told me that I was to accompany him and the Aboriginal stockmen on this venture. I was mounted up on Tote, an ex-racehorse, so was able to keep up with the mob even though I didn't have a clue what I was doing! Four blissful days followed, discovering the life of a stockman on a large, isolated cattle station. The Kimberley scenery was magnificent, with the red country and limestone hills — these latter terrible to ride on as very slippery for the horses.

We had a very congenial time and got to know each other fairly well, sharing a lot of common interests and also our origins, but not our swags in case you are wondering.

Tim had been born in December 1939 in India where his English father, James, had gained a post in the Indian Medical Service, which he held until Independence in 1947. Tim and his sister Sarah and their parents lived in a Mutiny Bungalow not far from Delhi. According to the customs of the English expatriate community, the children were looked after by ayahs, who were told not to speak English to the children lest they pick up unfortunate accents!

During the early years of World War II, their mother Jane had a severe stomach illness that could not be treated in India. As the voyage to England was too risky, she and the children went to Melbourne. After an operation, Jane decided to send Tim and his sister to what passed for a boarding school at Panton Hill, outside Melbourne, but for some inexplicable reason, she soon took off to India then back to England, leaving the children stranded in Australia.

Tim was about four at the time, and his independent sister decided to run away from the school. They were picked up by the police many miles from the boarding school — a dreadful experience for young children isolated from their parents.

At the end of the war, Tim and Sarah were sent back to England on the *Dominion Monarch*, then a troop ship, in the care of an inexperienced girl. They ran riot on the ship and, according to Sarah, they ended up like "wild animals".

In 1947, Tim's father bought a private practice in Gisborne, Victoria, sight unseen, after seeing an advertisement in the *British Medical Journal*, thus the family's permanent ties to Australia began. The family travelled to Australia on a Lockheed Constellation, a four-engine piston aircraft that was the first on the Qantas Kangaroo Route from England to Australia. It carried twenty-nine passengers and eleven crew, and stopped in six cities, including two overnights. It was the first pressurised aircraft, so was able to fly above storms and avoid bad weather. It was still a noisy, vibrating, never-ending journey, which Tim never forgot.

James liked to "do the right thing" by his children, and also liked to be "seen to be doing the right thing", thus Tim was sent to Geelong Grammar School, arguably the best boys' boarding school in Australia at the time.

He was lucky to have been able to spend a year at Timbertop, the mountain education precinct where boys learnt independence, bushcraft and survival techniques. This was probably a good thing, as amazingly the boys were allowed to take off for a weekend hiking in the mountains without having to notify anyone of their plans. They certainly learnt survival and self-sufficiency.

Tim mated up with a friend, Con Gration, whose family had a property on the Murray River, and Tim would spend holidays with them. This, coupled with his Timbertop experience, gave him a love of the bush and resulted in his applying for a job with Vestey Brothers, the privately owned English company that had international food product businesses all over the world, including cattle stations in Brazil, Venezuela and Australia. They began in 1897 from a family butchery in Liverpool, England, and pioneered refrigeration.

They purchased large tracts of land in inland Australia when no one wanted it owing to isolation and cost of development. Over the years they owned the following stations, but not necessarily at the same time:

Northern Territory stations:

- Helen Springs
- Willeroo
- Kirkimbie
- Limbunya
- Nutwood Downs
- Delamere
- Birrindudu
- Wave Hill
- Manbulloo
- Waterloo

Western Australian stations:

- Flora Valley
- Ord River
- Mistake Creek
- Gordon Downs
- Margaret River
- Nicholson
- Turner River
- Sturt Creek
- Spring Creek

Queensland stations:

- Morestone
- Doongmabulla
- Avon Downs
- Oban
- Fitzroy Vale
- Archer
- Cooloolah
- Lake Learmont

It can be seen from the above that there was plenty of opportunity for transfers and the ability to learn a variety of skills and different methods from the various managers.

At one stage, Tim was even sent to the Vestey-owned abattoir in Darwin for three weeks to further his education, but ended up causing a strike as he didn't have a union ticket, unions being very strong at the time.

It is interesting to note that the general manager at the time, Mr Morris, also went to Geelong Grammar School, so he and Tim always had a good rapport.

It is reported that by 1930 the company had 30,000 employees worldwide. To transport their product, they also owned the Blue Star Shipping Line. They were a great company to work for, and everyone who was employed on a Vestey cattle station had nothing but praise for them.

Tim had previously applied to join an Antarctic expedition but was not successful, so when a friend told him about the great life on a Kimberley cattle station, he immediately applied to Australian Investment Agency, namely Vesteys, and within two days an airline ticket to Wyndham was in the mail.

His first posting was as a jackaroo on Ord River Station, approximately 180 kilometres south of what is now Kununurra, a 2600 square kilometre station incorporating the southern part of the Bungles. Wild, beautiful and unfenced, it was running nearly as many donkeys as cattle and hundreds of cleanskin bulls, so Tim was to get all the excitement a young and energetic man could soak up. In those days, mustering would take him to the foot of the Bungle Bungles.

Throwing bulls was a popular pastime. It involved running a bull for a short time to get it winded, jumping off the horse at the gallop and grabbing hold of the bull's tail. The bull would then turn round to charge the aggressor, and in that moment, the stockman would give it a tug, throwing the bull off balance then on to the ground.

Quickly the tail would be secured under one leg, and the man would sit on the bull while another stockman secured the head. The bull then parted company with some of his vital parts, namely horns and balls.

This operation was usually performed when other stockmen were around in case something went wrong or the horse took off. Usually the horse would "ground tie", as stockmen only used long reins that were not tied together, so the horse instinctively pulled up, though not always.

In those days, many stockmen carried pistols for control of bulls which were worthless at the time and hampered mustering. This changed when McDonalds discovered that Australia's bull meat was perfect for their hamburgers, so bull catching became a profitable enterprise.

From here Tim was transferred to Kirkimbie, where Graham was the manager and Rob, my old friend, the manager's wife.

Tim told me lots of stories about his Ord River days, but a couple that stick in my mind are as follows. Clarrie Wilkinson, an old Vestey pensioner, and another fellow named Alec Cadell shot 10,000 donkeys in one year on the Ord. Such a sad end for these gallant little animals who had performed so many arduous tasks in the pioneering days, pulling huge loads and fire ploughs to grade roads. After mechanisation, these animals, along with their camel counterparts, were just turned loose to breed up into the plague proportions that exist today.

Old Clarrie owned a Volkswagen Beetle, totally unsuited to that hot, dusty country owing to the fact that they had their engines where most cars have a boot. Clarrie didn't like driving it himself, so he would second unsuspecting drivers to take him to Wyndham or Nicholson Station.

All the red lights would be flashing, but that wouldn't worry Clarrie, he would just say, "Keep her going, keep her going!", and somehow it seemed to be able to do that without blowing up.

Norman Wellman was another old Vestey pensioner who lived permanently on the Ord. He died at the age of eighty-seven and was just buried there in the station graveyard, no red tape in those days. The day he died he said, "I think this is going to be the end of a perfect day." What a way to go.

The Ord River graveyard is a very historic place, but unfortunately not many people know its whereabouts now as it has almost disappeared under long grass and spinifex. It is somewhere opposite where the old homestead used to be and very hard to find.

The Aboriginals were given white man names such as Camel Foot Charlie, Mulga Bill, Tucker Bill, Bunda, Jimmy Jam Tim, Suleiman, Splinter, Rusty Walker, Molly, Polly, Sheila and Gracie, but they also had their Aboriginal names.

Two items kept in the station store and in the Flying Doctor medicine cabinet were much sought after by the Aboriginals. They were Californian Poppy hair oil, with which they loved to plaster themselves on special occasions, and what they referred to as "rubbing medicine", which was handed out of the first aid cabinet whenever there was an ache or pain. This was officially called Lin Methyl Sal, which stood for liniment methyl salicylate and seemed to be able to soothe any complaint.

They would hold corroborees at night, and you knew that they were happy after a hard day's muster. These dances could go on well into the night and usually celebrated some particular event. Sometimes they played cards. The stakes were usually items of clothing, so it was nothing to see some of them turn up for the muster next morning bootless, shirtless or hatless.

At the end of each mustering season, they would go wandering off into the bush with their spears, woomeras, boomerangs, coolamons and a bit of station tucker, but they mainly lived on bush tucker so they had the best of both worlds. Sometimes they would take a station packhorse to carry a bit of extra ration, but they always turned up back at the station when the mustering season was due to start, usually about Easter, and were happy to go back to work and a regular supply of food.

At that stage, Ord River, Wave Hill and Kirkimbie stations had 110 volt power, which is standard in America but unusual in Australia. Unlike 240 volt power, it is not lethal, so it seems like a good idea to me. Appliances that were used with 32 volt power were unable to be used with the 110 volts.

Straddling the border between Northern Territory and Western Australia created great difficulty time-wise as radio schedules, usually referred to as "skeds", were on Western Australian time. This made for some very long days at times as these stations' normal activities operated on Territory time.

THE PARTY

Rob and Graham organised a party — no ordinary party, as visitors came from all over the country. All the good-looking eligible young bucks from miles around (there were very few white women in the country at that time, and most of them were married) came to have a look at the new female from the south. It was an exciting introduction to Kimberley-style revelling, but during the night I only had eyes for Tim.

As the night wore on, the men became more and more intoxicated, so a game was invented to see who could run the furthest UP THE KITCHEN DOOR! Naturally, many a slip between the floor and the door, but fortunately no one was injured.

The amusing part, though, was that the floor had recently been painted and was not quite dry, so many footsteps appeared next day when everyone had sobered up a little. It was amazing to see the height which they achieved. Door running competitions were interspersed with verandah water bag fights, so altogether it was a hilarious night.

Rob and I decided to pay a little joke on Tim and pinch his riding boots. Next morning, we were surprised to find Tim well-shod, but Pompei, an Aboriginal who was employed by Ralph and Thea, was barefoot. We had raided the wrong swag!

A SAD GOODBYE

The three weeks at Kirkimbie went all too quickly and it was time for me to board the mail plane for the sad trip back to Adelaide. When I went to the quarters to say goodbye to Tim, he was sitting on his verandah doing a bit of saddling. All he said to me as farewell was: "See you, one of these days."

I was devastated, thinking I would never see him again. The flight to Wyndham was unforgettable — I cried all the way. Back in Adelaide, I determined to put him out of my mind, and once I settled down, I resumed dates with Marty but it was hard going.

I decided I had better go back to Gunnedah and see Tony, as we had still been corresponding. I spent a few lovely days back at "Ruvigne", during which time Tony and I decided we would just remain friends. I met Father Thomson's mother, a grand old lady, who was staying at Ruvigne at the time, and she welcomed me into the family, unaware that it was not to be.

I caught up with my old friends Mary and Louie, then it was back to Adelaide. When I arrived, there on my bed was a letter from — TIM! I was flabbergasted but overjoyed — after all that time, three months, there it was. Just when I had sorted it out between Tony and Marty, this most welcome complication suddenly confronted me.

Tim told me that he had to come to Melbourne to have an operation on his foot to fix a plantar wart that had been giving him trouble for some time, and he was wondering if we could catch up! Could we? I couldn't believe it and was terribly excited at the prospect of seeing him again. This would be no trouble, as I was often rostered to do Melbourne flights and overnight in the (then) plush Southern Cross Hotel.

A JOYFUL REUNION

So we met up again and it was bliss — Marty had no idea what was happening. Amazingly, he had been transferred to Canungra for a six-week course in jungle training, so there I was, two-timing again. Oh well, I suppose it all helps to choose the right partner in the end, and as the saying goes: "All's fair in love and war!"

Tim bought a car for courting — a classy old English Riley. One weekend, he took me to a property where he had jackarooed before going to the Territory, a lovely property with frontage to the Murrumbidgee River owned by David Tynan and his sister, Ginny. Days were spent doing cross-country gallops over plains and cultivation and through melon holes (small shallow waterholes), exploring the gorgeous countryside, overjoyed to be in each other's company again.

One day Ginny, a very capable and intrepid lady, took us for a walk along the river. The riverbank was frequented by numerous red-bellied black snakes sunning themselves in the early morning, but Ginny just stepped over these snakes as though they were mere pieces of stick. Tim followed then I bravely brought up the rear. The snakes took no more notice of us than Ginny did of them. Her only concession to their being poisonous was the fact that she carried a stick. Though poisonous they are not aggressive, not like their cousins, the blue-bellied blacks.

Another fun time we had involved catching rabbits along the levee banks of the river for the purpose of injecting them with myxomatosis and releasing them for spreading among the rabbit population, which was still in plague proportions in Australia. The rabbits would race to the end of the banks, and when they arrived at the water's edge we could pounce on them, but we still had to be fairly lively.

Poor little buggers, it was a horrible disease spread by insects, mainly fleas and mosquitoes, as well as the rabbits themselves. They eventually went blind and died, but I guess the means was a necessary evil to try to eliminate this pest that had caused so much destruction to the Australian landscape.

Rabbits had been introduced into Australia from England in 1859 for sport and hunting. By the 1920s, the population had reached an estimated 10 billion. Trapping, poisoning and shooting had been the only means of control, and even the rabbit-proof fence, built between 1901 and 1907, failed to make much difference owing to the fact that the rabbits were reaching the other side of the fence even while it was being constructed.

Sir Sidney Kidman, the Cattle King, maintained that rabbits had done more than any other single event to change the fauna and flora of Australia, as rabbits could even eat the roots of grass and shrubs.

In a desperate attempt to make some impression on the plague, myxomatosis was introduced in the 1950s, but was largely ineffective until it was discovered that the virus needed mosquitoes and fleas in order to spread from rabbit to rabbit.

Once this problem was rectified, ninety to ninety-nine per cent of the population was wiped out. However, resistance was developing, so a new disease was introduced, rabbit haemorrhagic virus (a type of calicivirus), which was spread by flies.

Farmers mainly keep the population under control now by ripping warrens, trapping and poisoning.

After four magical days on the property, we drove back to Melbourne in time for my flight to Adelaide. It had been a wonderful time and we were definitely falling in love.

Tim drove to Adelaide while I was flying from Melbourne — I gave him a wave as I flew overhead! We had some happy times in Adelaide, but I think Tim suspected who the FJ Holden that was parked in my yard belonged to, though he never mentioned it.

Our blissful time together was coming to an end and Tim was booked to fly back to Alice Springs, then Kirkimbie. I saw him off at the airport and he told me later that had he turned around he wouldn't have boarded that plane, but he reckoned that he had to keep a good job if our relationship was to flourish into something permanent.

On the station, it was back to work for Tim, but this time living in the homestead on his own as Rob and Graham had left, and Tim was caretaking and in charge of thirty or so Aboriginals.

One of the Aboriginal workers was a delightful old man called Hector, whose only job was to tend a small patch of Hunter Valley lucerne, which was grown as a treat for the horses. Hector was very proud of his patch and his days were spent lovingly watering and cutting the crop.

Another Aboriginal was well named "Mad Sandy". I think he must have been an epileptic. One time Mad Sandy attacked Tim with a crowbar, but the rest of the mob came to Tim's defence and no injuries occurred.

BOEING 727S COME INTO SERVICE

Round about this time, Ansett introduced Boeing 727s into service, the first pure jets, so I was able to experience flying on these magnificent aircraft, a far cry from the old prop jets. We were all issued with new uniforms, pale green frocks with darker green caps. Sydney to Melbourne flights now were so fast that we were still hauling in trays as we were landing, and obviously this was unacceptable.

The solution? Make the flight time longer! So it was extended from about forty-five minutes to fifty-five minutes and the problem was solved. We still had to move fairly quickly, though, to complete the cabin service before landing.

ANOTHER CHANGE OF PLAN

At the end of 1964, I decided to give up flying and return to Sydney, where I got a secretarial job with the CSR Company in O'Connell Street. During this time, I shared a flat with Uncle Ted in Potts Point. Not sure why I gave the flying away as I loved it, but anyhow I moved on. Tim and I were writing to each other virtually every day, but as his mail service was only fortnightly, there would be a pile all at once. Joy, oh joy!

We planned that I should go to Kirkimbie and spend some time with him so we could consolidate our relationship. This was to be in about March 1965, but I was a bit dubious about this arrangement. There would be no other white people on the station as Graham and Rob had left and Tim was the relieving manager. We had no choice if we were to get to know each other better, so arrangements were made.

The best laid plans of mice and men …

Out of the blue, Marty turned up on my doorstep in Sydney looking all handsome in his officer's uniform and asked me to marry him! I was blown away, and unbelievably I said "Yes." What on earth was I thinking? More accurately, you could say I wasn't thinking. I had just been swept of my feet by this romantic act, flying all the way from Adelaide to pop the question.

So then I had to contact Tim to tell him the awful news — not easy when the only contact was via telegram through the Wyndham Outpost Radio with the whole country able to listen in.

I said, "Have decided definitely for Adelaide, now unable to come. Joce."

I still can't bear to think how this must have affected Tim living without the company of Rob and Graham and in isolated circumstances. How could I have been so cruel?

Invitations were sent out for our wedding in Sydney, parties were organised and all the usual pre-wedding revelry, including having a wedding dress made.

However, I was getting more and more unsure. In fact, I gradually spent a lot of time crying, agonising with myself that I had done the wrong thing. My parents were very supportive, but didn't try to influence me either way and I became despondent and convinced that I was marrying the wrong man.

It is interesting that Tim said of Marty, "I'm sure if I met him I would like him", but Marty referred to Tim as "my cowboy friend" in a rather derogatory manner.

I had allowed myself to be swept off my feet by a handsome officer in uniform and a romantic proposal.

Two weeks before the wedding, Marty and I sat down and wrote to all the prospective guests advising them that the wedding "had been postponed".

This, of course, was a lie, as I had no intention of going through with a marriage to Marty, now or ever. I would be finishing off with him forever, though he didn't know this at the time. I think he still thought he could talk me round. No way, I had learnt my lesson and realised I didn't really love him.

So then I was faced with the prospect of contacting Tim again, but would he want to have anything to do with me? I had no idea, but I had to try. I knew he was THE ONE and I had to set about diplomatically reversing the damage I had done.

I wrote to him and said something along the lines of, "Dear Tim, I have called things off with Marty and if you feel like writing to me, I would love to hear from you", and a bit more news. I didn't really expect to receive a reply, but I was wrong. Before long there was the longed for letter in his beautiful and familiar writing.

ROMANCE REKINDLED

He said he had never completely lost faith and knew that some day he would hear from me again.

I was overjoyed, and he must have been too as he suggested that I go ahead and make plans to fly once again to Kirkimbie — what bliss!

Actually, Marty had done us a favour. Had I continued with the original plan, we would have virtually been living in sin (so the rest of the country would have thought). In the meantime, new managers Mick and Hazel had been appointed, so we had our chaperones and I was greatly relieved.

This time I flew to Wyndham and caught the Connellan mail plane to Inverway, and now we come to the preface in my book, that magical time when we met again. In fact, Tim never asked me to marry him, there was such a strong current between us that we both knew, as soon as I stepped off that aircraft and our eyes met, that it would come to pass. In fact, neither of us ever said, "I love you", we didn't need to, it was just another wavelength that we were on together.

Also on the plane with me was Judy, a bookkeeper going to Limbunya Station to work, and I remember feeling so smug when this handsome stockman came to meet me at the airstrip with an "Aren't I lucky?" stamp all over my face.

I will never forget the trip back to Kirkimbie with Tim in the Land Rover, the way he handled the narrow, winding road so casually, with one arm resting nonchalantly on the door frame and negotiating the corners at high speed. I had never been so happy, and I could see a wonderful future stretched before us.

I met Mick and Hazel, a delightful, salt of the earth couple from Maryborough in Queensland. Six magical weeks ensued with Tim and this hospitable and entertaining couple, during which time I had a good insight into life on a Kimberley cattle station. To say the least, I was wrapped.

I used to go out on the run with Tim and we would stop at a set of yards on the way and have long, lingering kisses. Years later, we would remember these kisses, which were always referred to as "Number Eight Kisses".

One day we went out on the run. It was a drought year and the waterholes were drying up. Tim pulled up at a beautiful spot called Rainbar and suggested we go for a swim. The water was inhabited by a large number of crocodiles, but Tim assured me that they were only freshies so I confidently followed him in, having one hundred per cent faith in his judgement.

I went out in the stock camp with Tim and the Aboriginal crew, who were all smiles at Tim and his new "Cudgerie".

"'Im got 'im Cudgerie, that Maluka," they were saying.

We were mustering in an area called Hedley's Creek when a beast broke from the mob. Tim said to me, "Go after him, Joce." So off I went on Finch, but Tim (a man of few words) had omitted to tell me to keep the horse front on to the beast if it charged, as side on the horse could get horned, which is exactly what happened.

Fortunately, it was only a tickle in the ribs, but enough to make the horse "drop its head" and I was deposited ignominiously on the hard ground. Unhurt but sheepish, I got to my feet and remounted Finch, realising that I had inadvertently provided all with a bit of entertainment. Tim was most apologetic.

One day, Clancy, one of the Aboriginal stockmen, was riding a mule as it was towards the end of the year and stockhorses were in short supply. Mules are marvellous, sturdy little weight-bearing animals, hardy in stamina and not needing to be shod. They are bred by putting a jack donkey over a mare, and are terminal, that is, they are unable to breed themselves.

They were mainly used for bronco branding and as pack mules, but not sought after as riding animals as they have notoriously difficult mouths. This particular day we were heading out on a muster when Clancy's mule suddenly took off totally out of control and was last seen disappearing over the horizon! He eventually made his way back to the mustering team.

As we were setting up camp that night, a "Happy Jack" came out of the blue and disrupted the proceedings rather disastrously. A Happy Jack is a sudden, narrow, severe storm with rain and strong winds. Lasting only a few minutes, it was enough to put the camp in chaos, some horses hobbled, some half hobbled, billy cans and camp ovens, dampers and corned beef strewn over the flat, saddles and swags all drenched. Tim and I rolled out our swags under the truck that night.

Evenings at the station were spent playing games on the lawn — games of balance and strength, head-butting and fly. It was a delightful period.

Kirkimbie was a very isolated station, and any sound of a visitor coming was met with enthusiasm and curiosity. Any of us who were at the station would rush into the garden to see who was gracing us with their presence.

The twice-yearly visit by the hawker, usually from Queensland, would also bring much excitement to everyone on the station. These travelling salesmen sold everything from belt buckles to boots, saddle cloths to shirts, pocketknives to pannikins, as well as "stuff", which was a four-foot length of material highly prized by the Aboriginal women as they made it into colourful dresses. These hawkers, sometimes husband and wife, made a welcome change in the entertainment circles and happily joined in the evening revelry.

One night, Tim and I were invited to Nelson Springs, a government research station with one scientist living there alone. Way out into the bush we drove, I not having a clue where we were going. I don't think Tim was too sure either, as on the way home he seemed to have trouble finding the correct route, so it took ages.

To this day I do not know whether he took a circuitous route to prolong a lovely evening or if he really was "bushed"! Anyhow, eventually we did arrive back at the station. I will never forget that we had ice cream for dessert, way out there in the Never Never.

One weekend, Ralph and Thea decided to put on a party at Gordon Downs. In those days, everyone in the country attended parties, from the manager to the stockmen, the bookkeeper and the bore mechanic. As staff were not as transient as they are today, everyone would know everyone and these parties were great affairs. Beer was hung in wet bags in trees so there was plenty of "Kimberley Cool" alcohol.

Tim and I decided to camp between Gordon Downs and Nicholson on the way home very early in the morning, so we rolled out the swags on the side of the road. Not long after daylight, just as we were surfacing, Hilly (Len Hill, manager of Nicholson) came along and in his usual cheeky way made the comment to Tim: "I see you are wearing your restrainers today, boy!"

He had noticed that Tim was wearing underpants and was aware that they weren't part of Tim's usual attire. Cheeky fellow!

Len Hill is recognised for writing a book titled *Droving with Ben Taylor*, which describes his trips up and down the Canning Stock Route at the age of eighteen. They took horses up and came back with cattle, a memorable feat for one so young, especially as he somehow found time to keep a diary.

Six glorious weeks were coming to an end. My first departure from Kirkimbie was marked with terrible sadness, my second time with overpowering joy — I was on my way back to Sydney to make our wedding plans! I considered true love was made up of four main ingredients — physical attraction, love, friendship and respect — and we had all four in abundance. I suppose without the initial physical attraction there is not much point in going further with a relationship.

Tim must have asked my father for my hand, but I have no recollection of this except to say that Dad would have been most willing to give his permission, as he was extremely impressed with Tim.

WEDDING PLANS

On the event of our engagement, we received a letter from Cec Watts, the pastoral inspector. I quote some of it:

> *Dear Tim, I received your most interesting letter this morning, may I be the first to extend my congratulations to you both. I am glad to hear that you are entering the ranks of wise men, all men become much wiser after marriage.*

I flew home via Alice Springs, Adelaide and Melbourne, where I was met by Tim's parents, who were going to take me to their home at Mount Macedon, a delightful area in the Macedon Ranges. This was like a Little England, where properties consisted of huge mansions on large acreages of beautiful, well-established gardens. James and Jane's property, Tremac, was also in this mould. Although not quite as grand as some of the dwellings, it was beautiful nonetheless.

My meeting with the Dorans was a happy occasion and Jane was soon on the phone to her friends saying: "Come and meet my new baby!" Interestingly, Jane's maiden name was Bird and her parents had given her the Christian name of "Nesta", so it was no wonder that she changed her name to Jane. Fancy being called "Nesta Bird!" What could they have been thinking?

They put on a party for me, and no doubt guests were keen to meet the prospective new addition to the family. It was a rather overwhelming time, but lovely to meet all the locals, many of whom spoke with a distinct English accent. I also met Tim's sister Sarah and her husband Bill, who was a barrister in Melbourne. They had three boys.

Tim's father took me to Melbourne one day to buy me a diamond brooch, and to meet his friends at the exclusive Melbourne Club.

The time had finally come to go home to Sydney and organise the BIG DAY, which was to be on Wednesday 19 January 1966.

Tim was never one to stick to protocol and so preferred a plain wedding — no dinner suits or tails, just a plain lounge suit and tie. This was also the reason for having it on a Wednesday instead of the usual Saturday. I didn't care, I just wanted our happy day to come as quickly as possible.

While I was doing this, I got a job with a secretarial agency that provided temporary staff to relieve while permanent staff went on holidays. This was really pleasant work as postings were about three weeks. One job I remember in particular was to work with the "Manly and Port Jackson Steamship Company", in other words, the Manly Ferry Company. The name still fascinates me.

I booked the wedding ceremony at St Swithun's Church at Pymble, which I had attended while at school at PLC. The reception was to be held at The Crest, Wahroonga.

THE WEDDING

It was a memorable and happy day, but that was the time when the relationship with my mother-in-law did a U-turn. Nothing, however, could dampen my elation at becoming Mrs Timothy James Doran. I think it suddenly dawned on Jane that I was stealing her beloved son and that he would now belong to someone else.

She didn't smile once on our special day, and rarely smiled at me later until not long before she died. She developed dementia and forgot to hate me. So for a short period we had a lovely relationship — so sad that it was only during the last years of her life. In-law relationships can make things very difficult for all involved.

At one stage during the dancing at our wedding, Tim's shirt was hanging down below his coat and a message was passed to me to tell Tim his shirt was hanging out! Who cared? I didn't pass it on, just loved him the way he was.

One telegram we received from a Territory character, read: "Sorry, unable to attend rodeo. Keep spurs, tapes and reins tight. Filly soon be camp mare! Best wishes to you both, Brodie."

It was usual then for the bride and groom to change into "going away outfits" before the final farewell, *Auld Lang Syne*. It is such a shame that this custom has now been abandoned as it was such fun.

We then set off in our Holden ute for the honeymoon suite at a nearby motel, with many of the wedding guests accompanying us. This we didn't mind as we were going thousands of miles away and would not be back in civilisation for a couple of years. About three o'clock in the morning, they all left. At last we were beginning our life of adventure together.

Tim's life is chronicled in the book *More of the Privileged Few* by Jeff Hill. This is the third of three books Jeff wrote about people who had lived and worked in the north during the days of Aboriginal labour, horse mustering and droving. We were lucky to have experienced this period, as the changeover to mainly white labour, helicopters and road trains occurred during our time up north and the country was to change forever.

Tim had been offered the job of overseer of Helen Springs Station, a 2082 square mile (5887 square kilometres) cattle station on the Barkly Tableland of the Northern Territory. (This was small by Territory standards — Wave Hill was about three times the size, and next-door neighbour Newcastle Waters the same.) For this, he was to be paid the princely sum of one thousand pounds — $2000 per annum. Interestingly, we later found out that the Helen Springs bookkeeper was actually on a higher salary. Never mind, he was a nice bloke.

THE HONEYMOON

Our honeymoon was the trip to the Territory, and exciting it was too. It was the middle of the wet season and roads were vastly inferior to the present day standards.

As the company supplied everything except toothbrushes and soap, our luggage in the back of the ute was sparse — I had a suitcase, a saddle, some coat hangers and my dog, Stormy. Tim had a canvas roll with his clothes, as well as a swag and saddle, and that was the sum total when we set off on our new life together.

The second night we spent in the Bourke Motel, then it was on to Cunnamulla where we had a night with my old grooming friend, Crick, who had become a governess when we parted and finally married the boss's son. They were on a beautiful sheep property in the "Salad Bowl" of the area, so named because of the excellent pastures and high standard of wool and properties.

The road between Cunnamulla and Charleville was a wide, sandy road that was more like a river from many flat gradings but no formation grading. At Charleville, the Warrego River was in full flood, so we were towed across by an obliging gentleman who was no doubt making a good wage as I think the charge was about $10 and he was kept busy all day.

A little ditty about Charleville comes to mind here. "Why did AdaVale marry CharleVille? Because he couldn't WinDorah!"

After Charleville, we encountered a narrow, one-lane bitumen road that made passing oncoming traffic difficult as one had to get off the side and be careful not to get bogged or break a windscreen.

On through Augathella, Tambo, Blackall, Barcaldine, Ilfracombe then Longreach, the last major centre before Mount Isa. Just before Winton, the Jessamine River was in flood and this once again necessitated a tow. This time the towing vehicle was a truck, and he hitched up three vehicles at a time. We were the third vehicle and the water was up to the bottom of the windows.

Had he stalled, I think we would have been submerged as the bow wave was all that was keeping the water level lower. There are several channels of the Jessamine, but now there is high-level bridge and this river no longer holds up the traffic. It was so exciting navigating it in 1966.

After Winton, there was only thirty kilometres of bitumen before we were at the mercy of the — mud! We were the first travellers to go through, and I have a movie of Tim almost building the road in places. He had to get out with his trusty shovel and rearrange the mud somehow. Without his expert driving we certainly wouldn't have made it, but eventually we got to Kynuna where a night at the Blue Heeler pub was most welcome. Fairly primitive but hospitable nonetheless. A night-time visit to the toilet involved stepping out the window and using the long grass!

On to McKinlay of Crocodile Dundee fame, thence to Cloncurry, where we once again picked up the bitumen to Mount Isa. The last town in Queensland is Camooweal, still a frontier town then. Then to the border and finally we were in the NORTHERN TERRITORY. I still have pangs of nostalgia when travelling on this road as it brings back such sentimental memories.

Across the Barkly Highway to the Three Ways via Barry Caves and Frewena, both primitive roadhouses that, sadly, no longer exist. In their place, radio repeater stations dot the landscape all the way along this route.

Tennant Creek was established because of a gold rush, but not where the town was originally planned to be. Evidently the bullock wagon carrying the grog and supplies broke down seven miles south of the actual creek so the wagon was unloaded and the town was established there. They had to get their priorities right after all.

OUR FIRST HOME TOGETHER

One hundred and fifty kilometres north of Tennant Creek we arrived at Helen Springs. Only a few kilometres off the bitumen of the Stuart Highway, it was a very civilised place compared to the Kimberley stations. Tim and I were shown to the visitors' quarters, a substantial and attractive building set among green lawns, athel pines, oleanders and poincianas. Three bedrooms and a large living–dining room, all enclosed with a fly-wired verandah. Right in the middle of all the station buildings, it was not the most desirable place to spend the first days of marriage, but fortunately it was only for three weeks while our permanent accommodation was being refurbished.

This was to be four kilometres away on the Stuart Highway at the company's Maryville Road Train Base. This had been rented to Noel Buntine of Buntine Roadways (now Roadtrains of Australia) fame, but the company had retained the use of the manager's residence, which was a lovely building perfectly designed for the climate. It had louvres along both sides of the bedrooms and living areas and substantial verandahs on either side, which made living conditions reasonably bearable in that climate.

It was to be a totally different life for Tim, pulled away from his beloved stock camp and horses, and it wasn't till years later that I realised what a sacrifice he had made.

Not long after we were married, Tim decided to compete in the buckjump event at the Renner Springs Rodeo. He was a very good horseman but not a buckjump rider, so I guess he was just trying to impress me.

He mounted the horse in the chute and the gate opened. Tim's horse flew out at the gallop, right to the far side of the arena, then it dropped its head in no uncertain manner. This type of buckjumper is commonly called a "bolter", and makes for a difficult ride as the competitor doesn't know when it is suddenly going to "drop its head." Tim had no hope, he was speared unceremoniously on to the ground! Unhurt but shaken and dusty, he regained his feet and walked off the arena, and that was the last time he ever rode in a buckjump event.

The Barkly Tableland is mostly treeless and flat, interspersed with the odd tongue of desert (red, scrubby, anthill country) thrown in, and big tracts of low-lying bluebush country that in big floods could cut the station in two. In the big wet season of 1974, this water went all the way to the Corella Waterhole on Brunette Downs, roughly 180 kilometres to the east. Only the top of the windmill in the Bluebush Paddock on Helen Springs could be seen above the water.

The only consolation was that the Helen Springs horses were known for their high standard and ability, and this factor helped to make up for leaving the beauty of the Kimberley. As the station was at the time a bullock depot for the company's western steers, there was lots of drafting out bullocks on the open camp, another factor that pleased us both.

This differs from competition drafting as the cattle are held in the open. One man goes in and cuts out a bullock then the men on the face of the camp guide it to the cut, which is held by a couple of stockmen away from the main mob.

Usually the cutting was done by the manager, overseer, head stockman and occasionally a jackaroo, but being the overseer's wife, I was occasionally allowed to partake in this most stimulating activity. Working on the face of the camp was also fun, but the worst places to be were the back of the cattle or holding the cut.

At the beginning of every mustering season, the manager would attend the drafting of the horses through the yard to allocate each man with his horse plant for the first six weeks or so of mustering. He would sit on the rail with the Horse Yard Book and mark off each horse as it went through: overseer, head stockman, stockman, jackaroo, camp horse, night horse, breaker, brood mare, pensioner etc.

Night horses were kept especially for watching cattle at night when no yard was available. They had to be good stock horses, quiet, sure-footed and equipped with excellent night vision, and were used for nothing but night watching.

When there was no yard available for the cattle, they would have to be watched, two stockmen riding round the mob all night, usually singing or making some noise so the cattle were less likely to be spooked and rush.

The night horse would be tied up all night in the event of a rush happening. Tim recalls one time when the cattle rushed and, when it was over, it was found that the night horse had rubbed the bit out of its mouth, but had done the blocking job basically without any guidance from its rider.

Each man would be allocated six horses, which would be given a trial if a horse was known to be inclined to buck. Great entertainment followed as the horses would be very fresh after a four- to five-month spell on good country over the wet season. New jackaroos were given an opportunity to show their skill or learn how to fall off!

Then the hard work came — everyone had to shoe their plant. A steep learning curve if you were fresh from the city, but the head stockman or experienced jackaroos would lend a hand to a green horn. Later on when females started to make up large members of the workforce, they too were thrown in the deep end at the end of a shoeing hammer.

Naturally, Tim would shoe my horses, but I did later learn how to do it myself. My shoeing was not pretty and I struggled to hit the nails accurately, but at least the shoes stayed on. Tim was an expert — he could nail on four shoes in twenty minutes, which must be somewhat of a record.

Now I believe some of the larger stations employ a contract farrier to shoe the entire plant.

After six weeks or so in the mustering camp, the horses would be pretty well burnt out, so they were bushed and another plant mustered.

Wally and Ivy were the managers, and Wally allotted Tim with a horse plant and gave me a great old horse, a big black gelding called Sambo, and a lovable and reliable chestnut gelding called Two Bob. Soon after we arrived, Tim took me out in the stock camp to join a muster.

MY FIRST MUSTER

We were mustering out from No 12 bore in a bit of desert country on the edge of the blacksoil plain. It is normal to ride in a group, not single file like "Brown's cows", so I was riding along quietly with the mob. Suddenly, I found myself on my own, left behind with nothing but a cloud of dust! They had spotted cattle and the rush was on to be the first to wheel the lead. I had no idea what was happening or where they had gone, and Tim, as I have said before, a man of few words, had told me nothing.

I tried to follow but even the dust disappeared. What to do? Not familiar with the country, I just sat and thought for a while, hoping someone would turn up. But no one did. I suppose I didn't know the rules of the bush then, which are when lost, stay in the one place. I rode around hoping Sambo would know where to go, but where was that? With the knowledge that I have gained since, I could have easily tracked the musterers as they were all riding shod horses, but I was basically just a city slicker then.

Eventually, I came across a cattle pad leading into a bore and followed that until I came to — the stock camp! This was some hours after I had got lost, the manager had been summoned and they were in the process of lighting up a pile of tyres so I could locate them.

Once again, I was feeling a bit sheepish. (I wonder where that expression comes from, after all sheep are SUPPOSED to be dumb, aren't they?)

The other episode that sticks in my mind is craving for water on another muster. The stock camp buggy usually goes along ahead of the musterers to set up "dinner camp", when everyone has a break and a change of horses if necessary. On this particular occasion, the camp cook got bushed and we weren't able to partake of the usual drink of water and pannikin of tea.

Thirst comes quickly in that country, even if not mid-summer. We set off to ride back to No 1 bore but I, not used to the conditions, soon became very thirsty — after all, we had been going since just after daylight. In fact, I became so thirsty that I started to get off my horse and try to find shade behind clumps of grass, impossible of course, but this is the sort of thing that thirsty people do. None of this was helped by the fact that we could see the windmill at No. 1 but it never seemed to get any closer.

My gallant husband to the rescue. He trotted in to the bore, leaving me and the other musterers (who weren't suffering as much as I was) and came back with a Land Rover and plenty of — WATER. My only experience of this nature and one I didn't want to repeat.

It came to my attention towards the end of the season that someone had complained about my being in the stock camp. In those days, it was pretty unusual for a female to be in the camp, but I just couldn't sit around and miss out on all that lovely horse work. I felt I got on well with all the jackaroos and the head stockman, Des Stenhouse, and when he enquired no one claimed responsibility for this act.

In fact, I think they were more than happy to have me there as I usually arrived armed with Anzac biscuits and fruit cakes to supplement the cook's rations, so I continued to enjoy life in the camp.

It was years later that I found out who had complained, and it came from a most unexpected quarter. Neighbour Allan Hagan, who was on Muckaty Station, told us that it was the manager's wife who had complained. I think she was probably jealous that I was out there having all the fun while she was stuck at the station doing the cooking. I didn't blame her really. We got on well with Wally and Ivy socially, and would usually have a drink with them at knock off time. I was relieved that it hadn't been one of the stock camp men.

I BECOME THE MANAGER'S WIFE

1966 was coming to a close when Tim was offered the management of Cattle Creek Station, an extremely isolated station in the Tanami Desert, seventy kilometres east of Wave Hill Station and some five hundred kilometres from Katherine. This was pure joy to us as at last we could be more or less on our own, as there were only a few Aboriginals there and one jackaroo. It was the company's bull breeding depot and incorporated blacksoil plains as well as lots of desert country.

I now became the MANAGER'S WIFE!

The bull breeding was a rather hit and miss affair, and the operation ceased not long after we were there when Cattle Creek became an outstation of Wave Hill. The Vestey homesteads were built with the extremes of weather in mind. They mostly consisted of two or three bedrooms, a lounge room, dining room and kitchen in row, with wide fly-wired verandahs on either side.

The lighting plants were 32 volts and these only provided lights at night as they were turned off on retiring. Fuel stoves and kerosene fridges completed the domestic requirements — cooling was just an occasional breeze if one was lucky.

We had a delightful Aboriginal couple working for us at Cattle Creek. Captain Major and Amy were their names and they had their own quarters and kitchen. Each afternoon, Amy would come to me for rations and I would give her beef and vegetables.

One time she said, "You gott 'im dat shold, Mishus?"

"What 'that shold', Amy?" I asked.

"Shold, Mishus, shold."

Eventually I figured out that she wanted salt! Amy would cook their meals in her kitchen, and they would sit up with a tablecloth and knives and forks while Tim and I roughed it with no such trappings. Except on Saturday nights.

Social life was very limited at Cattle Creek, so every Saturday night we would give ourselves a dinner party. Place mats, candles, three courses and wine, it was like going to a restaurant.

Occasionally a jackaroo was sent over from Wave Hill to give us a hand, and the bookkeeper came once a month to do wages etc. His name was Ben Winston, nicknamed Furry Fingers. I don't know whether this was because he had hair on the back of his fingers or because he was a bit light-fingered, as he was later sent to gaol for adding a zero on to the wages of the Aboriginals. However, we always enjoyed his visits and the bottle of whisky he plied us with.

Later on he stayed with us at Manbulloo on his way to the lockup in Darwin.

CAPTAIN MAJOR GOES TO CANBERRA

At this time, after unrest at Wave Hill, Aboriginals were being more involved in decision-making. To this end, our Captain Major was summoned to Canberra. Poor Major, he didn't have a clue what it was all about, but all the same he became very excited. Tim fitted him out with a white shirt and tie and he became all puffed up with shy importance. We drove him to Wave Hill where he caught the plane to Katherine and on to Canberra.

He came back a couple of weeks later, still the same, delightful Captain Major, totally unaffected by the experience. Later that year, we sold him our honeymoon ute as we needed a station wagon, and he became more "puffed up" than ever.

At one stage, we were isolated for six weeks owing to a big wet season. The only perishables we had left were a few potatoes and the outside leaves of cabbages in the vegetable garden. (Plenty of hard rations in the store though.)

The general manager, Mr Peter Morris, somehow heard of our plight and flew in with a planeload of luxuries. We weren't worried, though, as long as we were together we were happy, and we always had plenty of beef. We sat round the fuel stove that night chatting amiably with Mr Morris.

Cattle Creek was a weather station, and I would do the observations three times a day, at six and nine in the morning and three in the afternoon, then relay this over the two-way radio to Darwin. I can still remember — "Cattle Creek Obs. Synop. (Observations Synoptic) …", then send details of temperature, maximum and minimum, rainfall, cloud type and height, and wind. It's interesting that these weather stations were dotted all over the north, and still play an important role today.

One of my enduring memories of Cattle Creek is of the many flocks of budgerigars — millions of them — that would weave endlessly in their fascinating patterns in the blue sky. Evidently, they do this for protection from predators.

THE KOOKABURRA TRAGEDY

Cattle Creek became famous when the aviators, Anderson and Hitchcock, became lost in 1929 while searching for the missing Charles Kingsford-Smith and the *Southern Cross*. They had taken off in the *Kookaburra,* a single engine Westland Widgeon, from Richmond in New South Wales and headed north via Broken Hill and Alice Springs.

The *Kookaburra* had engine trouble and was forced to land on Cattle Creek just east of the station, but then, after doing repairs, they were unable to clear a suitable area for take-off. They were ill-equipped for such a journey having limited water and food, so they perished — one under the wing and one some distance from the aircraft, apparently hoping to find help.

The plane was finally located in 1978 by businessman, pilot and adventurer Dick Smith after his second attempt, and the remains of the aircraft were moved to a public display at the Central Australian Aviation Museum. Such a tragic story and one that created much bad publicity for Kingsford-Smith.

You may have heard of raining fish? Well at Cattle Creek we experienced it first-hand. Numerous trees had been planted and they had rings of dirt built up around them for the purpose of retaining water. One time we had heavy rain, and there they were — each tree surround was full of tiny fish. Quite amazing to have experienced such a phenomenon which we experienced once again later on at Helen Springs.

During the early part of 1967, I became pregnant with our first child. Joy, oh joy! The extreme isolation didn't worry us. I just bought a book called *You and Your Baby* and it became my bible throughout child-rearing. There was no one around to give advice and I was totally ignorant about everything connected with the process. I still have this treasured book in my library.

The Flying Doctor called once to give me a check-up and declared everything was going well after a brief consultation on the bed in the plane. I was terribly ignorant about the procedure and didn't even know it was called "confinement". So I wrote to the Katherine Hospital asking to be booked in for "hospitalisation for childbirth". I have such a laugh about all this now.

Two weeks before the due date, I moved to Manbulloo Station, another Vestey station about ten kilometres out of Katherine. Here I mated up with Sue Mackey, who became a close friend till her death from cancer at the dreadfully young age of thirty-nine. Our paths were to cross many times during the next seventeen years.

ANDREW COMES INTO THE WORLD

On the morning of the baby's arrival, after the waters broke, Sue took me into Katherine Hospital. I had never been in hospital before and thought the sensible thing would be just to stay in my nightie and brunch coat. Not surprisingly, I attracted a few stares, and I still feel embarrassed at the thought.

Andrew was born at one o'clock in the afternoon after a reasonable birth. I won't say it was without pain, but my only concession to assistance was to have oxygen, which seemed to help along with correct breathing techniques. Andrew, however, was not so keen to come out. The cord became wrapped round his neck and the doctor was obliged to perform an episiotomy. I always had the feeling that he had been unnecessarily savage with the knife when he performed this operation, so I never did feel comfortable with him.

This caused me more trauma than the whole birthing procedure, as climbing into the high bed every day for a week afterwards was particularly painful. The nurses would haul you out of bed at about five in the morning after barely any sleep to change the sheets. I think hospital procedures might be more compassionate these days.

Tim was able to come in the next day and was I glad to see him. Strangely enough, I envisaged that the hairs on his arms had grown thicker, but I think this might have been a figment of my fuzzy imagination.

After a week in hospital, we were allowed to travel back to Cattle Creek. Andrew spent his first night out of the hospital camped in a meat safe cot on the bonnet of the car so the ants wouldn't get him. Tim and I had our swag, of course.

During the heat of the day, it was October and getting towards the wet season, the only way we could keep Andrew cool was to put his cot out in the cement gutter surrounding the homestead. On the southern side of the house, this was quite effective.

ANOTHER TRANSFER

After only a year at Cattle Creek, Tim was offered the management of Manbulloo Station after Bernie Warren had taken over the management of Mountain Valley Station, owned by an American Company, Dillingham Corporation. Bernie's nickname was "Big Eye", and most of the staff went with him, leaving Tim to start with a new broom in the labour department.

I was told of an amusing incident that took place when Bernie was manager. He had built a tennis court beside the homestead and had his Land Rover inside while he hitched up the last of the wire. His wife Jess was watching him from the homestead verandah but made no attempt to let Bernie know that he had just fenced himself in. She just stood there with an amused grin on her face until Bernie woke up and had to cut the wire again.

To take over from Tim at Cattle Creek was a fellow called Bill Petrie, with his wife Ina. They came and lived with us for a week or so while we showed them the ropes. Bill was an expert on the guitar and the only man I ever knew who could play the "Moonlight Sonata" on that instrument. I had a pet peewee at the time, and strangely enough, this big strong man was afraid of the bird. It had a habit of landing on people's heads and Bill became quite agitated. The bird eventually joined its bush mates.

Just before our departure for Manbulloo, we were invited to a farewell party for Tom Fisher, the manager of Wave Hill. Tom had been with the company for decades and had earned the nickname "The Tropical Frog" owing to his short, stout stature.

As Tim had more or less handed over to Bill, he let him drive the one and a half tonne Bedford that was our means of transport the eighty kilometres to Wave. That was okay on the way over, but on the way home Bill was a bit full, and it was a very nervous manager's wife who clung on for dear life on the back of the truck, swaying from one side of the road to the other. I had been hoping that Tim would take over, but as he had already handed over the management to Bill, he just sat it out on the back with me. Fortunately, we had left Andrew with Amy.

The fellow taking over the management of Wave was a colourful Territory character, Frank Wilmington. Frank had been Vesteys' droving boss and he was able to navigate by the stars. He had innovative nicknames such as "The Hollywood Cowboy", because of his habit of turning up his collar when the ladies were around, "The Bush Cockroach", probably because of certain habits these insects displayed, and also the plainer "Jambar" — I have no idea where the latter came from. Ever the gentleman, he was quite a hit with the ladies.

The transfer to Manbulloo was a considerable promotion as it was a much bigger management than Cattle Creek. The company was about to embark on a big pasture improvement program. For this enterprise, Tim was to be paid the grand salary of $4000 per annum, but I wouldn't be on the payroll. Who needed to be paid to live an idyllic life?

Manbulloo was 3800 square kilometres, in a beautiful location perched on the bank of the Katherine River, to which it had about seventy kilometres of frontage. Immediately below the homestead was a deep, green, mysterious looking waterhole where we would swim every afternoon after work. I would have to be very brave to swim there now as crocodile numbers have increased exponentially since they became protected, but in 1968 they were rare.

Crocodiles can inhabit salt water, fresh water as well as land and are protected, whereas sharks can only survive in the ocean and most species are not protected. Crocodiles now occur in almost plague proportions as they have no predators, so it is an anomaly to me.

The approach to the Manbulloo homestead was a very pleasant vista. There were sweeping lawns interspersed with eucalypts, tamarinds and jacarandas festooned with bougainvillea, all fighting each other to reach the top branches of the trees. Bernie had installed monsoon sprinklers so no matter what the season, this was always an oasis.

First the tennis court, then a sprawling, gracious homestead and outdoor smoko area, then bookkeepers quarters, top dining room, kitchen, men's dining room, laundry, then men's quarters, both old and new.

On the other side of the entrance road there were horse and cattle yards, the store and office, workshop and vehicle parking bay, and a very substantial vegetable garden. Further on, about eighty metres, was the Aboriginal camp of substantial buildings.

The country was typical Top End country, that is, long grass, very protein deficient but supporting millions of trees. It was very poor cattle country and it was a testament to the Shorthorn breed that they survived at all.

Shorthorns had been the mainstay of the cattle industry, basically since settlement, and in uncontrolled herds where outside genetics were rarely introduced, their ability to not "run out" made them superior to other breeds at the time. Despite the protein deficiency, they continued to have high fertility rates and reasonable carcase attributes.

Manbulloo was running about four thousand breeders. To enable them to survive the dry season, calves were weaned very early and sent to Helen Springs to grow out and fatten.

The introduction of Brahmans into Northern Australia greatly increased the profitability of the cattle industry owing to their adaptability to the extremes of climate and their resistance to ticks. The Beebes at Ucharonidge Station on the Barkly Tableland were among the first to introduce this breed into the Territory in the mid sixties, after which bulls were imported in their thousands.

Owing to Manbulloo's proximity to town, it had unique features compared to other Vestey stations. Two-forty volt power was a very welcome improvement over the western stations. Owing to the many company visitors who traversed the Territory on their way to and from Darwin or the western stations, we rarely had a night to ourselves and were constantly entertaining.

A bomber strip had been built at Manbulloo in May 1942 after Katherine had been attacked by the Japanese in March of that year. Amazingly, only one man was killed in that attack. When we were there, the only evidence of this was the runway, as all the buildings had either been destroyed or fallen into disrepair.

The other notable wartime construction was an abattoir. This was built on the banks of the Katherine River on a twenty-five-hectare site. It was a pretty substantial affair, with forty-six buildings including mess huts, barracks, mess halls, freezing works and, of course, the abattoir itself. Poultry yards and market gardens completed the picture, and up to seven hundred head of cattle a week were slaughtered. The meat was made into bully beef and used to supply the army. Labour was supplemented with a camp of about one hundred Aboriginals.

Owing to the fact that the buildings were dismantled or pushed into the river, there is very little left as a record of this important contribution to the war effort. Tim and I were once shown its location, but it was very hard to find and only cement pillars and slabs remained.

NEW STAFF

We were able to gradually assemble around us a capable and loyal staff. Des Stenhouse, the head stockman from Helen Springs, joined us. Graeme "Wixy" Wicks, who came up by bus from the Kingaroy area, Jim Scriven from Melbourne, Patrick Gaffney from Brisbane and Warwick Bates, nicknamed "Scales" owing to his penchant for collecting snakes, also from Melbourne, made up the team of jackaroos in the stock camp along with about half a dozen Aboriginals.

Scales was passionate about his snakes. One time, I saw him ascend to the top of a tall eucalypt, braving bougainvillea prickles and all, in order to capture a snake. Don't ask me what kind though, it didn't matter to Scales, he loved them, poisonous or harmless.

He used to love to sleep with a snake in a chaff bag. He would have a peaceful night in the swag as, not surprisingly, no other members of the stock camp would go near him.

Tim caught the bug a bit, too. One time, he allowed a huge python to wrap itself round his arm, but the snake had such a grip that he had trouble disentwining the reptile.

Other members of the white staff were Sue Mackey, who had come up from Helen Springs to do the cooking, Warrie Wegert, a mechanic, Stan Wilson, the horse breaker/saddler, and Jim Jackson, the bookkeeper/storekeeper, after whom the racecourse in Katherine is named.

Warrie was an amazing man. He could stop a motor by laying his forearm over the spark plugs, didn't seem to feel a thing.

Sadly, he had a nasty accident that affected him for the rest of his life. The Aboriginals had asked if he would give them a lift to Edith River, north of Katherine. Instead of driving himself, he let one of them drive, but they ran off the road somewhere on the Stuart Highway. Warrie had a badly injured arm. They all fled into the bush leaving Warrie for the first motorist that came along.

He had to have the arm amputated, and for the rest of his life, he suffered terrible phantom pains in the stump. Even copious quantities of rum could not ease the pain. He was not a vindictive man and never held any ill-feeling towards his passengers.

He soldiered on, though, and became the gardener. His only concession to being handicapped was to agree to use a Ladylite wheelbarrow, which only needed one hand.

Warrie and Nellie had a twenty-one-year-old grandson who lived in Alice Springs. Mark lived with his lovely girlfriend, had a successful career as a chef and didn't appear to have any lifestyle issues. One day, he mysteriously disappeared and there was nothing to indicate where he might have gone and why.

Six months later, the outcome was revealed when his body was found in the front of his utility many kilometres out in the desert country north-east of the Alice. Suicide and murder were both suspected, but as the body was in an advanced state of decomposition, no conclusion was ever reached. It was a terrible shock for his devoted family. (Postscript: on a recent trip to the Territory I was informed that it had, in fact, been suicide.)

In those days, most stations had two dining rooms, the "top" dining room was for the manager and his wife, the head stockman and jackaroos, bookkeeper and any visitors. The other dining room was the "men's", and was for all other staff, quite a class distinction in the old English style.

The top dining room would be set up with white tablecloth and meals would be brought from the kitchen in large serving dishes, which were then ceremoniously dished out by the manager. Earlier on, everyone would attend the evening meal adorned with shirts and ties, but this practice has largely been abandoned today. After a two-course meal, all would adjourn to the large creeper-covered smoko area for coffee. All very formal.

Bernie, the previous manager, had had an altercation with a man he found trespassing on the station with a rifle. Bernie had grabbed his rifle and bent it over a tree and told him to remove himself in no uncertain terms. Months later, this fellow snuck into the station and took a pot shot at Bernie in the dining room, but Bernie had been able to flick the rifle so the bullet lodged in the upper wall of the dining room, the mark of which can still be seen today.

The following few pages are excerpts written by Wixie from his experiences at Manbulloo while he was with us.

START OF WIXIE EXERPT

WIXIE'S STORY – MANBULLOO

I arrived in March 1969 at the end of the wet. One of the first jobs (stock camp had not got together yet, before Des's arrival) was to cut and brand a mob of mickeys (young male calves) that had been mustered (trapped) before the wet, but were too poor to process at the time.

Our "camp" consisted of Blucher, Manbulloo Pat, Greg Crawford, Tim, Patrick Gaffney and myself. It was at this point Tim's and my close relationship developed because, although a first year jackaroo, I was able to scruff any mickey that escaped the calf cradle while the allegedly more experienced hands couldn't.

As the dry was approaching, Tim took me to look around the run. We only got just beyond the old bomber strip when the Land Rover went down to the floorboards. I ran back to the homestead to get the tractor to pull us out.

It was during these first interactions that our bond began its unbreakable trend.

Continuing the bogged theme – Des Stenhouse and stock camp were mustering down at Laiger's Yard. We were riding along as a group, yarning, when suddenly we all found our horses floundering in quicksand in the middle of the bush. We had to dismount, give the horses a spell, then hoosh them along to get them out.

Des, being the character he was, was always using (to us louts) big words, which was apparently catching. Warwick Bates had a big brown horse that kept throwing him, so Des suggested a more competent rider take the sting out of him. Picking himself up, Scales retorted that it was his "prerogative" to ride the horse. Hence, Des and all of us made much out of this, and "prerogative" got a good workout from a vocabulary and physical point of view.

Scales had an issue with bulls, or they had an issue with him. At Bottom King, a big young bull broke and Scales and Des Dessai went to throw him. As Scales grabbed the bull's tail, the bull kicked up and Scales landed flat on his back with the bull standing over him, hooking his green jumper this way and that until Des clowned the bull off him. Scales never spoke for the rest of the morning and was pale as a ghost.

Prior to mustering to Laiger's Yard, Tim came on our first muster out. We were mustering in the vicinity of the old army camp. Des, Tim and I were riding out quite a distance from the coachers (quiet cattle), doing a wide sweep. Des and Tim were yarning amicably, with me (the boy) trailing behind. It was an overcast day and we rode past a concrete slab (old army hut) with the remnants of an old Crown stove on it.

A couple of hours later, we rode past the same old stove! Directions are a bit confusing on a cloudless day in that featureless country, and Tim and Des, yarning as they were, hadn't really concentrated on their whereabouts. We eventually caught up to the coachers.

On one other occasion, mustering down towards the Scotts Creek boundary, towards the river from Limestone, again it was an overcast day. We had just had dinner camp and Des was going to lead us back to camp. He headed in the opposite direction until Larry came to the rescue.

Manbulloo is notoriously poor horse and cattle country. Our horses would come in fresh, but with pot guts and ribby. Tim, being a very good husbandman, always made sure the horses used in the camp were well supplied with a jam tin of oats, half a jam tin of meat meal and a bit of coarse salt in nose bags, then Townsville lucerne hay on the horse camp each day. After six weeks mustering, the horses were let go fit to run a Melbourne Cup, and shining in prime condition.

Tim was the easiest man to work for. Greg Crawford had dislocated his shoulder from memory, so his "light duties" were to paint the store roof. I had dislocated my left collarbone in a horse fall while mustering. My "light duties" were driving the old Bedford truck, picking up bulls the stock camp had thrown and tied in the bush.

As I brought one such load into the Katherine Meatworks, Des was fortunately with me. As we got to the top of a rise on the bitumen, the police had a road check set up just on the downward slope.

A big old copper strutted out into the middle of my path, summoning me to pull up. Fortunately, I had started gearing down when I topped the rise as I suspected the brakes weren't the best. The policeman held his ground, but we were still travelling down the hill fairly fast. As he encountered the bull bar, Des yelled out, "Got no brakes."

I was in a flap trying to control the truck, and terrified, envisioning a long "holiday" in Fanny Bay Gaol. One hundred metres further on, we pulled over. The policeman had scrambled sideways off the bull bar, and now came to the window. At an impressive one hundred words a minute, Des tried to explain the situation while I mentally examined my underwear. All's well that ends well. The copper survived and I had to front up on Monday with my truck licence, only recently acquired, and the repaired truck to the police station. I was sent home with a whole lot of relief and education.

So much for light duties and a strong sense of obligation to my new-found family, Tim Doran and stock camp.

The Aboriginals were undeniably the most loyal, good-humored and trustworthy people I worked with. Manbulloo Larry was the best horse tailer, tracker and bushman I have ever come across. When he was with the cattle, he always rode in the lead of the coachers. All the while he'd be looking for fresh cattle tracks and would always be first to spot cattle.

He would sign to Des, having pulled up, and indicate direction by pointing with his lips to "something" probably three to four hundred metres in front. No matter how hard we whities looked, we could not see anything. On faith, two or three of us would ride a wide circle in the indicated direction and sure enough, there would be a small mob of cattle.

Larry took me under his wing and gave me lessons on tracking on a number of occasions. He taught me to look for as small a thing as a disturbed leaf or broken straw of grass, and if the track disappeared, to cut a wide circuit hoping to pick up the track a bit wider out.

Manbulloo had a mob of unbroken Ord River horses. These were slowly brought into use, being broken in seven at a time each week and sent out for us to work. There were no fences, so the horses were always hobbled out at night. On a couple of occasions, two or three of these youngsters would take off back towards Ord River, six hundred or so kilometres to the west. It was nothing for Ben or Larry to be gone for two or three days following, catching and bringing back these youngsters. They took no food or spares. Just lived off the land and always returned with the horses.

Dave Molloy was one camp cook we had. There are several names given to camp cooks, as they are a rare breed with unusual habits. We had a young fellow who used to like to sit on the camp ovens. Dave did not approve of this but said nothing. One evening, just after we had let our horses go and washed ready for tea, Dave filled the camp oven with hot coals. I'm sure even today you could identify that fellow by the scars on his nether regions.

Two of Dave's specialties were Burdekin Duck and Mysteries in Their Overcoats, which in fact turned out to be the same thing only on a different night — corned beef in batter.

Larry's wife was Nida. Nida went to the store one day to ask storekeeper Jim Jackson for a "milk trowsher". Because of the language barrier, Jim had difficulty understanding her, and asked her a second time what it was she wanted. Obviously now partly frustrated, Nida responded "milk trowsher, milk trowsher", vigorously cupping her hands under her pendulous breasts.

END OF WIXIE EXERPT

ABORIGINAL STAFF

There was a substantial camp of Aboriginals who had a very large compound of two-bedroom huts, an ablution block and a combined kitchen–dining room some eighty metres of so from the homestead complex. Most were on the payroll, but there were also pensioners and children, and all were fed, clothed, and supplied with blankets and nikki nikki or chewing tobacco, which was an essential requirement. In other words, whether they were on the payroll or not, they were all supplied with the essentials of life.

I have read stories in some sections of the media stating that they were fed "bones and offal". This may have been true when a beast was killed for rations, for on that night EVERYONE, both black and white, scrambled for rib bones and offal such as kidney, liver, brains, curly gut and sweetbread, all of which were considered luxuries.

They were always well supplied with tea and sugar, bread and beef and other rations, as well as luxuries on Christmas day such as lollies and soft drink.

They were a wonderful workforce, totally suited to station work. The men were great stockman, horsemen and trackers, and their ability in the bush is legendary. In the early days, the women also did stock work, but for some reason unknown to me that practice became illegal. They had a great sense of humour and readily laughed at the smallest joke.

It is tragic that a stroke of the pen in Canberra resulted in the majority of this workforce ending up in towns. Now many can be found dejected, drunk and unemployed. Subsequent reunions with previous workers result in expressions such as: "Ah Missus (or Maluka), we bin miss dat station life." They were a lovely people with a great sense of humour, and mostly a pleasure to work with. Honest as the day is long, you could leave $100 on the dressing table and nothing of any value would ever be touched.

Mob fights were not uncommon, but usually took place down at their camp. One time, I heard a commotion outside the laundry, and on investigation found Ellen and Ruby getting stuck into each other with sticks. Not much damage was done, but the commotion and screeches would suggest that there would be serious injuries, although this usually wasn't the case. When there was a death among them, they would beat their heads with stones till they bled, thereby creating "sorry wounds" that would have to be patched up.

Aboriginal laws were very effective in keeping law and order, and also preventing in-breeding. During initiation, some of the men would have an operation that would render them unable to reproduce, as well as the usual chest scars etc.

The young boys were also circumcised at the ceremony without any type of anaesthetic, apart from making them run until they were knocked up. Sometimes they would turn up days later with terrible infections and in awful pain.

Anyone breaking Aboriginal laws could be boomeranged in the legs, resulting in breakage and a permanent disability. Other punishment could be more severe, that is bone pointing and death.

The Kadaitcha Man or witch doctor had enormous powers, and if the bone was pointed at someone, death would inevitably result and no amount of care or nursing could save them. They had been "sung".

When white man law was introduced, it was very conflicting for them. Sometimes, when appearing in court, their limited understanding of some of the terminology resulted in great confusion.

The Aboriginal children on Manbulloo, of which there were about seven, all attended school, and it was my job to transport them there in the back of the ute to Katherine, a service for which I was paid by the government.

Owing to our proximity to town, there were constant problems with alcohol and the Aboriginals, who were not supposed to drink at that time. As their camp was perched on the banks of the river, it was easy for townspeople to sneak grog into the camp, and disruptions were many and violent. To help alleviate this problem,

Bernie had set up searchlights that could be switched on from the homestead.

On these occasions, it was amusing to see figures running in all directions, both black and white, mainly for the river, which provided a handy escape route. Occasionally a taxi would come in and deliver grog by that means if it managed to sneak through without being intercepted by Tim.

The grog factor presented us with labour problems and we would end up with a skeleton staff. No one had to work hard, but all were an essential part of a forever turning wheel, and absences were difficult to accommodate.

One time, Tim and I made the mistake of holding back the beef ration, and we had a real strike on our hands! That was a lesson to us, bread and beef, tea and sugar were their most important staples, and ones that you didn't use as bargaining tools.

Most of the Aboriginals were on the payroll and, when sober, were a great workforce. There was Larry and Nida, Pat and Queenie, Albert and Ruby, Alec and Burrundilla Ruby, Blucher and Daisy, and Jimmy and Ellen.

Nida and Ellen were in the laundry and taught me how to iron a huge tablecloth, Ruby was in the kitchen and used to make the daily bread by kneeling on the kitchen table in front of a huge tub of dough, kneading away with her hands. Burrundilla Ruby was in the visitors' quarters and kept everything spotless for the numerous guests, including delivering early morning cups of tea, Sally was in the men's quarters and Daisy ruled over the homestead.

Daisy very kindly gave me a coolamon, which the Aboriginals used to transport food as well as their babies. They were usually made out of paperbark and were a very clever design, enabling a baby to sleep on them in complete safety and ensuring that the baby had a nice straight back.

On most Saturday nights, Queenie would sidle up to me and say, "Missus, we go dem pictures tonight?"

I could never say no, so the horse float would be lined up at the house and all were happily loaded in. It was always amusing to watch the faces of the open-air theatregoers when we dropped the tailgate and unloaded our rather unusual cargo!

CLEANSKIN BULLS

There were still a lot of cleanskin bulls and mickeys roaming around. When the opportunity arose, Tim would knock one over with the Land Rover bull bar, and while they were pinned to the ground, would leap out, put a rope around their horns and tie them to a tree (trees were everywhere). They were not hurt in the knocking down process, but owing to the nature of the country, the chase was extremely exciting.

Later on, the station's truck would come along and pick them up and take them to the meatworks, which was then functioning in Katherine.

In this manner, Tim sent many bulls to the meatworks, and occasionally I was lucky enough to accompany him on one of these wild dashes through the scrub after a bull. It was fairly dangerous work owing to the nature of the country, long grass littered with ant hills and shrubby trees. But it was terribly exciting and I couldn't resist.

Tim managed to pay the running expenses for the station for one year from these bulls, though I don't think the company would have been impressed as it wasn't exactly company policy for the manager to be bull catching.

One time, Warwick Bates was going to leg rope a tied bull when the head rope break. Warwick had to leave the scene in a considerable hurry.

The bull was fairly angry and breathing down his back, and its horns were hooking him either side of his ribcage. Then Warwick fell over! It looked as though a disaster was unfolding, but the bull just galloped over the top of him and took off into the scrub. It had only wanted to escape.

Originally, bulls were either shot or thrown from a horse and cut, dehorned and released, but when the Yanks discovered their meat was perfect for hamburgers, a whole new strategy regarding bulls was developed.

At the beginning, they would be knocked down with a specially developed short wheelbase Toyota. This was then made more sophisticated with the use of the "bionic arm", which made for much safer and more efficient handling of the animals.

In 1963, the Hooker Company opened a meatworks in Katherine called Northmeat to accommodate this trade, which thrived. The meatworks burnt down in 1969, but were rebuilt in four months. In 2002, the meatworks closed for good after years of ups and downs for various reasons too numerous to document here. It had been such a boon for Manbulloo, as the bulls only had to be carted nine kilometres for processing.

ANDREW

Andrew was an easy baby and settled into station life very quickly. I was lucky to have two willing babysitters — Sue loved Andrew and was happy to look after him whenever she was able, and Daisy was constantly in his path making sure that no harm came to him. She also gave him his night-time bath. This enabled me to go out on the run and enjoy the odd muster still. I had Bernie Warren's horse Cindy in my plant, and built a set of show jumps that gave Cindy and me endless pleasure.

TWO BOB

We had contacted Wally Atkinson, manager of Helen Springs, to see if he would send up my horse, Two Bob. To this he agreed, so I had a good horse plant again and Two Bob turned out to be a great kid's horse.

Later on, Two Bob somehow contracted the dreaded colic. I would leave no stone unturned to save his life, and for three days and two nights there was either Tim or I or one of the staff watching over him. The vet dosed him with paraffin oil and we propped him up with hay bales to prevent him from lying down, as this can result in a twisted bowel and quite often death.

Miraculously, he survived and lived for many more years. I really thought he was going to die and I didn't want to go through that again.

Manbulloo had a substantial set of horse and cattle yards at the station, as well as numerous small paddocks, so it was eminently suitable for the popular rodeo and campdraft held a couple of times a year. Tim was made president of the rodeo club and I eventually became president of the pony club, as Manbulloo was convenient for all the townspeople to compete and spectate.

There were three substantial, beautiful lily-clad waterholes on Manbulloo, named Cowai, Wongalla and Longreach. These had been fenced and traps set into them to catch any elusive cattle. Towards the end of the year, Tim would send out someone to pump out any small waterholes that remained, thus forcing cattle to water in the trap yards.

THE PARTY

Tim and I decided to have a party one Saturday night and, to quote a line from a famous poem by AB Paterson, "All the toffs gathered to the fray." Apart from staff and people from surrounding stations, a couple of notable Territory characters were in attendance.

Shorty Hayes, or Lyn, was a popular, well-known, lovable Territory rogue. A brilliant horseman and cattleman, he spun many colourful yarns and could go well into the night plying his audience with copious quantities of grog and stories. At our party, he was getting a bit wild, so his wife Patsy grabbed him by the scruff, marched him down the hall and into the shower, then she turned on the cold water!

If you stayed on the right side of Shorty, he was a loyal friend, but heaven help anyone who crossed him. One unfortunate fellow did just that, so Shorty got in his bulldozer and flattened some of his buildings.

We were great mates with him, and Tim turned a blind eye when he got the odd "killer" from Manbulloo. It was not uncommon practice in those days for battlers to help themselves to a bit of beef from the large company stations. Not that Shorty was a battler, he ran many successful businesses round Katherine, but he also went broke a few times!

His older brother Ralph managed Vesteys' Wave Hill Station for many years, and Ralph's wife Thea has become a well-known author publishing her popular books *An Outback Nurse* and *A Country Nurse*.

Younger brother Milton managed Vesteys' Gordon Downs Station in the Western Australian section of the Tanami Desert, and all three brothers were well-known throughout the north. We attended Milton's wedding when he married Madeline, and it was another memorable Territory occasion, lasting a few days.

Along with Rob and Graham Fulcher, we all remain close friends.

The other legendary character present at that party was Jack Vitnell, immortalised in the book *The Gun Ringer* by Geoff Allen. He was utterly fearless and excelled at rough riding, bull throwing, roping, whip cracking, campdafting, fighting and boozing.

This last attribute, however, led to his undoing. In January 1970, Jack and his mate had been doing some fencing outside the newly established town of Kununurra when they went on a bender.

After two weeks on the rum, they suddenly found they were out of water. His mate took off for Wyndham, but was arrested for apparently being drunk and put in the clink for the night. This delay had a bad outcome, for when his mate finally got back to Jack he was dead.

A tragic end at the age of forty for one of the Territory's unique characters.

We had two unexpected visitors during that party. Unannounced, Mr Roy Bell, the general manager from Sydney, and Mr Cec Watts, the pastoral inspector from Darwin, suddenly appeared from the smoko area. To say we were stunned was a complete understatement.

The only place quiet enough to conduct business was in the men's dining room, so that's where the four of us adjourned. Such a shame to have to leave a beaut party, but we were able to return after a couple of hours, considerably soberer.

Roy Bell was a far cry from the previous general manager, Mr Peter Morris, who would advise exactly what time and date he would be arriving. Then all station staff would be thrown into a tizz polishing and cleaning, sweeping and mopping. We treated him like royalty, and he was a great bloke and much respected by all company personnel. Mr Bell, also a beaut boss, took a much more casual approach to his visits and would arrive sometimes with barely a day's notice.

Towards the middle of 1968, I became pregnant again. Don't let anyone tell you that you can't get pregnant while breastfeeding, because it's just a big lie!

"AUNTIE LISA" COMES INTO OUR LIVES

Meantime, head stockman Des Stenhouse had returned from Melbourne with a wife — Elisabeth. I will never forget my first meeting with this lovely lady — she turned up at the homestead wearing a skirt and blouse and — thongs with socks! I think I might have stared a bit, but soon regained my composure.

Elisabeth had been born in Germany in 1932, and had suffered many awful deprivations during the war. Her family life was a very unhappy one, made so by a mother who left them at an early age and a controlling father who beat the children. One brother was killed in the bombing of Dresden, and another brother was seconded into the Hitler Youth then later handed over to the SS. Fortunately, Elisa had a loving grandfather, so her early life was probably made bearable by the kind acts of this man. It is amazing that, despite all these hardships, she was always cheerful and positive. We became good friends and stayed so till her death in 2018 at the age of eighty-six.

She had married a German in Australia but eventually divorced him, met Des, married and lived a much happier life in the Northern Territory.

Hardworking and always cheerful, Elisabeth set about making a comfortable and attractive home out of the old men's quarters, which were fairly primitive to say the least, but the only accommodation we had available for a married couple at the time.

She had three sons. The oldest, Christian, was killed in a helicopter crash, but her twins are both still alive and well and living in New South Wales. Christian's death was a great blow to Elisa, but she managed to soldier on, through the death of husband Des, until her own departure from this earth.

SOPHIE COMES INTO THE WORLD

Confinement time was approaching for me again in February 1969. Des was amazed that I was still planting trees in the garden the day before our beautiful daughter was born. He thought I would be in hospital for a couple of weeks prior!

The doctor in the Katherine Hospital was a bit slow attending to the birth, so Tim had the pleasure of performing that task. I was very grateful as the doctor who eventually arrived was the same doctor who had attended to me at Andrew's birth, so I was very happy to have Tim there instead and fortunately there were no complications this time.

Meanwhile Sue, our cook and close friend, met Des Smith, a contractor working on the huge pasture improvement program on the station.

He was contracted to plough thousands of hectares in order to plant Townsville lucerne (now called Townsville stylo), which had to be very carefully managed to enable the new pasture to survive the rigorous growth of the inferior native pastures during the wet season.

On a visit to Manbulloo during the 2000s, we were informed that the improved pasture had succumbed to some bug and was no longer evident. The Townsville stylo did, however, survive along the roadsides, and can now be found on thousands of kilometres of roadside verges.

A VERY MEMORABLE WEDDING

Des and Sue's wedding on the station will never be forgotten by those who attended, and even many who didn't attend but heard of the memorable occasion. The reception lasted for three days, with guests coming from all over the Territory and from Western Australia.

Ralph and Thea Hayes and sons, plus Milton and Madeline and their young son Danny, all drove over from Gordon Downs Station in Western Australia. Ralph, being in the Vestey mould of economising with expenses, decided they would all go in a Toyota Land Cruiser ute together.

As Madeline had a new baby, Danny, she had prime position in the front, with Ralph driving while Thea sat in the back with her three boys, along with Milton and all the luggage, including their swags. You could say they were fairly heavily laden.

They called in to Wave Hill to pick up Nita Beebe, whose partner was Don Hoare, a well-known Territory character and fencing contractor about whom a book could also be written.

Tim and I put them all up at the homestead, apart from Nita, who had gone to Katherine. That night we had a hens' party for Sue, while the bucks party for Des was conducted in the old storeroom out the back. In true Territory style, the bucks party was a wild affair. At some stage, some innovative character welded Des's leg to a post, rendering him out of action for some time. They must have cut the link, as Des made it to his nuptials the next day in one piece.

There were six girls, including Des's sister who had flown up from Perth for the occasion. A fairly conservative lady, she appeared to be fitting in quite well when we heard a sudden noise and turned to see Graham Fulcher wandering unstably towards us. He parked himself down in our midst then rose and said, "Greetings ladies!"

and let go with a resounding fart, not once, but several times! We Territory girls shrieked with laughter, but not our Perth friend — she was not amused.

At the wedding, the organist started to play "Here Comes the Bride" and everyone turned to look. Des's sister was heard to gasp in horror when she saw Sue — she was resplendent in a red chiffon dress with white spots, while we bridesmaids wore white dresses with red spots! Unfortunately, Des had omitted to inform his sister that Sue had been married previously, and the poor woman never really recovered from the shock of seeing the bride in red.

Sadly, only a few short years later, we followed Sue down the same aisle, only this time in a coffin. She died of cancer at the too young age of thirty-nine.

Next morning, everyone adjourned to the Katherine River, where we swam and lay around on a lovely sandy beach. There was a terrible scatter when Jim Jackson, our bookkeeper, drove down the riverbank and nearly ran over baby Danny, who was asleep in his coolamon.

All good things come to an end, and next day Ralph decided that the Gordon Downs crew had better make a departure. They picked up Nita in Katherine and had gone about eighty kilometres down the Stuart Highway when their ute suddenly slowed down, then stopped. They were unable to do anything, but fortunately a road train was coming towards them.

It turned out to be Jack Beebe, Nita's brother, with a prime mover and three trailers, returning from one of the stations. (Jack later came to a sad end when he fell asleep under his Toyota and was run over and killed).

Jack suggested they chain Ralph's ute to the last trailer, so everyone climbed into the first trailer, except Madeline and Danny, who rode in the cabin, and Ralph, who stayed in the driver's seat of the ute. What a drama he was about to experience.

They took off — dust and manure were billowing all round the people in the back, who had to bury their heads in their laps in order to breathe. Poor Ralph was being thrown from one side of the road to the other. The only saving grace was that no vehicles came from the opposite direction or goodness knows what Ralph's fate might have been.

Fortunately, after a few miles, Jack decided he had better check on Ralph, an act which probably saved his life. So they left the Toyota on the side of the road, much to Ralph's relief, and all climbed into their life-saving road train and returned to Manbulloo, where Tim and I had beds waiting.

The ladies and children rested at the station while the men returned and towed the ute back to Manbulloo for repairs. Ralph became very irate when he located the problem — someone had tampered with the rotor button, a very important part of an engine without which a vehicle is unable to function.

Someone had decided they didn't want the Gordon Downs mob to leave as it would break up the party. They never found out who the culprit was, but I had my suspicions that it was Shorty, Ralph's brother, who was quite capable of performing such trickery.

After the men had a bit of a camp, they all took off again, but had only travelled about two hundred kilometres when Nita suddenly cried out, "My suitcase is missing!" She had inadvertently left it on the side of the road, so back they went, eighty kilometres, and there it was, still propped up where she had left it.

The next drama for the poor souls was flat tyres when they were still 150 kilometres from Wave Hill. Milton and Thea walked the few kilometres to the Top Springs roadhouse around midnight. Fortunately, the proprietor, the well-known Mrs Hawkes, greeted them warmly and offered rooms for the women and children while the poor men repaired the tyres. They must have been pretty buggered by this time. Station people are made of tough stuff, but these events would have tested their endurance to the limit.

They took off once again in the early hours of the morning and finally arrived at Gordon Downs, just as the sun was coming up, to be greeted by a buzz of activity. They wondered what all the commotion was about — and soon found out.

"Ralph, Milton, dat bushfire, him bin get away and come dis way!" came the chorus from the Aboriginal staff. So the poor men had to go firefighting for the rest of that day and part of the next.

Thea thought that sometimes it was good to be a woman. Ralph considered that the bushfire was most likely caused by a lightning strike.

DES AND SUE

Des and Sue and Tim and I formed a pretty close relationship, and would congregate every night and have "cocktails". Des had been employed by the company to plough thousands of acres in preparation for the planting of Townsville lucerne, now called Townsville stylo.

Sue had previously formed a relationship with Stan, the horse breaker/saddler, but when she married Des, Stan became very angry and threw acid on Sue and a friend in Katherine one day. Fortunately, there were no serious repercussions, but it was a very disturbing time.

Life continued happily at Manbulloo with our two beautiful children, who always had willing babysitters. Apart from Daisy, Elisabeth doted on Sophie and was always there if I had some function to attend, and Sue was Andrew's mate so life was pretty good.

Manbulloo had a well-established, lovely tropical garden of large proportions, and it was customary to enter this in the local show, usually winning one or two of the prizes. It was such a delight to live in a tropical paradise.

The constant stream of visitors, however, was starting to affect our private life, as we barely had a moment to ourselves, something that was very important to us.

We always had to maintain a generous supply of alcohol for entertainment and would book a certain amount down to the company.

TIM GETS ITCHY FEET

At this stage, Tim was getting itchy feet to do his own thing. When we received a note from the company secretary in head office suggesting that we were debiting too much alcohol to the company, this was the trigger for him to write the following letter to the secretary:

> *Owing to the location of Manbulloo, it seems to be necessary to keep a supply of "grog" on hand at all times. Various people, not appearing in the diary, such as numerous groups looking at the pasture improvement program, panels of judges looking at entries in the local show, as well as outside company personnel sent from Darwin, have all contributed to June being a heavy month.*
>
> *My wife and I not being alcoholics, I can assure you that the said "grog" is being used in a discreet manner, however, this practice shall cease as desired.*

On the same day, he wrote to Mr Roy Bell, the general manager, the following:

> *I would like to tender my resignation from the company as of 1 October 1969 or thereafter until such a time as a replacement can be found.*
>
> *As you know, we are not settled here at Manbulloo and I have for some time been considering doing something on my own, and it is towards this end that I resign.*

I think this was a bit of a shock to Mr Bell (a most likeable boss) and he responded to Tim with these prophetic words, "You will be back in six months."

How true those words were, almost to the month.

So we loaded up all our gear and said goodbye to the north, not without mixed emotions though, as basically it was a pretty good life, but Tim had been nurturing a burning ambition to "do his own thing" for some time.

We had $6000 saved, but no job or job prospects, so it was a pretty brave (or foolhardy?) move. We did have a home to go to – my parents had a second cottage on their farm at Quakers Hill and this is where we headed.

Primitive was an understatement. A fibro cottage with one bedroom, lounge room, kitchen–dining room and a tiny little closed in verandah, which would be the kids' room.

Quite a culture shock after our lovely homestead and gardens, and staff to help with all the day-to-day tasks. The place was so cold in winter that we used the clothes dryer to keep the kids warm at night-time, yet still Sophie's cheeks would be red with cold.

Tim did a bit of horse-breaking, shoeing and saddling, and I took over my sister June's egg run round the local district, but we had to be very frugal.

When Christmas time came, I offered my egg clients dressed chooks at $2 each. I received many orders, as this was a fairly poor district. We both got to work killing and dressing the chooks, and I duly delivered them on Christmas Eve.

Next time I went on my egg round, I was greeted with stony faces, and I wondered what on earth was wrong. It turns out that we had omitted to clean the wheat out of the birds' crops, and when people placed their carcases on the festive plate, the wheat spread out over the dish. How ghastly! I was mortified.

Anyhow, they forgave us and continued to buy eggs, fortunately. We also sold Christmas trees on the side of the road but, Oh! How I missed the Territory!

WE BUY TWO HORSES

We went to the Homebush Horse sale one week and bought a couple of horses, for which we paid $140 each. Otherwise they would have been destined for the knackery.

The Count was a beautiful bay gelding, but forever on the bit. In the many years we had him, I could never really let him go except on a racetrack. Sure-footed and comfortable, he was a cheap buy. The other horse we called Temptation, as we were tempted to keep him but had to sell him eventually.

Almost six months to the day since we had left Manbulloo, Tim rang Mr Bell to see if there were any jobs available with the company. He received the following reply:

> *Confirming our telephone conversation this morning, I very much regret that I have no position which I could offer you at the moment. I have asked you to let me know of any change in address so that I can communicate with you if a vacancy does occur. Yours sincerely, Mr FRM Bell.*

About six weeks later, we received the offer of the management of Spring Creek Station in the Kimberley. Joy, oh joy! We would be going back to our beloved Kimberley country. Tim's salary would be reduced to $3600 per annum, and I would be paid $20 per week if I was willing to take on the cooking. Would I! Anything to be back on the payroll after our stringent lifestyle, and it would be so much better for Andrew and Sophie.

As the management didn't become vacant till the beginning of August, we had a bit of time to fill in. We went to Cairns to stay with my sister Mollie, her husband Geoff and their three children. We had six riotous weeks there as our kids were roughly the same age, and we adults all liked to party fairly well.

We then returned to Sydney to pick up our gear and The Count. Tim had built a horse float while we were there (he could seemingly turn his hand to anything), so we set off on the approximately 4600-kilometre trip to Spring Creek, located off the Duncan Highway 150 kilometres south of Kununurra, which was then in its infancy.

We had bought a Holden station wagon for the trip and this would be the kids' beds. Tim and I had our swag. We spent a night once again with Crick, then it was camping out all the way. How we had enough room for all our gear and the horse's food I have no idea, but it was so exciting to be going back, I would have done anything. I know I used to dry wet nappies out the window as we were travelling as we weren't in a position to wash them.

When we were approaching Bourke, however, disaster struck. The diff in the Holden was starting to run red hot, and we were forced to hole up in Bourke for a couple days while it was repaired. Being on the Darling River, it was not hard to entertain the children (and ourselves for that matter) and we took The Count to the showground.

We went on our way again through western Queensland to Camooweal and the Georgina River, where we camped a couple of nights. Here I took the opportunity to give all the nappies a thorough wash in the river, as well as our own bodies, and to generally recharge our batteries.

The Count was a marvellous traveller, and throughout that arduous trip, never once bailed up on going into the float. On across the Barkly Highway to the Three Ways, Elliott, then Katherine and Manbulloo. Here a few days respite were welcomed by all, and we enjoyed the hospitality of the new manager Arthur Garrard and his wife, another Jocelyn. Tragically, Arthur was later killed when his quad bike hit a fence.

The bitumen lasted seventy kilometres from Katherine then it was on to a BAD ROAD. Bulldust, corrugations and potholes all made this a challenging drive through to Timber Creek on the mighty Victoria River.

This area of the Victoria River is the infamous site of the 1987 murders of five people, mainly tourists, during a ten-day reign of terror that ended with a fatal shoot-out with police. The perpetrator was a German tourist, and the motives for the murders were never explained. He had been spotted concealed in the scrub by Peter Luetinikker, owner of Fitzroy Helicopters, while he was mustering cattle in the area. Peter later became Andrew's boss.

We proceeded on to Kununurra, which had only recently been established for the building of the Argyle Dam. At that time, 1970, the town consisted of only a store, a post office, a school and a pub.

Here we stocked up with supplies before heading off on the last leg of our journey. Back to the Golden Gate (the junction of the Victoria Highway and the Duncan Highway, now the Duncan Road), then through Rosewood and Argyle, which are now partially under the waters of the Argyle Dam. Finally we arrived at SPRING CREEK!

We had traversed forty-six hundred rugged kilometres of varying road surfaces with a horse, a son aged just under three years and a daughter aged eighteen months, and we had arrived unscathed with no major incidents occurring.

A NEW START AT SPRING CREEK STATION

Our new home was based on the standard Vestey manager's accommodation, the living rooms and bedrooms all in a row, with wide fly-wired verandahs on each side. The kitchen here was a separate room, unlike Cattle Creek where it had been part of the main building.

Our only connection with the outside world and the Flying Doctor was Wyndham Outpost radio run by the amiable Everett Bardsley. Our call sign was SPU.

Spring Creek was a very small, rough place, with uncertain boundaries, part of the Mistake Creek lease. To augment the scope of brandings, the stock camp would unofficially venture into the unfenced Texas Downs and Lissadell. This practice had probably been going on since well before our time, but with fences and modern mustering techniques, it probably no longer occurs.

There was a considerable Aboriginal camp over the creek from the homestead, and once again we had a sustainable workforce. Old Joe and Dolly, Limbunya Jimmy and Shirley, Linda and Jacky were some of the names I remember.

We settled into the homestead, once again back to thirty-two volt lighting plant, hot black fuel stoves and kerosene fridges. As the wet season came on, we were to experience the hottest climate we had encountered so far, although Tim had experienced hotter during his time at Ord River Station.

Nights would find us constantly moving from one area of the station complex to another trying to keep cool. We would start off in the bedroom with no bed attire of any kind, then we would move out into the carport on wire stretchers, then finally in desperation, we would move on to the lawn, stretchers and all. The only thing that put us to sleep in the end would be sheer fatigue!

Fortunately, the kids were good sleepers and seemed to be able to survive through the night in their bedroom.

We hadn't been at Spring for long when we met our neighbours at Mistake Creek Station, the amiable Buddy and Alan Johnson. We shared much in common, both adults and kids were about the same age, and we all loved to party. Buddy was a capable and efficient nurse, which was a very handy profession in that isolated country.

As our friendships grew, we found we were needing greater supplies of alcohol, and as Kununurra was 150 kilometres away and Mistake Creek 200 kilometres, we decided to order a seatainer of beer to reduce the cost per carton. This we collected from Wyndham Port, but I don't think we ever drank it all, and I don't remember how many cartons it contained!

One year, 1971, when going on holidays from Spring Creek, we travelled via Normanton in the Gulf Country. I still remember standing on a corner outside the Purple Pub with the children, then aged four and two and a half, when a motorbike went past. The children stood there with their mouths open in total awe! They had never seen a motorbike before.

BARBECUE AT ROSEWOOD

Our neighbour at Rosewood Station (now underwater), Peter Harpham, commonly known as Lord Ted, decided to put on a party, so we girls dressed up in pretty dresses and the men wore white moleskins and RM Williams boots.

When we arrived at about four o'clock, Peter announced that we now had to CATCH THE BARBECUE! So we all piled into the Land Rover, with Graeme Wicks on the running board — fortunately Wixie was with us, otherwise we might have gone hungry. Peter ran the vehicle up beside this poor unsuspecting goat, and the active Wixie dived off and captured the animal doing about forty kilometres an hour. Fresh goat has never been my favourite repast, but it was a case of eat it or go hungry.

We shared many happy weekends either at Mistake or Spring. One evening was particularly memorable when Buddy and Alan's daughter Rachel fell on a broken glass and had a large gash on her back. Buddy's nursing skills jumped to the fore immediately and she had Rachel sewn up in no time, no anaesthetic or anything. Rachel bore it like the trooper she was.

Rachel's brother was christened Gregory, but he was always known by the name the Aboriginals called him, Goorie.

Other Vestey managers with whom we became firm friends were Robin and Len Hill, managing Nicholson Station. Robin's nickname in the Territory was The First Lady, and she ran the place like a five-star hotel.

I will never forget my first introduction to the Nicholson top dining room. Tim had taken me over for a visit before we were married, so I was pretty nervous meeting all these people for the first time. I guess there were about fifteen in the dining room, and I was suddenly struck with a terrible shyness. No one else seemed to be game to start up a conversation, so the atmosphere was very formal and stilted. It would have been a different story in the men's dining room no doubt, everyone would have been yack-ai-ing and carrying on.

THE NEGRI RACES

The Negri race meeting was held once a year and had had various locations over the years. This was Vesteys' own race meeting. People from other stations were also invited to attend, though most of the surrounding stations were owned by Vesteys.

The very first meeting was held on the Negri River on Mistake Creek Station in 1948, and it was later moved to the Linnacre River, then eventually to a location on Nicholson Station after a riot broke out among the Aboriginals. These races were always referred to as "The Negri".

Because Vestey staff had two months holidays every two years, it was felt that a break was needed after the busy winter mustering season. Long hours in the saddle and nights watching cattle made for a pretty strenuous work schedule and there was no such thing as overtime in those days, you just worked when there was work to be done. These race meetings afforded at least a week off from the busy routine.

The races were grass fed, that is, horses had to be paddocked under supervision for a month then they could be put on hard feed and be in training for a week before the races commenced. This was supposed to make it fair for everyone and station horses were the order of the day.

It would take at least a day to pack up and travel to the venue, another day to set up and catch up with everyone from the surrounding district, then the event itself, two days racing and two days rodeo, campdraft and jumping events. A couple of stockmen would walk the horses to the racecourse, sometimes hundreds of kilometres.

Novelty events such as one hundred metre sprints, broom throwing and rescue races were also held.

Shelters were set up made up of bough sheds with hessian walls, primitive but effective (unless it rained, which it normally didn't). In later years, Robin Hill, The First Lady, would take the red carpet, fridges, washing machines and silver cutlery. She knew how to do things properly, did Rob, but she also knew how to join in a good party. Later on, Thea Hayes became known as "The Duchess".

Congeniality was the order of the day, along with much drinking and socialising. A race ball was held on the night of the Cup, and everyone managed to dress up in amazing finery.

Before I came to the Territory, my usual alcoholic drink was brandy, lime and dry ginger, but I soon found that combination was very inconvenient in the north, where both refrigeration and glasses were in short supply. Consequently, I learnt to drink beer from a can before advancing to a stubby, and this habit has stayed with me until today.

The Aboriginals had their own camps and corroborees, and also competed in the rodeo and Stockman's Purse.

On the night of one of the dances, which were held on a wooden floor erected under the stars, Frank Wilmington (The Hollywood Cowboy) decided to play a joke. He inserted into his mouth a piece of fake sick, and was planning to disgorge this on the dance floor. The joke backfired, however, when the presence of this fake sick in his mouth stimulated the ejection of the real thing!

He happened to be dancing at the time with Mrs Peg Underwood, a very proper lady who, with husband Pat, was the owner of Inverway Station. She showed her disdain by immediately vacating the dance floor, followed by a few other revellers who were trying to get away from the smell. Not to be upstaged, Frank quickly extracted his hanky and whisked the sick off the floor and deposited it in his pocket! All done in one very suave manoeuvre, though the original action was anything but suave.

After the races, it was then a recovery party and packing up before the return journey, so everyone had had a really good break.

FORMER STAFF JOIN US

Staff who had been with us at Manbulloo, Graeme Wicks and Rod Polla Mounta, joined us, and Andy Martin augmented the team.

The Spring Creek cattle were notoriously hard to yard up. As soon as they got near the wings of the yard, they would start to bail up and break. I would hear them coming and mount The Count to go and join in the "fun".

Eventually we filled twenty-litre tins up with stones, placed them strategically in front of the wings, then rolled them along behind the cattle. They usually went into the yard before they realised what had happened.

We had a really good team of active, capable and keen young fellows who took every opportunity to hone their skills in the buckjumping field. Every time we had cattle in the yard, the flank girth would be produced and any likely buckjumpers were brought into the arena. Tim would be pickup man riding his faithful horse Bomber, and great fun was had by all.

Tim had carried a movie camera with him ever since his arrival in the Kimberley, so we have many great movies of these stockmen and some rather exciting exploits, both on the horses and unexpectedly dismounting them. Bulls would also be bucked out, and some of the escapes from the yard with a bull hot on the hammer made for some memorable photography.

One fellow we had working on the station at the time, Oscar, had been employed to build a new store. Anxious to join in the fun, he was determined to ride a steer, but his ride was very short-lived — he was dumped almost immediately. He was a carpenter not a buckjump rider!

Sadly his life also was short-lived. He later disappeared leaving all his tools at the station. We hung on to these, hoping one day he would return to claim them as we had no idea where he had gone and what had happened to him. We could only assume that he had committed suicide. His body was not found for a long time. We felt immensely sad as he gave no indication of unhappiness and he was great company.

Another death occurred while we were at Spring, this time one of the Aboriginals. Dolly, a pensioner, was a great old stick and much loved by both black and white. She died of old age, but her hut remained empty as Aboriginal superstition prevented it from being used again. Her husband, Old Joe, was bereft.

ANOTHER WIXIE EXCERPT

SPRING CREEK

Bells Creek was one of the small holding paddocks on Spring Creek. In our time, it was accessible only by packhorses. We arrived to muster the very rough area only to find the paddock fence torn down and two camels in the paddock.

Packhorse camps are minimal — axe, .22 calibre rifle, horseshoes and shoeing gear, tea, flour, camp ovens, swags and little more. On finding camels and broken fence, Tim handed me the pea rifle with the instruction to have no live camels in the paddock.

I had not so much as seen a camel prior to this, so when a large bull and young bull camel came trotting straight towards me, I very quickly appraised the height of the snappy gum trees and soon realised that even at the top, I would probably not be safely out of reach.

On standing my ground, I found they were curious, not hurtful. However, when you look at a curious camel at one hundred paces with a .22 rifle, you realise you will only get a nostril shot, not a brain shot, so again one must find an alternative. Suffice to say that eventually a heart–lung shot did the job.

Packhorse camps made me realise what true freedom was. No terrain could stop us. We had plenty of beef, no fences and no communication with the outside world, so absolutely no constraints. Apart from the incredible countryside ranging from volcanic basalt to great sheets of limestone, there were springs of water everywhere and conkleberries, a sweet grape-like berry that grows on a shrub and supplies the Aboriginals with plenty of Vitamin C.

The Negri picnic races were held at a bore on Nicholson Station. Spring Creek didn't have a truck to cart our sports horses on, so Joe Kelly and I were appointed to get our team the 180 kilometres to the venue. Again, with packhorses, we set off down through Ord River Station on the two-day trek. Spring Creek being all rock did not have good racehorses, so by the time we were almost ready to depart, the last of our horses was still coming home! However, put the pampered racehorses on Spring Creek and they would be crippled after the first muster.

We had a yellow bay mare called Orbit, named for good reason, and on days when we weren't riding horses for work, we rode horses for fun! Tim encouraged us all to ride in the rough stock events and Orbit helped us hone our skills.

It was at this time our Spring Creek mob went down to Mistake Creek to help the stock camp there with one of the first helicopter musters. Stewart Skoglund was to muster the Stirling River area. The portable yard was erected and a kilometre of wing was run out and camouflaged with branches cut from bloodwood trees. The result was unbelievable, with many cleanskin bulls and old piker bullocks yarded. A great success.

END OF WIXIE EXERPT

SHIRLEY

Shirley loved the kids and was a great babysitter. She could be found pulling Sophie, sitting regally in a billy cart, while poor Andrew had to pedal alongside on his bike. Oh well, I suppose it helps to be the younger.

Shirley was a very attractive girl, about sixteen I would say, and she had been "promised" to Limbunya Jimmy, a much older Aboriginal. This was their custom and should not be interfered with, but we did just that, allowing Shirley to sleep with the kids on the verandah. I know this was wrong, but we felt sorry for her as she wasn't keen on the arrangement.

After we left Spring Creek, she married Jimmy. We met up with her in Kununurra during a visit there in 2002, when Shirley would have been about fifty. Hugs were shared all round, but Shirley was not the happy, carefree girl she had been on the station. Town life didn't fit in well with her and she had obviously been drinking. We left feeling very sad.

One time, the stock camp was going to muster round Bells Creek, a very rough area about ten kilometres out, and as the only vehicle we had on Spring was an old one and a half tonne Bedford truck, we borrowed Alan Johnson's Land Rover.

I couldn't resist attending this muster, so I rode out with the men on my trusty steed, The Count. He was the perfect horse for mustering in this country as he was so sure-footed in the stones. Anyhow, the stock camp was to camp out that night, but I had to come home to be with Andrew and Sophie (I had left them in Shirley's care). This meant riding home in the dark, a prospect that didn't appeal to me greatly as I was no explorer.

Fortunately, my horse had a good sense of direction and got me home all right, but I can still remember arriving back at the spooky station which was clothed in moonlight and shadows. Then I had to venture into the dark homestead, as I didn't bother to start the lighting plant for such a brief time. All was well though.

We had a terrifying time in the old Bedford one day. Spring Creek was a very hilly, rocky place, and on this occasion, Tim was ascending a steep hill when the truck ran out of puff and at the same time the brakes failed. So Tim had to steer it backwards down the hill, ever gaining speed, until he was eventually able to guide it into a fence line and pull up.

Between the homestead and the men's quarters was a barbed wire fence that hadn't been strained up for a long time. Andy used to leap this fence when he came over for meals, but one day Tim strained the wire and Andy didn't see this in the dark. He came a terrible cropper and arrived at dinner clutching some rather precious parts! (Andy, I'm sure you will get a laugh if you ever read this.)

ANDREW GETS SICK

Andrew was attacked by a gastric wog and suffered terribly for about four days. He had violent attacks of vomiting and diarrhoea at the same time, but he never complained and suffered till the disease ran its course. Nerve-racking for us, but we didn't want to call the Flying Doctor and have him evacuated to Kununurra Hospital, where he would have been given drugs to suppress the symptoms and make it harder for his little body to fight the disease. Fortunately we were able to nurse him back to good health and he was never sick again.

We were given two very cute white pups of unknown origin. They became great mates to all of us, especially the kids. One day they went missing and, on searching, we found their bodies at the mailbox. Someone had obviously laid some 1080 poison baits and both dogs had suffered that awful fate. So sad.

The young fellows were very competitive. One day, we were driving home in the Bedford truck. We could see by the shadows that the lads in the back weren't hanging on, obviously seeing who could last the longest. Tim mischievously started swaying the truck from one side of the road to the other, until eventually one of the lads fell off. Chastened and scratched he climbed back on to the truck with a sideways glance at Tim.

I GET SICK

In December 1971, I started to have unexplained pains in my abdomen. Thinking they would go away, I ignored them, but they became progressively worse.

During this period, I received a letter from Dad to tell me that my precious Auntie had died. I was absolutely bereft, as she had been my saviour in my childhood years. Had Dad even sent me a telegram to tell me that she was sick, I would have flown immediately to Sydney, but I guess Dad didn't realise how strong our bond was.

This was a very anxious time, so I decided I had better see the doctor. We all piled into the station wagon for the trip to Kununurra. The doctor investigated me and asked for a bit of my history. When I told him about the loss of Auntie, he jumped to the conclusion that my tummy problem was stress.

I knew this wasn't the problem so we took the opportunity to phone Tim's father, who was then in charge of the Heidelberg Repatriation Hospital in Melbourne. He instructed me to fly immediately to Melbourne, and arranged for me to see the top gynaecologist in that city.

This probably saved my life. My situation was becoming so serious that the doctor consulted me on 23 December and operated the next day, Christmas Eve. He only had to put one finger in the right place to diagnose an ectopic pregnancy, that is, a pregnancy outside the uterus. In my case, it was in the fallopian tube.

He asked me if I wanted to have a hysterectomy, and when he informed me that it was possible to still keep the ovaries and thus have normal hormones, I readily agreed.

Not as simple as that though. In those days, it was necessary to gain husband's approval to have this life-changing operation, and the only way to contact Tim was via Outpost Radio, with the entire Kimberley region able to listen in. I had no choice. Tim was sent a telegram and approval was given, though I have no recollection of the wording of that memorable epistle.

I spent a week with Tim's family recuperating before the arduous trip back to the Kimberley. A stopover with my family in Sydney gave me a bit more time to recover before I started on the long trip back to Spring Creek. Coming into Darwin, we encountered stormy weather and had to circle for half an hour before landing.

Then on the final leg to Kununurra, the pilots lowered the landing gear while we were still flying at cruising altitude. I became extremely worried that something was wrong, as I had never encountered this before in all my years as a hostess.

I never did find out the reason for this, but we landed safely. I will never forget the moment when I spotted my beloved family. Tim wasn't waiting until the passengers disembarked. He barged out through the terminal gate and was at the foot of the aircraft steps as soon as we landed. We hugged and kissed with tears in our eyes.

He had dressed the children in special clothes, and to this day I can remember what they were wearing. Soph had a pretty white frock and a blue ribbon in her blonde hair, and Andrew had on a smart shirt and shorts — and they were both wearing SHOES! In our six years of marriage, Tim and I had never been apart before, making my homecoming all the more emotional.

We settled back into the routine of station life, and everything proceeded peacefully with a good wet season and the usual heat and bush flies. These flies gave the horses a terrible time, and would eat large holes in them in various parts of their bodies.

I had a horse called Petite, and every year after the wet, she would come through the yards with a huge hole in her chest — big enough to put your fist in — created by these tormenting creatures. The hole always appeared in the same place every summer and healed up during the dry season. We tried all sorts of treatments, but nothing was successful. Mostly the horses were attacked round their eyes and terrible sores would appear.

They also had a disastrous effect on the Aboriginal children who would not brush the flies away and nearly always had what we called "bung eye". Andrew and Sophie were lucky in that I cut up my entire wedding veil to make fly veils for them.

Later on, dung beetles were introduced into the north and the bush flies largely disappeared, but not long after, they were replaced by buffalo flies, which drove the cattle mad but didn't affect humans and horses so badly.

When I first went to the Kimberley in 1965, the bush flies were so bad that, if eating out in the bush, you had to be very quick to get a mouthful of food into your mouth before it was black with the marauding creatures.

ANOTHER TRANSFER

Early in March 1972, Tim received a telegram from the pastoral inspector, Cec Watts, summoning him to Darwin. Such requests were unusual, and naturally we were very excited to know the outcome. Left at the station alone with the children, Andrew then aged four and a half and Sophie three, I found the suspense of those few days almost too much.

Tim's news on return brought great joy and excitement to us — he had been offered the management of Helen Springs Station on the Barkly Tableland, the same station where we had spent our first year of marriage in 1966. His pay would be the grand sum of $8000, double his present rate of pay.

Helen Springs, as previously stated, was 5887 square kilometres (1,332,480 acres), and in 1972, was divided into seventeen main paddocks, two holding paddocks, two major drafting and trucking yards, and thirty-five bores mainly connected to windmills, and carried an average of 25,000 bullocks. There were also three hundred horses, including thirty broodmares and a stallion.

The station was the bullock depot and fattening property for the company's male cattle travelling from the western stations to their abattoirs in Townsville and Rockhampton.

This is an interesting comparison to the Bohnings day, when they relied on one well and the springs, which weren't very numerous. The station was well-equipped with a little windmill (which was still standing in 1979), and pumping water though this was continually recycled. The homestead was made of mud bricks and the floor pounded antbed.

The Bohning family had taken up the Helen Springs lease in 1917 and lived a primitive existence, which made the women folk very capable and self-reliant, doing all the work round the station themselves in the absence of menfolk. Jack Bohning supplemented the family income by well and tank sinking with his horse team.

Jack and Esther Bohning had two daughters, Edith and Elsie, and these women later on drove their turnoff bullocks to the railhead at Alice Springs, and so became known as "The Petticoat Drovers".

One time during the war, when the American army was upgrading the Stuart Highway, a couple of army recruits came into the station and threatened the women, who were alone.

They didn't bargain on the reception given to them by Mrs Bohning, a very resourceful and capable lady, who gave them short shrift until they were taken away by the Military Police.

The Bohnings sold the station to the Vestey family in 1943, and I believe they only inspected as far as the No 1 bore, twenty-five kilometres from the homestead, and bought the place for a reputed nine thousand pounds (eighteen thousand dollars). Mainly beautiful Mitchell/Flinders grass grazing land, interspersed with tongues of red desert country and bluebush swamps, it only needed capital to further develop the place.

The Aussie battler didn't have the resources to drill and equip bores and install fences and yards, thus it was left to the big companies to do this, and the Vesteys made a fine job of it too.

Tim and I were particularly happy at the prospect of this move for, although we loved Spring Creek and the life there, we knew that Helen Springs was top grazing land, with good improvements and, of course, excellent horses.

Before our departure, which was to be as soon as we were packed, we wished to say goodbye to our good friends at Mistake Creek, Buddy and Alan Johnson. As our RFDS radio was out of action at the time, we piled into our old station truck, the old Bedford, and headed down the road, only to find that the Negri River was in flood and impassable.

We went back to what was called the Barytes Road (owing to the mine there), which passed through Mistake Creek, and fortunately were able to negotiate the Mistake Creek itself. (I think it had been called this as it had been mistaken for the Negri River many years ago.)

However, we were once again halted by the Negri, but at this point it was only about one and a half kilometres from the homestead.

We had left Andrew and Sophie in the care of Shirley and Linda, but had in our company a young jackaroo who had been trying to get from Kununurra to Mistake Creek, and a young lady by the name of Lindesay Crawford, who had been staying with us at the time. Lindesay was a relative of John Vestey, so was like Royalty!

After a conference by the river, which must have been about seventy-five metres wide at this point and flowing swiftly, we decided to swim the river then walk up to the homestead. Bravely, my dog went in first, so we were able to judge the current, then Lindesay and I, followed by the men, who weren't as confident in their swimming ability.

We ended up about 150 metres further down the river as we swam with the current. Our friends were much surprised to see us and gave us a very good party before we had to make the return journey.

A truck was sent over from Helen Springs to help move our gear, as well as my horse The Count and my dog Stormy.

GOODBYE TO THE KIMBERLEY

It was not without some trepidation that we faced our new position, as Helen had a large staff of about twenty Europeans and fifteen Aboriginals, and the station had been run by the same manager for ten years. We were to find, as time went on, that it was necessary for a new broom to sweep practically clean.

The Aboriginal staff was made up of Lucy in the kitchen, Dixie in the house, Lady in the visitors quarters, Jillian and Mollie in the garden, Ruby in the laundry and Connie in the men's quarters. Newcastle David and Wauchope (pronounced Walkup) Jack were the mainstays in the stock camp, along with a few others whose names escape me. George assisted the mechanic and Ned Ambrose's favourite spot was the vegetable garden, which he tended with much love and care.

David and Jack had stock-handling skills that few white men could match. During the turnoff season at the end of the dry, alone they were able to tail out five hundred bullocks all day then yard them at night-time, an amazing feat of stockmanship.

They were able to achieve this owing to their patience, and the fact that they let the bullocks spread out wide and get a good feed so they were content to be yarded at night. This they would do for three days while the rest of the stock camp was mustering the next mob of turnoff bullocks.

Every year when the season was favourable, Helen Springs would turn off eight thousand fat bullocks to the company's meatworks at Ross River, Townsville, or Lake's Creek, Rockhampton.

The bullocks had to be mustered, dipped, held for three days, scratched by the stock inspector for ticks, then dipped again. The very first mob of fats Tim presented to the stockie was knocked back as he maintained he had found a tick (his nickname was "The

Tick"). We always reckoned he had concealed a tick in a matchbox to make things difficult for Tim, as for some reason The Tick had it in for him.

So the bullocks had to be held for another three days and inspected again, but this was the last time Tim had any trouble. Later, we had more congenial stockies, especially Graham Coleman, who was based at Elliott for most of the time we were at Helen.

After clearing, six double-decker triple road trains lined up ready to be loaded for the trip to Mt Isa, eight hundred kilometres away. They were then spelled in Mt Isa for twenty-four hours before being loaded on the train for the coast, a fairly gruelling trip for the poor beasts. During turnoff, five hundred bullocks left twice a week, so it was a busy time for all involved.

The bullocks were loaded according to the number of "Ks" that had been ordered, a K wagon being the name given to the railway wagon the bullocks would eventually be loaded on to. So for five hundred bullocks at sixteen to the K, for instance, you would need approximately thirty-one Ks — this removed any confusion between cattlemen and railways.

On one occasion, we were notified that there was a strike at the meatworks just as the cattle were being loaded, so the loading was stalled and the truckies came into the station to wait it out. In those days, they lived on "million milers", tablets which would enable them to drive for days without a spell.

When they came into the station, they started to relax. One of them actually went to sleep in the men's dining room with his head resting on his arms in the dessert. They were a great bunch, though.

There is a famous photo I have seen in many varied places in Queensland, including in doctors' surgeries and on walls in friends' houses. It is a photo of seventeen road trains consisting of one hundred and two decks with 3060 head of cattle loaded at No 5 bore on Helen Springs ready for transport (this was after Vesteys time and I won't guarantee that my figures are totally accurate!)

SETTLING IN AT HELEN SPRINGS

The first couple of years for both of us involved a lot of hard work and some trying times, until we gathered around us employees who suited our style and didn't refer to "the way we used to do things".

During those first years at Helen, I rarely saw Tim home from the run before eight o'clock at night, and weekends spent relaxing with the family were a rarity, almost non-existent. I would collect our dinner from the station kitchen and keep it in the oven, no matter what time he arrived home.

Sometimes the waiting became a bit tedious, so we brought a piano back from Sydney after one of our annual leave holidays (they were yearly now, not two yearly as previously). This I found very relaxing while waiting during the long hours after Andrew and Sophie were in bed, but I needed it less and less as Tim got things running more smoothly on the run and it was not necessary for him to be away so much.

Mr Roy Bell gave me open slather to order new furniture and soft furnishings for the station, which I did with great relish, and these arrived with the next loading.

There were eight gates on the way out to No 8, which was one of the main trucking yards. Truckies had a pretty torrid time having to walk past three trailers every time they had to open and close a gate, and of course, it always led to the possibility of gates being left open and cattle boxed.

Tim installed grids at each of these gates, and these were appreciated by truckies as well as station staff. Later on, he installed lights and sprinklers at the yards, but I jump ahead a bit.

From my own point of view, I tackled the garden, which had the potential to be somewhat of a parkland with a few modifications to the water supply and a bit of digging here, planting there. When we arrived at Helen, there was an excellent bore at the station equipped with a Mono pump, but the storage tank, though elevated, was very small, and what's more, it leaked!

There used to be a joke told by the mechanic, whose house was at the end of the pipe, that if he turned his bath on in the morning, it would be ready for him by the time he knocked off work at five o'clock in the afternoon!

Keeping lawns watered was a constant battle, in fact, it was a losing one. There just wasn't enough to water the large area comprising the introduced trees in front of the homestead, so this area just became brown in the dry season, green in the wet season. The garden is quite well known for the magnificent poinciana tree that had reached enormous proportions in the front garden and could be seen many miles from the station.

I was told by Miriam Hagan, who had been born in the Territory and was our neighbour at Muckaty Station that the tree had been brought from Darwin by bullock wagon in 1906. Sadly, the tree had to be destroyed in recent years owing to the presence of white ants or termites, that scourge of the north.

However, back to my task. The first thing I did was to order fifty trees from Darwin, then set about planting them round all the station buildings and quarters which, apart from the homestead area, were devoid of any trees at all. Watering them was a major task, but was achieved with a few improvements to the plumbing.

POP AND NANNA

One day in 1974, we were visited by a delightful old couple whom we called Pop and Nanna (Fraser), friends of our bookkeeper. Old Pop was such a blessing for, though seventy-one at the time, he could work like a Trojan. No matter what the mercury soared to Pop would just keep working out in the hot sun, always wearing a woollen shirt, which he said kept him cool.

He had cut his teeth on the Sandy Hollow railway line in the Hunter Valley in 1937, when it began as an unemployment relief scheme of the New South Wales Government. It gained infamy for having no modern mechanical devices used on it, other than trucks carrying concrete for the five tunnels and bridge piers. All other work was done with picks, shovels, hand drills, horses and carts.

Pop and Nanna would visit regularly during the dry season, and Tim would put him on the payroll doing odd jobs for a few weeks. His first job on Helen was to dismantle and re-erect a twenty-thousand-gallon (seventy-five thousand litres) squatters tank, sheet by sheet, bolt by bolt, on top of a hill about five hundred metres from the station. It was hot, tedious, repetitive and difficult work, but Pop was made of tough stuff and he persevered until every last bolt was in place — and there would have been thousands of them.

Tim then installed two-inch poly pipe from the bore to the tank, and from that day on we had unlimited supplies of water, all at high pressure. I was able to run five sprinklers at the same time all day in the homestead area alone, and the mechanic didn't have to turn on his bath until he finished work!

I set about planting extensive lawns, happily assisted by the Aboriginal women. They who would spend afternoons digging away with their digging sticks, chatting and laughing all the time. These sticks would normally be used for digging yams, but they were removing the native grass so I could plant couch seed and buffalo runners.

We then removed the untidy old fence from around the homestead complex and fenced off the entire station area, thus preventing the milking herd from finding holes, as they seemed to have a preference for established gardens. We built a tennis court, which later became a great source of entertainment after work.

This became a green oasis, appreciated by all who worked on the hot and treeless Barkly Tableland. Lawns were later planted round the men's quarters and the three married quarters, and the earlier planted trees flourished, giving the entire area a much cooler atmosphere.

The two lighting plants were a constant thorn in the side. Vesteys, in their wisdom, had transferred these plants from one of their Blue Star Shipping Line vessels, and they thumped away day and night making noise pollution a constant and annoying feature of station life.

At sixty-five KVA, they were quite large enough to power a town the size of Elliott, but with no noise-reducing insulation round their tin shed, they were a bugbear the entire time we were there. Chewing up huge quantities of diesel, they had been a false economy when the company had decided to send them to Helen.

One time, both plants were out of action, and we had to use a small seventeen KVA emergency plant that the company kept on hand. Placed on the flat outside the workshop and totally underpowered for the job required of it, we could see it glowing red in the dark at night-time. Amazingly, it kept us in power for the couple of weeks it was pulled into service.

When we first arrived at Helen, the manager was a man of great economy and would turn the lighting plant off at half past nine every night, then on again at six o'clock in the morning. The result of this was that all the fans would go off at the same time, waking everyone on the station, and we would then be invaded by hordes of mosquitoes. Everyone would be up wandering round trying to get some peace.

Tim and I were not immune to this so the system was soon changed and we had twenty-four hour power and a much larger diesel bill.

WARRIE AND NELLIE

Warrie Wegert and his wife Nellie had transferred to Helen. Warrie was working as the handyman, and with his Ladylite wheelbarrow and one arm, he built a lot of the sandstone paths round the station area and cemented them all in place. Nellie became our ever-faithful station cook, and remained a friend until her death many years later.

There was a sandstone ridge behind the station containing many Aboriginal rock carvings. We would take all our visitors up to the site as they were pretty impressive, but I never knew an Aboriginal to go near them. Years later, when we visited the station, the area was fenced off and a sign said: "No entry, sacred site!" I often wonder who made that decision, some "seat polisher" in an air-conditioned office down south probably.

Tim continued to make many improvements round the station, including installing Mono pumps at most of the bores instead of the unreliable windmills (I should say the wind was unreliable, not the mills) and cumbersome pumpjacks. He built holding paddocks at all the bores so numbers in the stock camp could be fine-tuned, and he installed sprinklers and lights at the two main trucking yards.

Tim or the overseer was always present when cattle were being trucked or untrucked, and as road trains often arrived in the middle of the night, there were many disturbed nights. The presence of the lights enabled cattle to be processed when they arrived, which was easier on man and beast owing to the high daytime temperatures. In our busiest year, Tim supervised the trucking and untrucking of twenty thousand steers and bullocks, so he was not home much during that year.

When road trains first replaced drovers bringing cattle from Wave Hill, 550 kilometres away, owing to the terrible road and frequent breakdowns, cattle could sometimes be on the trucks for forty-eight hours.

Helen Springs was also a staging place for herd bulls en route from Queensland to the west, and at one time we looked after two hundred head of Brahman bulls when the company first changed over to this breed. The Brahmans were so easy to handle. Pastured in the Aerodrome paddock during the day, they were yarded each night and we would only have to point them to the yards and they would file in. Very civilised and intelligent.

One time, a mob of eighty Shorthorn bulls arrived at Helen covered in Noogoora burr, despite the fact that the permit stated that they were free of burr! Tim and I didn't like to think of this pest spread over the western stations, so we got to work with a pair of scissors each and cut every burr off the bulls using the crush at the station yards.

STATION STORES

When we first arrived at Helen, non-perishable groceries and all other station requirements — beds, kitchenware, bore casing, saddlery etc. — were delivered to the station every six months by road train, having been ordered previously via Sydney office. Originally, station loadings were delivered by camel or bullock wagon, so we had come a long way by the 1970s.

Before we left Helen Springs, I asked Dita, the road train driver, if I could drive his road train a few metres just to get the feel of such a massive vehicle. His answer was quick and blunt: "I don't want my clutch buggered!" Huh!!

Perishables were delivered weekly by Co-Ord road trains, which collected goods from the Ghan train in Alice Springs and took them to delivery points all along the Stuart Highway to Darwin. In this manner, we were able to keep up a good and reliable supply of fresh fruit and vegetables. In this respect we were very lucky, as in most Territory places, these items could be in short supply due to geographical factors usually.

I once heard a joke about the old Ghan which was notoriously slow. A lady got on the train and after a while she asked the conductor to stop the train as she was going to have a baby. The conductor replied: "Madame, you shouldn't have got on the train if you were pregnant." "Sir", she replied, "I wasn't pregnant when I got on the train!"

In later years, we bought all groceries from Peter's Place in Tennant Creek, as well as most other station requirements that could be purchased locally, the balance still being ordered from Sydney.

The owner of Peter's Place was a real character. Coming from Nimbin in New South Wales, he fitted well into the mould of your typical hippie. He had a thing about fat people, and had a huge poster above the checkouts saying: "CSR Poisons People for Profit" below a photo of a huge overweight lady. He was not beyond taking sugar and sweet things out of people's trolleys, and was quite happy to point out that sugar was bad for you.

When I became the bookkeeper/storekeeper in 1978, it was my job to take the station ten-tonne truck to town each month for supplies, and a very tiring day it would be too, as everyone would approach me with their personal shopping lists. I would arrive home absolutely buggered and sometimes in the dark, but not to rest, as the perishables had to then be unloaded. However, a big freezer and cold room refrigeration was a far cry from Mrs Bohning's time, so we really didn't want for much.

PETS

I will take a few paragraphs here to talk about the many and varied pets that lived on the station from time to time during our ten years at Helen.

The smallest was Cocky Paul, a delightful character, a Major Mitchell cockatoo belonging to Shona, our governess. Cocky Paul entertained all the staff with his antics, the most memorable of which was to let residents' car tyres down! He couldn't resist the flow of air past his face when he depressed the valves, an action that rarely impressed the unfortunate owner of the vehicle.

One time he escaped too high into his favourite tree and Jack, the head stockman and Shona's boyfriend at the time, was obliged to scale the tree to restore Cocky Paul.

Later, Jack Chambers from Renner Springs Roadhouse gave us a white corella, which naturally we named Cocky Peter. He was as mischievous as Cocky Paul, but his penchant was car dashboards. One day, Little Jude (our gardener) came to Jack and said, "Bad news, Jack, Cocky Peter has eaten a hole in your car dashboard."

Jack was understandably annoyed, but when Cocky Peter started chewing the electrical wiring (240 volts) going to our house, Tim got the shotgun and blew him out of the sky.

Actually, corellas were a constant problem, as their favourite pastime over the wet season was to chew all the wiring going to the cattle yards from the thirty-two volt plants on the outstations.

Next in size was Crony the crow. Another character full of intelligence, he delighted in going into the workshop where George, the long-suffering mechanic, would have all the nuts and bolts from the engine of the grader laid out carefully on the bench. Crony loved to rearrange these, but George wasn't so impressed. One day Crony mysteriously disappeared. It wasn't hard to guess what had happened.

Then came Bertie the eagle. Bertie had been given to me by Noel, who was living on an outstation called Eaglenest, one hundred kilometres from the homestead. Noel had removed him from his nest when he was quite young, but as he grew he failed to be able to fly properly.

I didn't find out the reason for this until it was too late, and Bertie never mastered the art of proper flight. In the absence of Google, I finally contacted the zoo in Darwin to be told that he needed calcium in his diet, so he was fed meat and ground eggshells forthwith, but sadly Bertie remained largely a ground bird.

Unfortunately, Bertie killed and ate Cocky Paul, which was distressing to all as he had become quite a favourite. Later, Bertie met a sad fate himself while we were on holidays one time. He somehow got into the twenty-thousand-gallon squatter's tank and drowned.

Then we had Eric the emu. Eric had been given to me by Harry Bennett, the camp cook, as a cute little grey and white bundle of fluff. Much easier to rear, he grew into a fearful bird strutting round the station area to his heart's content. He was able to use his tiny brain to great advantage, for whenever we fed the horses, Eric would turn up and polish off his share of horse nuts.

He was not averse to sharing smoko with us either. This was served in a creeper covered outdoor area, so it was very easy for Eric to raid the sugar and toasted sandwiches. One day, one of the girls was about to insert a sandwich into her mouth when Eric snatched it straight out of her hand!

Honky Tonk was a cute, miniscule white donkey that was brought in to me after his mother had been shot. He settled into station life very quickly and spent his first night in the girls' goondi as though he had been there all his life.

When he got a bit bigger, the kids took great delight in leaping on to his back and urging him to buck or bolt or whatever took his fancy.

We also acquired a dingo, Vern, from someone, but I was to learn that dingoes don't domesticate like the usual house dog, and she was always a bit aloof. While we were at a race meeting/rodeo at Daly Waters in 1975, George had to shoot Vern as she was killing his rabbits!

It was during this event that we lost our beautiful dog and kid's guardian, Dougie. We would normally take our dogs with us, but we had heard that there were 1080 poison baits laid around the area, so we thought it prudent to leave Dougie with George in our absence.

We never saw him again. He obviously went off trying to find us and must have been picked up on the highway or perished somehow. We were all devastated as he had been a loving, faithful, child-minding dog. We left no stone unturned trying to find him — not easy in that sparsely populated country with no local newspaper or radio.

Finally, we had Little Man, the kangaroo who started off little but became extremely large, and could be a bit threatening to strangers. We had him castrated (which should have calmed him down a bit), but he was still somewhat of a liability when we had visitors. Fortunately, no one was ever hurt.

ANDREW AND SOPHIE BEGIN THEIR EDUCATION

Andrew started school in 1973 and Sophie the following year, so I undertook supervising their lessons during these first two years in a light and airy school room that had once been the men's quarters. In that year, correspondence lessons came from Adelaide, but soon everything was changed over to the Katherine School of the Air.

I was most impressed with the way the correspondence lessons were set out. I consider our children are lucky to have had this form of education as a ground work to their learning.

We were also lucky that the Isolated Children's Allowance in its present form was introduced in 1975 when we employed Shona, our first and very capable governess. It would have been hard to find a better governess than this young lady, and she stayed with us for three years before going overseas. We are still friends.

After she returned from England, one night the cook had put on a roast dinner. As we mainly killed bullocks, the shoulder that came out of the oven was so huge that Shona had to get her camera and take a photograph. Such large joints of meat were rarely seen in the UK, which had been her abode for the previous twelve months.

We had three more governesses before Andrew went to boarding school, Churchie (Church of England Grammar School) in Brisbane. Kez and Jenni were two of them who remain good friends. I taught Sophie Grade 6 before she also went away to school at St Margaret's in Brisbane.

Sophie still recalls how miserable she was at boarding school. She missed Tim and me and the station life terribly, and this was reflected in her letters, which I still have. Thank goodness for letter writing in those days or I would not have this priceless record from both children.

BOARDING SCHOOLS

Travelling to school was an epic trip for the children as there was no flight from Tennant Creek to Mount Isa, so they had to travel from Tennant to Alice Springs, then Mt Isa, Cairns, Townsville and Brisbane. It was just a miracle that they could do it all in one day, but the poor little things would be worn out by the time they arrived at school.

Surprisingly, the children had lots of little friends in the surrounding area or children belonging to staff, so they were not starved for the company of their peer group during the periods when they were on the station. They learnt to ride at an early age and this occupied a lot of our spare time, as I was also keen to partake of the daily ride.

The kids also used to go out some afternoons with the Aboriginal women who taught them about bush medicine and foods. They never wore shoes until they went away to boarding school, so developed hardy feet like their Aboriginal tutors. Bush apples, bush bananas, bush passionfruit, bush soap and conkleberries were some of the native plants they learnt about.

Sophie and I had a great time playing cowboys and Indians on our horses in the vast paddocks. The previous manager had brought Two Bob back from Manbulloo after we left, so we were reunited with this great little chestnut gelding. Andrew learnt to ride on Wattle, a lovely black mare that had been retired from campdrafting, so both children were well mounted.

We had two by two wheeled kids' motorbikes, and Sophie and Veronica Hagan, a friend from the neighbouring station, were out cross-country riding one day with all 1.3 million acres to ride in when they had a head on collision. Fortunately, neither was badly hurt, only scratched and sorry, but one of the bikes was bent and never the same again.

Sophie had a very close little School of the Air friend named Andrea from another station. Andrea and her brother would sometimes stay with us on the school holidays. One day, she was out mustering with her family when her horse tripped over a concealed ant bed and Andrea was speared into the ground. She never regained consciousness and her loss is still lamented by family and friends. I still have a cry when remembering this lovely girl.

STAFF

We had a very loyal and capable white staff who had a great respect for Tim, with one or two exceptions. Two of these were the bookkeeper and his wife, who was the storekeeper. The bookkeeper I think resented Tim as he was much younger. This gentleman always maintained that he could have managed the station, even though his knowledge went no further than double entry bookkeeping and answering phones — he knew nothing about cattle.

There were cartons of Surprise dried peas and beans in the store which had been there for ages, and didn't look as though they would ever be consumed. Tim and I decided to take them into Peter's Place in town and swap them for something more suitable for the station. This we did and came home with some seagrass matting, which we laid on the floor of the overseer's house.

Enter the bookkeeper — he dobbed us in to Sydney office, probably thinking that we would get the sack, but Mr Bell was on our side. Tim just received a token "rap over the knuckles". Many years later the aforementioned gentleman was charged with fraud and ended up in gaol.

On another occasion, the storekeeper wanted to go for a ride so I put her on Two Bob, our quiet horse, as she was no horsewoman. Two Bob took exception to the huge weight that was suddenly deposited on his back and dropped his head in a very determined fashion, throwing the poor lady forward on to the knee pads and leaving her with the most colourful bruises on her thighs.

She never forgave me, as she thought I had done it on purpose. Fortunately, they were later transferred and we had congenial bookkeeper/storekeepers subsequently.

Another employee who resented Tim was G, an old drover. Tim was many years his junior and G considered himself a better stockman and thought he should be running the place. He was posted out to Eaglenest to look after the one thousand square kilometre

Mon Mona block. His great delight was to saddle up his horse and packhorse and ride into the station during the wet so that his horses had to flounder through one hundred kilometres of mud.

They would arrive at the station in a terrible state (the horses that is, I didn't care about the rider), so I would put the horses in the stables and give them a good feed ready to flounder back to Eaglenest. He had no reason to come in, he had plenty of tucker, I think he was just trying to attract a bit of attention as his droving days were well and truly over.

The Mon Mona block was an amazing piece of country — not a tree on it. Not surprisingly, one of the four bores was named Paradise! Judy recently told me that when she was stock camp cooking in this area she nearly pulled the pin a few times as conditions were unbearable — no shelter from the Barkly "breeze", no refrigeration and no creature comforts at all. Evidently I talked her into staying on a bit longer, which she obligingly did.

The mechanic, George, and his wife Marcia were a great couple. George was twenty-three stone and showed every bit of it. Their main ration was beer, of which they consumed, between the two of them, nearly a carton a day. George compensated for this by being a most capable mechanic — there was nothing George couldn't do, and at the end of the year he would put on a New Year's Eve party. He even made the dresses for his grandchildren who came down from Darwin for the event.

If you saw George's fingers you would marvel at this, they were like little plump sausages, but that didn't handicap him in his work — not like Crony the crow, who made things very difficult rearranging his nuts and bolts. Most nights, we would go to their place and play 500 till all hours.

Marcia was extremely tall and slim and George used to boast that he had "the only woman in the country with two backs". Marcia took it all with good humour and was always a delight to be around. Sometimes she would say to George: "Give us a kiss!" and George would respond: "What! Put me off me beer!" They were great mates.

One day, a young fellow blew into the station asking to see the manager. He was a very personable, good-looking fellow and he wanted a job as a handyman. As we needed someone to fill this position, Tim put him on the payroll.

A few weeks later, Tim's ute disappeared and was later located on the Stuart Highway near Elliott, one hundred kilometres away. Our charming handyman was in fact a very able conman — he had even conned the storekeeper to fill the ute up with petrol on some pretext that he was doing a job for Tim. We were lucky to get it back, as well as our saddles and some other gear that were still in the back, when the police located it.

On another occasion one of the men went on a rampage down in the men's quarters, brandishing a .22 rifle and quite terrifying everyone in his path. Tim was summoned and in his cool, calm and collected manner persuaded this gentleman to surrender the firearm. A very tense time culminated in no further drama thanks to Tim's capable handling of a tense situation, though no doubt his heart was making a few extra beats!

CYCLONE TRACY IN 1974 AND THE BOMBING OF DARWIN IN 1942

The infamous Cyclone Tracy occurred on Christmas Day in 1974, two years after our arrival at Helen. The Stuart Highway was wall to wall with cars escaping the almost total destruction of this vibrant city, as women and children were evacuated south.

The whole area consisted of piles of rubble, bomb craters, bent and twisted corrugated iron, shattered timber and miles of broken glass.

Cyclone Tracy was the last in a series of disasters to hit Darwin, but the attack by the Japanese beginning on 19 February 1942 was a destructive force of a different kind. Eight ships were sunk, many more were severely damaged, the surface of the water was on fire with burning oil and the sky was dark with the billowing smoke from the entire conflagration. Hundreds of people were killed, but the true number was never known.

THE END OF AN ERA

In 1975, a series of incidents culminated in a major change to the running of the station — the departure of the Aboriginals. It was a busy time of the year, with mustering in full swing and the men away most of the time except for the married bookkeeper and the single mechanic at the time, Frank.

The head stockman's wife, the overseer's wife, the governess and I were all alone at night in our various residences. One night, Raelene, the overseer's wife, was attacked, despite the presence of her supposedly savage dog sleeping in the house. (The overseer, Christie, who was always boasting about the prowess of this dog, received much light-hearted banter after this incident!)

The intruder groped for the bed and felt his way to Raelene's neck, then fled when she screamed. A few nights later, the same incident occurred to the head stockman's wife and the drama was really on. We women were all starting to get very nervous at night, despite the fact that we all had a firearm. All sorts of suspicions were going round the station and it was a very unpleasant time.

The poor man who came under most suspicion was Frank, the mechanic though none of us believed that he could do such a thing. The police were notified, but of course it was largely a problem for us to solve among ourselves.

The girls slept in the homestead with me until the matter was cleared up, as we all felt quite safe with our dog, Dougie, on guard.

A few days later, Tim noticed down at the camp an Aboriginal man who did not normally reside on Helen Springs. He was not employed by the station though he was a relative of George, an Aboriginal employed to be the mechanic's offsider. On enquiring with the police, Tim found out that this particular fellow had been previously charged for similar offences. Tim went down to the camp and told George that the culprit could remove himself and not return.

George's reaction was very quick. "He go, de whole camp go."

Tim, never one to be stood over, replied, "Well — go!"

In less than two minutes, our entire domestic labour force was just a cloud of dust disappearing up the road towards the Stuart Highway (they owned a couple of old cars).

When the few Aboriginal stockmen we had returned to the station (they were great old fellows and excellent stockmen), they too reluctantly rolled their swags and departed — George was definitely the head man.

The others came back later during the night and collected all their gear except for a few skinny cats, and that was the end of the Aboriginal labour force on Helen Springs. Some of them tried to come back as most of them did not want to leave, but it was a hopeless situation and we could see the writing on the wall. We even had a visit from a Department of Aboriginal Affairs officer telling us we were trying to make them come back against their will which, of course, was absolute nonsense.

I had the unpleasant task of going down to the camp and disposing of the animals they had left behind, including a clutch of scrawny kittens.

In subsequent years, we would see them occasionally in the streets of Tennant Creek, sullen and resentful, often drunk and usually unemployed. Once again, I felt terrible sadness, as I had much respect and genuine liking for them. On the station, they laughed and joked a lot and were always well-fed and clothed, but of course, the story is quite different now.

Round about this period a change in federal government legislation resulted in a mass migration of most of the Aboriginal workforce on the cattle stations into towns and communities. We were very sad to see them go and it represented the end of an era.

As a result, the stations were obliged to adapt to the new regime by employing contract musterers and helicopters, and increasing the number of jackaroos in the stock camps.

Roughly the same time droving came to an end and was replaced by road trains, and to some extent the helicopters replaced the use of horses for mustering.

So it can be seen that this was an era of major change from methods that had been operating more or less since settlement.

We immediately applied to the Mt Isa Commonwealth Employment Service for two domestics, a cowboy gardener and some jackaroos, thus a new era started on Helen Springs.

For the next seven years of our management of Helen, we had a variety of young, capable, charismatic men and women on the staff. I could write another book about these people and their antics, but suffice to mention some of the names here.

Wixie, who had been with us at Manbulloo and Spring Creek, was transferred from Flora Valley to be our head stockman, and he brought with him his bride to be, the most attractive and elegant Val, who had been born in Rhodesia (now Zimbabwe.) They had met on Nicholson Station where Val was working, while Wixie had been the head stockman there.

They were married on the lawn at Helen Springs in April 1974 with Tim as best man. Owing to Val's tall and elegant posture, we nicknamed her "Brollie", and the name has stuck to this day.

She went on to be camp cook and horse tailer, and at the latter she excelled, able to catch any difficult rogue.

Wixie was an excellent buckjump rider and fearless horseman. They were transferred to Mistake Creek in 1975, and Jack Wheeler took over the running of the Helen Springs stock camp. Jack's sister Jenni was our governess for a year and a very attractive addition to the staff she was too.

Judy Cruckshank (Little Jude) from Wee Waa in New South Wales was from time to time cook, camp cook, domestic and gardener. She arrived in 1975 and really jerked the garden into shape. We are great friends to this day.

The next Judy we called Bundy to differentiate between the two Judes. Another great worker, her main claim to fame was as stock camp cook, at which she excelled. She had a tractor and trailer to cart all her food and tools of trade, and did her cooking over an open fire with a bit of tin for a windbreak. All the stockmen had their swags and camping out was the order of the day.

Over the years, we had lots of capable, entertaining and conscientious young people working for us — I would like to name them all but for fear of leaving someone out, I will just mention a few.

Head stockmen after Wixie were Jack Wheeler, Willie Childs and Geoff Nixon. A great team of stockmen were with us from time to time. They included Shane Condon, Peter Mitchell, Keith Whiting ("Tiddles"), Guy Thomas, Keith Shearer, Andy Martin , Ricky Cruckshank (Jude's brother), David and Paul Brennan, Paul Brent ("Parrot"), Mick Bohning (descendant of the original owners of Helen), Paul Jones (nicknamed "Tiny" to reflect his rather large stature), and Jean Grimblot (nicknamed "The Blot"), who had once been in the French Foreign Legion.

A funny incident occurred with The Blot one day. Since he had been in the Legion, Tim reckoned he would be a good shot, so he gave him the rifle and asked him to shoot a killer that he had yarded at No 1. The Blot took careful aim and was about to pull the trigger when the beast charged him. The Blot threw the rifle in the air and raced for the yard rails! Evidently, shooting cattle was not his forte.

Not all managers fraternised with their staff, but we did in spades. We played tennis with them, partied with them, drank with them, had dances in the homestead, parties in the kitchen and rode horses after work (the girls that is). We played hard, but we worked HARDER!

Camp cooks could be a rare breed. Many in the early days were escaping from the law or alimony or some other dubious situation. There is a saying in the Territory: "Call the cook a bastard? Call the bastard a cook!" As we mainly employed young girls for this position, we didn't have any trouble.

Now elaborate set ups are common — demountable kitchens, dining rooms and sleeping quarters and horses are trucked out to the job each day, eliminating the need for a horse tailer.

This used to be an exacting job. The horse tailer would get up before daylight with the cook and locate the hobbled horses with his one horse kept back for the job. A horse bell would help him to locate them then he would bring the horses on camp, unhobble them and catch them for their rider for the day.

Most of the horses would be reluctant to be caught, so this job required a lot of horse psychology — some people had it and some didn't. Aboriginals had an exceptional talent in this department, as did Wixie's wife, Brollie.

Occasionally, some very bad tempers came forth during this exercise, and there was even a horse at Helen called "Axe in the Back" as this was what happened when some frustrated horse tailer was having trouble. This incident occurred under the previous manager who loved his horses, and no doubt that particular horse tailer either got the sack or was put on cooking duties.

Musterers would be usually gone at first light then the horse tailer would have his breakfast and take the rest of the plant on to dinner camp, where a change of horses was usually needed.

Tim and I were going out to the stock camp one day towing Tim's mare, Peggy, in a two-horse float behind. Suddenly we looked to the side and there was Peggy and the float — cruising along beside us, with Peggy looking as though she was riding a surfboard! The float had come unhitched, but settled gently with no injury or breakage.

WE GET NEW ACCOMMODATION

When we arrived at Helen, I was not very happy with the homestead we were to live in. It was the worst, I considered, of all the Vestey homesteads. I was told it had been the shearer's quarters on Oban Station in Queensland, but I don't know if this is true. Anyhow, it was a very primitive building.

The house we had lived in when Tim was overseer in 1966 was now empty again, and we put it to the company to move this to the station, but the man contracted to do the job just never got round to it. Finally, in 1975, it became a reality.

It was moved in two pieces while we were on leave, and what a joy it was to finally move in. Also moved down were the men's quarters, complete with a large recreation room and ablution section. This was also cut in half, and it was fascinating to watch the to-ing and fro-ing as the men manoeuvred the two sections to be a perfect join. Also moved was a cottage for the mechanic, George, and his wife Marcia.

We now had ample accommodation for everyone and each employee had a room to him/herself. With an all-white staff and busy years ahead as a result of the excellent seasons, these extra buildings proved to be a boon, though upkeep of the station area and buildings had by now become a major task.

Wes set up a club in the coldroom so staff could have a drink at night after work. This entailed an honesty system, so people just helped themselves and put a tick beside their name. At the end of the month, the bookkeeper deducted the amount from their wages. Most stations had adopted this system. Drinks were limited during the week, with a greater amount allowed over the weekend.

MY DOG DISAPPEARS

Stormy, my faithful little companion and dog I had owned prior to our marriage, disappeared one day. I frantically looked for him then everyone joined in the search. After three days, we found his little body down on the creek bank — the Aboriginals' dogs had killed him (Gillian later told me.) It is interesting that Aboriginals' dogs hated whites' dogs and vice versa.

I was devastated to lose him, he had been with me for over ten years.

Another animal to whom Sophie was very attached was Ginger, the cat. One day Jenni came to me and said, "Joce, did you know they shot Ginger last night?"

"No, that was only a bush cat in the kitchen," I replied.

But on further investigation, it turned out to be Ginger after all. Ginger happened to be in the wrong place at the wrong time and they had shot the wrong cat.

ACCIDENTS

A few accidents occurred during our time at Helen, but surprisingly few considering the nature of the work. The overseer was breaking in one wet season and one of the colts dropped its head, causing Johnny to "put the boots in" and mutter to the horse something like: "I'll give you buck, you bastard."

This the horse did with great gusto, too much in fact. It bucked right off its feet, landing on its side with Johnny underneath. Unfortunately, Johnny's foot had come out of the stirrup, and this piece of iron was jammed between the horse and Johnny's leg, breaking it in a very nasty way. He was in much pain. We gave him morphine, which could only be administered by Tim or me and had to be accounted for.

He was transferred to a station wagon and met the ambulance halfway into Tennant Creek, a total distance of 150 kilometres. It was a very nasty break and he wasn't able to use his leg properly for some years. Although we had a good air strip at the station, the Flying Doctor aircraft was not permitted to land there as it fell a hundred metres or so short of requirements, with a creek at one end and a small hill at the other.

Tim was one of the first managers in the country to employ jillaroos. One pretty young girl, Leanne, had a nasty accident, and Tim felt so awful that he vowed he wouldn't have girls in the stock camp again. He said he didn't mind if a hairy-arsed jackaroo got injured, but it was a different matter with a girl.

On this particular day, Leanne was working on the face of the camp while some cattle were being drafted. She took off at full gallop after a bullock on her supposedly trustworthy horse, High Tot. The horse dropped its head and Leanne was thrown heavily, unfortunately landing on her head.

She was in a coma and had to be transported the eighty kilometres or so into the station in the back of a rough little utility, well-padded with foam rubber mattresses. (How easy now with two-way radios everywhere able to summon a helicopter.) When she arrived at the station, she was delirious and nauseous and we were very concerned for her safety, as well as being sad that she had had to be transported in this manner.

Once again, the ambulance met us along the Stuart Highway and she was taken to Tennant Creek Hospital, where she stayed for some weeks, unable to even feed herself for a long time. She suffered slight brain damage that resulted in a minor personality change, but it was a long time before she could work again, and never on a horse.

My nephew Roger, nicknamed Cus, came up from Sydney to work in the stock camp for a couple of years. He had hardly been on a horse when he arrived, but became a fearless rider prepared to take on anything – galloping full tilt over any type of country that the holey Barkly Tableland country could throw at him. The jackaroos would sometimes practise riding a buckjumper when the horses were fresh at the beginning of the season, and nothing daunted Cus.

One time, they were a bit short-handed at Manbulloo and they asked if we could lend them a couple of stockmen. So Cus and another young fellow were put on the bus to Katherine. Being notoriously long grass country on Manbulloo, Roger's horse fell over a cow lying down in the grass and Roger was ejected from the horse. As he fell, the horse kicked out and its shod hoof caught him squarely in the face.

He was patched up in Katherine Hospital as best they could, but to this day he wears that scar and a slightly changed face shape.

Head stockman Jack had a nasty fall in the Bluebush Paddock, where the holes are big enough to bury a bike in. His horse took a tumble and Jack was speared into the dirt. When he landed, a piece of stick went through the soft part of his hand, protruding out each side.

Taken to Tennant Creek Hospital, the doctor proceeded to try to dig the stick out with a metal probe, but the anaesthetic wasn't working properly and as he dug in he was touching the bone. Jack kept telling him it was hurting but the doctor just told him he was making it up. Finally Jack told him to "Get your dirty mitts off me, mate," and walked out.

The sister who was assisting could see that it was hurting. She told Jack to come back the following week, which he did, but he was still fishing bits of bark out of his hand weeks later. Jack wasn't impressed when Tim told him, "You should have been more careful!"

Harry Bennett, the stock camp cook at one stage, cut his finger off when he was trying to put a belt on to a pulley to start the pump jack. Harry just put a dirty old white rag round his hand and kept on cooking the stew he was preparing for dinner. It didn't worry Harry, the finger was numb anyhow and he claimed he had been trying to get rid of it for years! When the men came in for a feed that night no one would eat the stew as they were worried about eating Harry's finger.

NED AMBROSE

Old Ned Ambrose, whose relatives once owned Banka Banka Station, was our gardener. He lived, talked and breathed vegetables, and we had to build more and more gardens to satisfy Ned's endless appetite for growing things. Although I had always maintained a vegetable garden, under Ned's stewardship, we had melons and vegies coming out our ears.

He was much appreciated and a real old character, but like many old characters in the north he had a problem — alcohol. When we discovered how bad Ned's problem was, everyone was forbidden from giving him any drink. He was allowed a well-supervised ration that he could handle.

One time, however, the system failed and Ned somehow got grog, too much of it. He kept coming to the homestead to tell us that "those 'blackfellows' were there again".

We would go out and have a look to placate him, but of course there were no "blackfellows" — Ned was hallucinating.

This went on for a few days, then Ned completely disappeared and didn't sleep in his quarters for two nights. We were becoming extremely worried about him.

Then Sophie came galloping home one day and said, "Quick Mum! I've found Ned."

We jumped into a Toyota and located him, cold and wet (it had rained during the night), over a kilometre from the station, obviously in the DTs. I managed to con him into the station utility to take him into the Tennant Creek hospital, much against his will. When we arrived there, he was very reluctant to go in.

They dried him out and sent him home after a few days, but he never quite forgave me for taking him to a doctor as he had a real thing about them. The poor old fellow died a year or two after we left Helen.

MORE CHARACTERS

Another type of alcoholic commonly found in the north is the man who can live in the bush and go without a drink for months, then go to town and spend three weeks in the pub — senseless. When dried out, these men are usually reliable and conscientious workers. We employed one such person, Noel, at Eaglenest, an outstation on the Mon Mona block.

After a year or two living in complete isolation with just the occasional visits to the homestead for stores, Noel acquired an Aboriginal lady, Margaret, who had once been part of the station labour force.

One day, Tim was doing his rounds and called in to see Noel. While talking to him, he noticed Margaret hovering shyly in the background carrying a cardboard carton. Curious, Tim asked Margaret what she had in the box.

"Me gott 'im piccaninny, boss!"

We hadn't even known she was pregnant, but they were amazing like that, they could just go down and squat in a gully, usually accompanied by a relative, and have no trouble at all giving birth. I wondered how Margaret had managed having only Noel as company.

At one time, Margaret had worked at the station, being employed to keep the visitors quarters in order. In the lounge room, there was a large, heavy circular coffee table, and I used to wonder how she polished the floor under this table. One day I spotted her doing it — she would turn the table on its side and roll it outside! Very impressive for a young, uneducated girl.

One day, Lucy, who worked in the kitchen, gave birth to a baby boy. When he was a few months old he became sickly and Lucy brought him up to me for nursing. His condition was beyond my capabilities, so I summoned the Flying Doctor and the baby was evacuated to Darwin. I never did find out the reason, but he later died and Lucy blamed me. In fact, she never forgave me, thinking that I had been the cause of the loss. Lucy remained sad and resentful for the rest of our tenure at Helen.

Another character we employed from time to time was Tommy the contractor. A lot of the new improvements on Helen Springs are a monument to Tommy, who would have to be one of the hardest workers I had ever met. Tommy would erect fences on his own, doing all the sighting alone and unaided. He got his fences so straight that Tim could look through the holes in the pickets and see right along the line! (So he said.)

Unfortunately, Tommy also had a problem — he was an addicted gambler. He would sometimes leave the station with $30–40,000 (a lot of money in the seventies) from his contract work, and return a couple of months later penniless. He was a great fellow and lots of fun, and kept everyone entertained on the tennis court, where he became the "leaping gazelle", streaking across the baseline to get a ball.

Sadly, a few years after we had left Helen, we visited Tommy in a hospital in Brisbane. He was an addicted smoker and died of lung cancer, a great loss.

One day, Wayne Taylor, alias "Spider", a reliable and hard-working employee who was the bore mechanic at the time, came into the station and announced to Tim, "I'll have to give me notice."

Quite taken aback, Tim said, "Oh, what's the trouble?"

"I pulled the mill over at Buffalo," he replied, very agitated and unhappy. (A windmill on the Barkly Tableland is a huge affair and we considered this no small feat.)

Spider (so called owing to his lean build) was expecting Tim to really blow his fuse, but instead Tim calmly asked him how it had happened. Spider explained that he had hooked the pulley up to the wrong leg of the windmill, thus bringing the whole construction toppling down.

Tim still remained calm and said to Spider, "Don't worry, we'll go out and have a look at it tomorrow. You don't have to resign though."

After he had gone, I asked Tim why he had taken it so mildly. He broke into a big smile and said, "Spider has just done me a big favour. I had been wanting to put a Mono pump at Buffalo for ages, and now the company has no choice but to approve the expenditure." Three cheers for Spider!

Another time, Tim hired a light aircraft to help muster some piker bullocks out of the scrub. The pilot of this plane was an ex-World War II US army pilot. He came to the office and held out his hand to Tim and introduced himself. "Howdy, ma name's Randy Man!" We got a laugh about this for a long time.

Another fixed wing pilot was told under no circumstances to land on the black soil plains. They look smooth from the air, but on the ground are anything but. However, this pilot chose to ignore these instructions and landed on the plain, almost wrecking the aircraft but escaping without injury to himself. It was a long time before the aircraft was removed for repairs.

When helicopter mustering began in the north, ex-Vietnam pilots were used to a large extent, but it was soon found that, though they were excellent helicopter pilots, they knew nothing about working cattle. The results were fairly devastating in that cattle were driven too fast, many became overheated, and a lot of calves were mismothered, so branding numbers were way down.

The problem was eventually rectified. Now helicopter pilots with stock experience take priority over pilots with little or no stock experience, in fact it is probably a prerequisite for the job.

THE FLOAT ACCIDENT

A dramatic incident occurred in 1974 when our old friend Sue from Manbulloo days and I decided to take two horses to Alice Springs to compete in the show. It was a day's trip for Sue from Katherine then we put both horses in our two-horse float and set off in our Valiant station wagon.

About twenty-five kilometres south of Tennant Creek, we had a blowout in one of the float tyres. The bang made the horses lurch (there was no division between them) and I found the whole outfit heading for the scrub on the side of the road. I instinctively felt that had I tried to correct I would have rolled both the car and the float, so I just hung on and watched the scrub loom up in front of us.

We came to a sudden and unexpected halt — the float had rolled, throwing out the two horses but saving us from a terrifying journey through more scrub. Thanks to the swivel on the ball of the tow bar the car remained upright.

Sue's horse immediately leapt up and she was able to catch him, but my horse, The Count, just lay there and I was sure he was injured. Sadly, I approached him, but he suddenly bounded to his feet, breaking his headstall, and took off down the Stuart Highway towards Alice Springs. I stood in the middle of the road watching him go and wondering if I would ever see him again.

Meanwhile, Sue saddled her horse and started to ride back to town. Fortunately, we had met Rhonda and Peter Clauson, managers of Tennant Creek Station, at the Renner Springs Races previously, so Sue was able to ride in there. Peter notified Tim then came to pick me up. Walking back alone along the highway wasn't much fun.

Meanwhile, Peter agreed to help us find my horse, and I silently resolved not to leave Tennant Creek Station until we had achieved this goal. Peter fortunately knew all the Aboriginals in town, and he was able to enlist the aid of an ex-station man who lived in Tennant Creek — "Lucky" by name and lucky by nature I reckoned.

Peter kindly supplied him with a horse, Rainbow, and for four days Lucky tracked The Count through country alive with brumbies, returning to the station each night. He would head out the next day and cut the tracks again south of where he had left off the day before. I had heard of their legendary tracking ability, but I was to witness it first-hand during these few days.

We were in turn very lucky to get Lucky, as he normally spent his days at the pub. I am always grateful to him for making this sacrifice, also lucky that Peter knew just where to find this amazing man. On the fourth day, Lucky was closing in on The Count (he was a very fit and active horse and was probably keeping up quite a pace), so when he approached the Phillip Creek boundary fence, I chartered a light aircraft.

Sue's husband, Des, went up to survey the situation from the air and was able to witness Lucky catching the horse and heading out to the highway. Peter kindly brought his truck and we loaded the horses from an anthill. It was amazing that he hadn't been killed by a brumby stallion, as they don't like geldings. Everyone was relieved that the drama was over and they could get back to normal duties, and Lucky pleased to have a bit of extra cash to spend in the pub!

Obviously, we didn't make the Alice Springs show. Sue and I later booked to go on a cruise to the South China Sea area on the *Fairsky*, but just before we were about to sail, the ship struck a submerged wreck and had to be run aground on a sandbar. No one was hurt, but once again our plans were thwarted.

The only favourable outcome from our float incident was the great friendship that ensued with Rhonda and Peter. We had only fraternised with them at race meetings until then, but now they were our constant dinner party companions whenever we went to town.

Tragically, Peter's life was taken far too early as a result of a freak accident.

At approximately seven o'clock on the evening of 28 February 1998, Peter had pulled off to the side of the road between Camooweal and Mt Isa to allow a truck heading for Mt Isa to pass. It had been a big wet season and there had been floods. He slid into the table drain and got bogged.

A man heading for Camooweal pulled up to help. He backed up to Peter's vehicle to pull him out, and parked his vehicle halfway across the road. He left his headlights on but didn't turn on his hazard lights.

Peter was attaching the tow rope when a vehicle coming in the opposite direction was confused and crushed Peter between the two cars. Despite the fact that there was approximately a one kilometre straight stretch of road, this man should have seen all the lights and slowed. Although he was totally negligent, he was never charged.

Peter died almost instantly, bleeding to death on the side of the road.

The truck driver who was first on the scene rushed into Camooweal to alert the authorities not knowing who had been killed. One of the people who went out with the SES was Pete's son, Steve. It was a terrible shock to Steve to be first on the scene of his father's tragic accident, but when he had been summoned, he had no idea who the victim was.

Peter was only fifty-four at the time. He and Rhonda had moved from Tennant Creek Station and subsequently bought the famous Middleton Roadhouse, optimistically called the "Hotel Hilton", between Winton and Boulia.

That she recovered from the shock of this tragedy and carried on the business at Middleton is testament to the character of this lady. She soldiered on with great help from her very capable daughter Margie, until the roadhouse was eventually sold and Rhonda moved to Camooweal.

Rhonda and I recently went through Middleton and I persuaded Rhonda to go in for a look. They say you should never go back, and Rhonda was reluctant. What a shock to see the place now. Rhonda and Peter had the place immaculate, with beautiful gardens, everything spick and span, and always a good-looking barmaid (or man) behind the bar. Now everything was run down and neglected and there was no sign of the once well-tended gardens. Rhonda couldn't get out of there quickly enough.

On one memorable occasion, Tim and I went to Tennant Creek to pick up a washing machine that had been ordered through the

Sydney office. This was something really special — a fully automatic machine to supplement the faithful old wringer jobs. We loaded the machine in town then called in to have dinner with Rhonda and Peter as usual and proceeded home.

We arrived at the back door of our homestead at one o'clock on a beautiful moonlit night to be greeted with a shock — there was no washing machine in the back of the ute! Tim was usually fastidious about tying down a load, but for some reason this time he must have just assumed the washing machine would be heavy enough to remain in its place.

Feeling very sheepish, we retired to bed to receive a phone call early next morning from the salesman who had supplied the machine.

"Did you lose a washing machine last night?"

"Actually, we did. Where is it?"

"It's on the side of the highway just north of the Three Ways."

"Okay, thanks, we will go and pick it up."

We went to retrieve the machine, but it was a wreck. Tim was only able to retrieve the motor, which still worked and we used it later on hooked up to a pump. Sydney office was very obliging and they were able to get insurance, so we received a replacement six months later. Not the most proper thing for the manager to be responsible for — perhaps the bookkeeper should have been in charge after all!

ON A LIGHTER NOTE

My days were not all spent organising the domestic side of things and gardening. Owing to my great love of horses and cattle, I was lucky to have a husband who allowed his wife to go out in the stock camp from time to time to attend musters and open drafting.

This is where the cattle are held in a mob on the flat and the horseman rides in and cuts out the required animal. It is great fun, and I was forever grateful that the men let me do the cutting from time to time. I often accompanied Tim on his rounds — all bores were checked every second day, which was a round trip of about three hundred kilometres.

Leisure time on Helen involved picnics at the Gorge, a beautiful and almost permanent waterhole about eight kilometres from the station, to which all staff would go loaded with eskies and children. We had lights installed on the tennis court, so this was a very popular after-work pastime, as well as drinks on the lawn. Race meetings, rodeos and campdrafts were well attended, and quite often ten or fifteen horses would be taken for competition.

Shona, the governess, is always grateful that we played tennis after work. Because she didn't play, she started dabbling in oils and water colours. Now she is a very successful artist, and this is her main source of income.

I became secretary of the rodeo/race club, which entailed a fair bit of work, but it was something I enjoyed doing, as well as riding in most of the events. Sophie rode in her first campdraft at Renner Springs at the age of nine and put in a sterling performance. Since that time, she has successfully ridden in many campdrafts.

At the dances afterwards in the Renner Springs Hall, Tim would be a show stopper with his rock-and-rolling, getting stuck into it with great gusto. I had trouble keeping up with him at times.

The Beebes from Ucharonidge had offered to give the Renner Springs rodeo some unbroken horses to use as buckjumpers. Tim took the station truck up the highway to collect the horses, about ten in all. It might give people a warm and fuzzy feeling to find homes for brumbies rather than shooting them, but I was to witness another aspect of this controversial subject.

The horses were happy to go on to the truck, but unloading them was a different matter entirely. No amount of coaxing, both gentle and more forceful, would entice those horses to vacate the truck. Eventually, they had to be skull dragged off, that is, putting a rope around their necks and dragging them out one by one using a 4WD. A terrifying experience for these animals, which Tim later handled so that they wouldn't have to go through anything like that again.

As buckjumpers they were a write off — they became too quiet and wouldn't buck!

A movie projector was supplied by the company, and feature films were screened once a fortnight, a very popular event. People came from all the neighbouring stations.

One of the highlights of the year was the Milla Milla Muster, which was attended by everyone — children, domestics, cooks, governesses and anyone who wanted to have a bit of time out bush and go mustering. Milla Milla was one of the very scenic places on Helen Springs where a few scrub bulls and piker bullocks still ran.

There were never large numbers of cattle, and though we tried hard to get what cattle we could, it was mainly a fun time, with plenty of excitement chasing piker bullocks through the scrub — some of them could be fifteen years old. The men would throw bulls if they got the chance. These musters are still remembered today.

One night, when the Station Creek was up, we decided to have wheelbarrow races over the creek, which had a narrow wooden plank across it about ten metres long. Husbands wheeled wives, boyfriends wheeled girlfriends and anyone else who wanted to join in the fun. It was a hilarious night. If your wheelbarrow driver lost his balance, the whole caboose ended up in the creek. Another memorable distraction from work.

One night, Tim and I were travelling home from No 1 when we saw a strange light in the distance where we knew there was no road. It appeared to be vehicle headlights, but never got any closer, just wavered around in a most peculiar fashion. We concluded that this was the mysterious Min Min light, for which no one has ever come up with a plausible explanation of its origins.

TIM BLOWS HIS TOP

Jack Chambers owned the Renner Springs Roadhouse and rodeo arena. A cantankerous old bugger, he sometimes made things very difficult for competitors and committee members.

One day, Tim was told that Jack had accused him of introducing ticks into the Barkly Tableland which, of course, was a lot of rot. Ticks had been there long before Tim's time.

I think that was the only time I ever saw Tim really mad. He strode out to the car and roared up to the roadhouse, stormed in and demanded to see Jack.

"What do you mean telling everyone that I had introduced ticks on to the Barkly?"

Jack back-pedalled, and stuttered and stammered his way out of it, but the relationship with him never improved. He had once owned Eva Downs Station with his pioneering family, but owing to his uncooperative manner, the brothers eventually sold up and went their separate ways after their parents had departed.

The story of his family's epic trip from Mungallala in western Queensland with all their worldly possessions — including chooks, wagons, sulkies, horses, a stallion and a baby — in the 1930s is beautifully described in the book *Battlers of the Barkly*, by Alf Chambers, Jack's brother. One stockman, seeing this cavalcade, galloped back to camp and told his boss, "A circus is passing by!"

In his book, Alf chronicles all the hardships and dramas the family encountered carving a station out of the wilderness. His father Sid and his long-suffering, hard-working, caring mother and the children — when they became old enough to be useful members of the team — all pitched in.

Alf wrote a second book at the age of eighty-five chronicling more stories from his Eva Downs days. Even then his memory was amazing.

DALY WATERS RACES AND CAMPDRAFT

The Daly Waters picnic race meeting and rodeo was a memorable affair, resumed in 1974 after a long absence. We were lucky enough to be able to camp in some old government buildings, with our horses in the yard underneath.

The campdraft was a wild event as, after the riders had completed the task of cutting out a beast and putting it through a figure of eight, the cattle were just allowed to go bush, and could have ended up on any station! The cattle were pretty rough also, any old thing would do — cows and calves, weaners, steers etc. Not exactly what you would call good animal husbandry.

During the bull-riding competition one of the bulls refused to leave the arena after having disposed of its rider. No amount of coaxing on horseback or on foot would entice the bull to exit. An old drunk decided he could perform that task, but ended up being tossed sky high at the end of the bull's horns. Being drunk, he didn't have much feeling so he landed unscathed, but the bull was still in the ring and fairly angry by this time.

Enter Billy Bright, a well-known, capable and fearless Territory stockman. Billy taunted, coaxed and hazed that bull right out of the arena, to the cheers of everyone present.

Our staff had many wins that day. Wixie won the buckjump and also rode the feature horse. Andy won the bullock ride and the barrel race, and Willy won the stockman's purse. Tim did the picking up on his gallant bay mare Sister. Nimble and sure-footed in both black soil plains and rocky desert country, she was his favourite horse, and carried him till we put her down many years later.

Picking up involves riding alongside a bucking horse and plucking the rider off — that is, if he hasn't been thrown. There were lots of minor placings, so altogether we had a most enjoyable weekend, the first of many at Daly Waters.

ENGLISH VISITORS

We had a couple of visitors from England, the aforementioned Lindesay and her friend Sue. They both wanted to go out into the stock camp mustering, and as we were unsure of their riding ability, we gave them fairly quiet, reliable horses. We needn't have worried — we subsequently found that Sue used to ride steeplechase horses in England!

One time, the stock camp had a very slow trip back to the yards with cattle and didn't arrive till nine o'clock at night. After a daylight start that morning, the men were all too tired to knock up a feed. Lindesay and Sue came to the rescue — they cranked up the fire and cooked scrambled eggs for everyone. They are made of pretty tough stuff, those POMS. (By the way, I believe this stands for People of Means not Prisoners of Mother England as is popularly thought). We have maintained a friendship with Lindesay and her Australian husband, who have bought a cattle property on Flinders Island, Tasmania.

Members of the Vestey family also occasionally visited the station. Ever humble, you wouldn't think they were some of the biggest cattle/business barons in the world. Mr Edmund Vestey, Lord Vestey's cousin, on one visit to Helen offered to help with the washing up. We had dined in the top dining room which was also the visitors' quarters and it was typical of the lack of snobbishness of this family.

CLOSE SHAVE WITH "THE COUNT"

I had a drama that I will never forget. I was riding The Count in the broodmare paddock (about sixteen thousand hectares), and for some reason I was riding in a hackamore, a halter with no bit and only a curb chain behind the chin for control of the horse.

The Count only knew one pace. This particular time, we were hacking along sedately when he suddenly realised I had run out of leverage and he could do just as he pleased, which was full gallop. I had absolutely no control, but stuck with him till he was heading for a steep, sharp creek bank. Being no Adam Lindsay Gordon, I decided discretion was the better part of valour and, terrified, I bailed out.

Not seriously hurt, I was able to limp back home. The Count wasn't waiting for me – he took off at high speed for the station. As no one knew where I was, Tim was very concerned for my welfare, but soon picked me up on the road back to the station. It was a while before I had the courage to board that horse again, but eventually I did.

The only time I had the courage to let The Count go was in a ladies' race at the Renner Springs Races, which were held every year. In case I couldn't pull him up at the finish line, a few of the stockmen lined themselves up to "rescue me" if necessary.

As I have said, The Count only had one pace. As soon as the starter's gun sounded, he was off like a bullet and I never saw another horse! Not everyone from Helen had enough faith in us to put some money on with the bookies. There were some well-bred horses in the line-up, but they didn't bargain on the "Knackery horse from Homebush"!

Later on, Andy Martin, who had joined us again to break in horses, rode The Count in a bareback race at the Negri Races and won again. I was very impressed, Andy was a great rider.

FIRE

There was a huge fire out on the south-eastern boundary, and all hands were needed to go firefighting. All necessary equipment was loaded on to the truck, including fire bugs (drip torches), bags and buckets, eskies of sandwiches and beer, water and just about the entire staff. When we got near the fire front, people were dropped off at various points along the road in order to back-burn.

We worked until about midnight when the fire appeared to be under control, and we left Jack to keep an eye on it during the night. He was last seen taking off at high speed towards the boundary in a Toyota, but eventually arrived home next day to report the fire was out. Once a fire gets going on that Tableland with a Barkly breeze behind it, it takes a bit of stopping. The Barkly wind is called "a lazy wind", as it doesn't go round you, it goes through you.

One grader driver on the Eva Downs boundary was not so lucky. While grading a break around a large fire, he decided the going was getting a bit hot, and for some unknown reason left his machine. He left his lunch on the seat, but the fire caught up with him and he was burnt to death. The tragedy of it was that, although the machine was caught in the fire, his lunch was unaffected.

Another time, Tim had to go out to a fire on the eastern boundary about eighty kilometres from the station to relieve Spider, who was driving the grader. I accompanied Tim in order to bring the vehicle back, but on the way home at Anjiwilli Waterhole, it broke a tie rod.

As no one knew we had gone out, I had no choice but to walk back to the station, a distance of about forty kilometres. I set off at about two o'clock in the afternoon, but walking through a mob of bullocks on the treeless plain was pretty scary as, with not a tree in sight, if one decided to get a bit proddy I had nowhere to take refuge.

Cattle are familiar with a man on horseback, but a lone figure walking among them is a different matter altogether. They could easily have taken exception to my presence. However I managed to reach No 1 bore safely, but the only food I could find was a packet of cornflakes and some powdered milk, which I ate with relish. Too hot to sleep with clothes on, I stripped off to my undies and attempted to sleep on one of the wire mattresses in the hut. It was a most spooky night as there was a fair wind up, and a flap of tin was banging against a doorframe all night.

After a fitful night, I set off at daylight for the final twenty-five kilometres back to the station. The shortest way was to deviate from the road and cut across through the air strip, which I was just doing when a light aircraft landed! It was Cec Watts, the pastoral inspector, coming to pay a visit.

He had assumed that Tim would be there to pick him up, so when I turned up, on foot, most dishevelled and with my dress on inside out, he wondered what was confronting him.

A TRIP WITH THE FLYING DOCTOR

One day when I was making one of the kid's beds I put my back out, as sometimes happens if you get into the wrong position. I soon became almost totally incapacitated, so Tim put a mattress in the back of the station wagon and drove me to Elliott, where there was a nursing clinic manned by Sister Barbara. This lady came to the station once a month and attended to all the Helen Springs medical needs.

When we arrived, she said, "I have a Flying Doctor plane due in an hour and I will put you on that to Alice Springs."

"Thanks, Sister, that would be good."

What she didn't tell us was that the plane had been ordered to transport an Aboriginal who had a broken hip. I was put on the plane and I have no idea what happened to the other patient.

All the way to Alice, I was grilled by the nursing staff on board, two sisters.

"Why was I on that plane and the other fellow left behind?" This went on and on, and I was so embarrassed. It was nothing to do with me, it was completely out of my hands.

Anyhow, we eventually got to Alice. I sat on a bed until I could be attended to, by which time it was about midnight.

Next day, after five x-rays, only one of which was looked at, I was put in traction. I have never been able to sleep in a comfortable bed, so I didn't get any that night. Trying to sleep with a brick hanging off your head is no laughing matter. Amazingly, the thing came unattached during the night, and though a doctor came to have a look, it was never reassembled.

I was returned to the ward, and it seemed as though bed rest was all I needed. After five days confined to bed I was allowed to go home. Bliss!

The back, however, continued to give me trouble, so I arranged to fly to Melbourne to stay with my sister Mollie and have a consultation with an osteopath. (Osteopathy is a type of alternative medicine that emphasises physical manipulation of muscular tissue and bones.) The man was brilliant, diagnosed my problem, and told me to hang from a bar and swim every day.

I followed his advice religiously, and have never had a major back problem since. Tim soon rigged up a bar, and every day I would go to the "boghole", a waterhole left by the roads department at the Helen Springs turnoff, and have a good swim.

HOLIDAY TIME

At the end of 1977, we took our month's annual leave. Holidays were becoming less and less appealing as we were obliged to live out of suitcases and stay with relatives and friends, which got a bit tedious after a while.

We decided it was time to look round for some small property in South East Queensland where we could put down roots for when we eventually left the Territory, and also where we could stay on holidays. In this endeavour, we were unsuccessful. As a consolation, Tim bought a sleek, maroon Mark 10 Jaguar, 1965 model, for $2000. This large, luxurious car was the British manufacturer's top-of-the-range saloon car for a decade, and we felt so grand driving back to the station in this beautiful automobile.

When holiday time came up again the following year, Tim decided to get some "million milers" from the truckies so he could get behind the wheel and drive non-stop to avoid the usual three days of our holidays just getting south. The truckies used to take these pills and could go for days without a sleep.

We headed off, but it wasn't long before Tim said to me, "You'll have to drive, I need a camp."

So we changed over. This went on until we got south thirty-six hours later, but when we arrived at our destination, the pills finally kicked in and Tim was unable to sleep! We didn't try that one again.

KURANDE, ALLORA

This time we found our dream farm outside the sleepy but scenically beautiful town of Allora, 130 kilometres west of Brisbane. It was the first farm we looked at with the agent, Harry Rubie, and I still remember sitting in the back with Tim, nudging each other at our first glimpse of this perfectly situated property, perched on a hill surrounded by creeks, trees and black soil flats. We thought this would be our dream holiday home.

The house was just right for our requirements. Referred to by the locals as the Chard Farm and built in the 1880s, it was a gracious old Queenslander with the typical bull nosed verandah all around, a rustic garden fence and a fabulous 360-degree view of the surrounding countryside.

It was very run down and fairly primitive, as water to the kitchen sink was provided by a hose through the window! Restoring rundown properties eventually became our forte.

We would get the 145 hectares for $35,000! So we approached the banks for a loan, as we needed another $18,000. Even though we were both on the payroll and earning a good yearly salary, none of the banks would touch us as they said we were "investors, not developers".

My Dad to the rescue. He lent us the money, and we returned to Helen to save up and pay off the loan. I had done rural bookkeeping by correspondence, and the company was prepared to give me the bookkeeping job at Helen, which enabled us to pay off the loan fairly quickly. We were privileged, as it was not normal policy for the company to allow the manager's wife to be in control of the wages and store purchasing owing to the possibility of fraud. I loved the job, and the knowledge I gained has stood me in good stead right up to the present.

While we were south, we decided to try to employ staff ourselves. Vestey managers were fairly autonomous and could hire and fire as they thought fit, so we advertised in the local paper and the *Queensland Country Life* for jackaroos on a Territory station.

We interviewed many people this way, and were able to find some really good employees until the company cottoned on to what was happening and put a stop to the practice. We had just employed a young man who later became known as "Big Foot", but the company wouldn't let him come to Helen. He was sent instead to Wave Hill, where he had a very successful career.

RETURNING HOME IN "THE BIG WET"

It had been a very big wet season, and getting back to Helen in the Jag presented a great deal of difficulty. We got as far as the Inca Creek west of Mt Isa, but it was running a banker, so we had to return to the city. There we left the Jag with Buntine Roadways (our trucking company), who agreed to keep it in their locked yard.

We then chartered a light aircraft for the 660 kilometre flight to Tennant Creek. Storms closed in on us all the way till gradually visibility was reduced to almost zero. The pilot had been following the Barkly Highway, but even that became elusive and he was having trouble finding his way.

Miraculously, he found the airport when a break in the clouds loomed out of nowhere, but a massive storm closed in on us and landing was a very nervous affair. When we finally made it, the pilot was congratulated by air traffic control for having set down safely. Whew, how lucky we had been.

Later that year, we went to pick up the Jag, but we hadn't gone far on the return journey before we discovered something was wrong. Being a very sophisticated car for its era, it had a lever on the dashboard that locked it into second gear. We now found that it was permanently locked in second gear, not a very desirable way to negotiate the Barkly Highway and the 810 kilometres back to the station.

Fortunately, we were able to go as fast as eighty kilometres an hour, but it was a very tedious trip, and the kids (and their mother) were getting pretty fidgety. It would appear that some of the truckies couldn't resist taking it for a joy ride and had somehow buggered up the gear arrangements.

It was a long time before we got it fixed, as we had to get a gearbox from Adelaide then find someone to put it in. We stuck to simpler cars after that.

BARKLY STOCK ROUTE TRAGEDIES

The Barkly Stock Route runs through Helen Springs, on which there are two Department of Interior bores — DI 4 and DI 5. (DI stands for Department of Interior). These bores were equipped with the massive windmills for which the tableland is famous, but a couple of tragedies occurred along this route during the droving days.

A doctor new to the country had been summoned to Rockhampton Downs, so he set off with his new wife from Tennant Creek in an old car — I think it was in about 1926. He went into one of the stock route bores, but couldn't find his way back to the road as thousands of cattle tracks obliterated his way in.

By the time Rockhampton Downs had sounded the alarm and a rescue party was sent out, it was too late and the couple was dead. This incident rocked the country for a long time and is still remembered today.

Jack Brady, or "Boomerang Jack" as he was known, was a well-known stockman who wanted to get home to Queensland for Christmas, so he set off across the stock route with an Aboriginal as his sole companion. Along the way, Brady developed malaria and died of fever on a desolate, treeless spot on Eva Downs. His companion covered him with his swag and rode all the way to the Anthony Lagoon Police Station to report the death. Many years later, Jack's sister erected a headstone and fenced the area off, a notable landmark to this day.

There is a quarantine paddock on Helen that was used during the droving days if travelling stock contracted pleuropneumonia and had to be held up until they recovered.

THE BTEC CAMPAIGN

Not long before our departure from Helen Springs, the federal government established the Brucellosis and Tuberculosis Eradication Campaign, always referred to as just BTEC. (Brucellosis is spontaneous abortion.) This massive undertaking was established to rid the country of these diseases, which hampered our export industries.

BTEC changed more than the health status of the cattle. It forced the introduction of much improved facilities such as fencing, yards and communication, and also the quality of station stock.

All cattle had to be tested, which involved taking a sample from the butt of the tail and holding the cattle for three days while the tests were interpreted. Hundreds of thousands of cattle and buffalo were shot. Some station owners were very bitter if they lost most of their breeding herds, as they felt sometimes compensation was not adequate.

On Helen Springs, along with the other cattle, our milking herd of about twenty head was tested, and our prize milker tested positive so had to be shot. However, an autopsy revealed that the test had been faulty and she was not in fact a reactor at all. Such is life (and death).

The scheme culminated in about 1985 and, though controversial at the time, it has resulted in enormous benefits to the cattle industry.

PART 2

My father Richard French (Kikang)

My mother Enid French (Gang Gang)

French family in 1956 L-R Roger, Mollie, Mum, Jocelyn, Dad and June

The miner's cottage that Dad bought at Yerranderie in 1942

Family adorning Studebaker on way to Yerranderie Cottage 1953

My precious Aunty (Lilian Douglas)

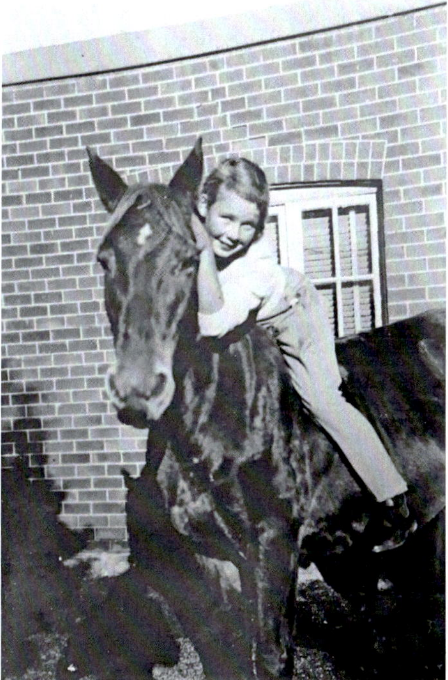

My precious Darran

Hoofs and Horns photo — mock hunt outside Sydney

Self on Darran and Fiona on Brando at Castle Hill Pony Club

Winning team of Four Lightweight Hacks with Rob Fulcher (right) at Sydney Royal 1961

Self and friend in Mollie's Messerschmidt

Rob Fulcher and I at The Entrance 1958

Exercising polo ponies at Ruvigne Gunnedah

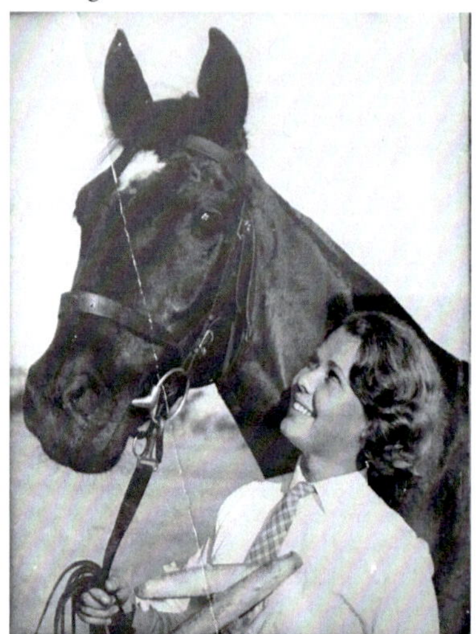
Self and Cloud at Gunnedah Polo Carnival

Plaiting Mr Thomsons polo horse ready for play

Hostess School in Essendon, Victoria 1963

Self in Boeing 727 uniform 1965

Tim when I first met him at Kirkimbie Sation in the Kimberleys 1965

Our wedding, Sydney 1966

James and Jane Doran, the newlyweds, and Dick and Enid French

Tim and I and baby Andrew, Katherine, N.T.

Daisy at Manbulloo Station

Andrew and picaninnies at Manbulloo

Tim and baby Sophie at Manbulloo

Tim and self at Katherine Races with Andrew

Spring Creek house with Andy and Stormy on lawn

Shirley and kids at Spring Creek Station

"Spring Creek 30 cwt. Bedford loaded for Negri Races

Our camp at the Negri Races (From left - Des Smith, Tim and Wixie with Soph at front)

Family dressed and ready for Negri Races

Signpost at Golden Gate en route to Spring Creek with The Count

Helen Springs Station homestead

Andy on Wattle at Helen Springs

Soph on Two Bob at Helen Springs

Tim's homemade float after accident en route to Alice Springs show

Helen Springs stockcamp on breakers. From left — Shane, Peter, Keith, Jack, Guy, Ricky and Mick

Andy with lubras on lawn outside dining room at Helen Springs

Self riding Metal in Renner Springs campdraft

Daly Waters Rodeo 1974 Helen Springs ringers in rescue race

Soph on post at Daly Waters Rodeo

Daly Waters Rodeo Tim picking up on Sister (who later came south with us)

WE LEAVE THE TERRITORY FOR GOOD

Since our marriage, we had had a very exciting and rewarding life in the Territory working for the Vestey family. Tim had spent twenty-one years working for the Lord (Lord Vestey), and I had been with him for fifteen of those. We had always longed for a property of our own, but as this was not financially possible in the Territory, at the end of 1981, we decided to make a move.

I would have preferred to wait until Andrew and Sophie had completed Grade 10 at their respective schools, but Tim was keen to go and nothing could change his mind. Andrew had a year to go at Churchie and Sophie two years at St Margaret's. As we only had $40,000 in the bank and no job prospects, we considered we would be unable to keep them at their expensive boarding schools.

Just before Tim resigned, he was offered the management of Wave Hill, as the current manager was leaving. Tim had no desire to take up a big management again, so he politely declined, at the same time giving Mr Bell our notice.

Wixie and Brollie, who had been managing Mistake Creek, were leaving at the same time, so we formed a considerable convoy for the big trip south, along with Bob Peterson, our friend and ex-copper from Elliott.

We had been able to purchase six of our favourite horses, five mares and a gelding, therefore had the pick of the horse plant. This was the last time Vesteys sold their horses, so we were very lucky as they were top quality and we only had to pay $150 per head.

My great old steed, Sambo, had earlier succumbed to Birdsville disease, a nervous condition caused by the consumption of the indigofera plant. Weakness, incoordination and swaying are some of the symptoms causing horses to blunder into anything at all.

Sadly, Sambo had to be put down, so that was goodbye to another dear old friend.

Owing to the fact that a horse abattoir was being built outside Tennant Creek, we weren't prepared to risk leaving all our old pets at Helen (they were now pensioners enjoying a life of freedom on Donkey Plain). Tim had the very unpleasant task of shooting them all. The Count, Two Bob, Wattle and Alpha were the lucky ones who didn't have to suffer the indignity of old age or the knackery. A very traumatic time for us but we knew we were doing the right thing by these wonderful animals.

A natural death for stock is not a very nice one — they can become bogged in a waterhole or just starve to death when unable to forage and there was no way we would risk that death for our beloved horses.

We had a six-tonne truck for which Tim had constructed a stock crate that just neatly accommodated the horses we had bought. Wixie had a truck for all his gear and was accompanied by their oldest son and Brollie drove their Toyota Land Cruiser ute with the other two young children. Bob accompanied us to cart all our possessions in his ten-tonne truck with a crane on the back, which proved to be a boon.

It was a harrowing trip for the horses, and I don't know how we managed to load them day after day. The first night we camped at the Mt Isa trucking yards beside the dip, then it was on to Longreach, but after this section of the road, the horses were fairly shell-shocked when we unloaded them, as the road had lots of nasty little dips, typical of the Channel country.

Finally, we got to Roma for the last night, but somehow I got the instructions mixed up (I was driving the horse truck), and unloaded the horses in the wrong yards. No mobile phones, but eventually the others located me and we had our last night by the campfire.

We had decided, as a bit of a bonus before we left Helen, we would butcher a steer to get us started in the ration department when we arrived at Allora. This was processed and frozen, then packed into tea chests lined with woollen blankets for the three and a half day trip south.

Amazingly, it survived, the outside parts being used for dog meat and the inside sections being perfectly preserved.

Naturally, the first thing we had to do on arrival was to buy a freezer, so Tim and Bob immediately set off for Toowoomba, leaving me to start settling in. Tim got a bit carried away though and came back with a cedar chest of drawers, for which he paid $800! To make the understatement of the year, I was flabbergasted considering we didn't know how long we had to make our $40,000 last. (He did buy a suitable freezer though.)

On reflection, it probably didn't matter. We invested spare capital with Graingrowers at ten per cent interest, but the company later collapsed and we lost $15,000.

SETTLING INTO KURANDE

After Bob had departed back for Katherine, I can still remember revelling in the fact that we were at last alone (no staff) and that we had the bliss of silence — no lighting plant!

Leaving 1.3 million acres to settle on 330 acres did take a bit of adjusting to, but we had no regrets, though I still miss the Kimberley.

After a couple of months, the kids came home from school and we all set about the mammoth task of making Kurande into a respectable property.

This was no mean feat, as everything was rundown. Rolling up old fences and replacing them with new ones, knocking walls out of the homestead and painting inside and out, closing in verandahs, sowing crops and hoeing out weeds were our daily activities. We replaced the hose that supplied water through a window to the kitchen sink. We bought a second-hand iron rolling machine, removed the bull-nosed verandah rooves and rerolled them into their original shape. It was all very satisfying.

We took the kids to pony club where we knew no one. The instructress was most unfriendly, so it was a rather unhappy time.

Both children were great little riders, but didn't really take to pony club in Allora owing to this instructress.

Enter Jean and Bob Burge. They were local farmers who felt sorry for us, and invited us to their home for dinner the following Friday night. This was a lifesaver, and so began a lifelong friendship. From then on, we had dinner at alternate places once a week where congeniality was the order of the night.

Nick Smith, an Allora dairy farmer who had married our last governess, Kez Sinclair, helped us with farming techniques, as we had no knowledge along these lines and Nick was an excellent farmer. He even acquired for us an old Sunshine harvester (every museum has one), and with this we harvested our first crop — canary for bird seed. It was not terribly lucrative, but some income all the same.

Being rather cash-strapped, we decided to brew our own beer as there was no way we could afford to buy expensive, ready-brewed stuff. Our home brew was eventually christened "Dorex", a play on our surname and the popular Queensland beer, Forex. Many a great night was had with the Burges, the Johnsons, the Smiths and any other Territory friends, as well as my sister Mollie and her family. Dorex was a fairly powerful brew though, and to this day Bob Burge won't touch it after we had a few good nights on it.

Mollie and Geoff had bought the Commercial Hotel in Allora, and this was the reason we headed there when we first went to Queensland.

Once again the Kendalls and the Dorans were reunited, and with our children and their cousins (Mollie and Geoff now had four children), lots of fun times were had.

To help make ends meet, we did work for local farmers, including mustering and potato picking. I reckon Tim and I must have looked a little incongruous turning up at a potato farm in a sleek Jaguar to harvest potatoes. We later sold it and bought a Mini Minor, so our status had definitely gone down in life.

We had a lovely old neighbour by the name of Stan Bischoff. He was a "salt of the earth" bushy, a great old bloke who still had a bullock wagon and the bullocks to pull it. He hitched them up for us one day and took us for a jaunt on the wagon. It was amazing to see what a tight circle those bullocks could turn the wagon in.

Stan gave us our first real working dog — Sally, a beautiful golden kelpie cross who was our faithful companion for fifteen years. She later had a litter of pups, and these were some of the best and most intelligent dogs we have ever owned. We gave two away, but we kept Lulu and gave Nuggett to Sophie. More about them later.

One farmer asked Tim to remove a cantankerous bull to another paddock, so Tim mounted up on Sister and went to shoulder the bull, but as he did so, it turned and hooked him right out of the saddle. The rotten mongrel!

Also acquired at that time was "Tojo", a short wheel based Toyota that had been used for bull-catching on Scott Creek Station, our neighbour with Manbulloo in the Northern Territory. It's a small world. Tojo was our work horse and stayed with us till 1994.

Bob asked Tim to conduct saddling classes as another source of income. This was another skill he learnt in his early days in the Kimberley — you had to be self-sufficient or you didn't survive. On Mondays, he went to the Toowoomba saleyards to help with cattle yarding and drafting.

Tim was multi-skilled, and did most of the plumbing repairs and minor electrical jobs on the place, as well as the fencing, yard and house repairs.

We had brought with us from Helen a great big old black fuel stove that had been in the Aboriginals' camp (luckily Bob Peterson had his crane truck). Every Tuesday was my baking day — I made a week's supply of cakes, biscuits and bread, and cooked everything on this great old stove, which we had placed in the garden. Obviously, rainy days were out and we had to tighten the belt so to speak.

We later bought a Jersey cow, which provided us with milk, and we also made butter, a very satisfying existence. Tim rigged up a bucket with a wooden lid and a hole in the centre, put the butter paddle on the end of an electric drill, and off we went butter-making the easy way. One day, the lid flew off in the middle of the high-speed drilling, and we ended up with half-made butter all over the kitchen walls and ceiling. It took us days to clean up the mess.

We acquired a grain grinder with which to make our own flour for bread-making, and grew fruit and vegetables, but we were to find that being self-sufficient, though rewarding, was very time-consuming and only saved a small amount of money.

We encountered a very dry year one time, so just turned our horses out on the road during the day and brought them in at night-time. It was amazing that we could get away with this, but we never had any dramas and they didn't wander far.

We also bought six young unbroken horses, which Tim and the kids set about breaking in, and which augmented the coffers somewhat.

While Soph was still at boarding school, we lent her horse, Melanie, which we had brought down from Helen Springs with us, to Little Jude in New South Wales in order to play polocrosse. Sadly for Soph, this had a bad outcome. One morning, Jude went to feed the two horses she had running in the paddock and found them both dead, side by side. It was concluded that they had been poisoned, which was devastating for Soph as Melanie had been her special horse.

Soph had bad luck with another of her special horses, Sapphire. For some reason, Sapphire had tried to negotiate the grid at Helen Springs and got her legs stuck between the bars. I happened to be on the phone to Mum at the time, so the mechanic was summoned.

This had a drastic outcome for, instead of trying to turn the horse sideways or get the oxy and acetylene and remove the bars, George, not a horseman, tried to lead Sapphire forwards. The awful result was four broken legs and a .22 bullet.

School time approached for Andrew and Sophie, and it was off to Allora State School. This was another shock for them after their fancy boarding schools in Brisbane, but they had no choice and eventually settled in. So we were Darby and Joan again, and knuckled into the workload with gusto once more.

After only a year at Allora State School, Andy went to Gatton Agricultural College to study stock and meat inspecting. He wasn't really interested in school work, so we considered it would be a waste of time to put him on a bus to go to the nearest high school, as Allora only went to Grade 10.

This course didn't tickle his fancy, so he applied for and got a jackarooing job with a cattle grazier from Guluguba, north of Miles in south-west Queensland.

The owner of the property really loved Andy, and even gave him his own brand — obviously he was going to let him start a herd of his own. Unfortunately, Andy must have inherited his parents' love of the wide open spaces, so he applied for a job on Ord River Station — Tim's old hunting ground.

He was successful with this application and was soon off to the Ord River Regeneration Scheme, where a government research station had been set up to fence and regenerate the land. So like father, like son, they both cut their teeth round the mighty Ord

River. Later, Andy found his true forte, but more of that in another chapter.

We were able to send Soph to Fairholme College in Toowoomba in 1984 to do her final years in secondary school. Here she excelled before going on to Gatton Agricultural College to obtain her Bachelor of Business majoring in hospitality management, which has been handy for her in her present life. She not only acquired a degree there, but also met her future husband.

She also joined the college polocrosse team, and this sport occupied a lot of her recreational time while at the college. She never did have much luck with horses though, as her polocrosse horse, Firefly, was later killed by a snake.

ANOTHER CHANGE

Though we loved Kurande, we couldn't stay as there was no way of making an adequate living unless one of us did off-farm work, which didn't appeal to us. We put the place on the market for the huge sum of $240,000.

After three years of hard work, it had become a bit of a showplace. Amazingly, we found a buyer and received $235,000. We now had enough money to buy ourselves a viable grazing property, which had always been our ambition. Two hundred thousand dollars was not a bad profit after six years.

My older sister, June, always reckoned the buyer must have had rocks in his head to pay so much for THAT place! She didn't allow for our charming colonial homestead, fabulous view, pretty gardens, post and rail fences, and good improvements on the run.

We then found Verona, a lovely property that was big enough for us to actually make a living from. The only problem was that it was a sheep property — cattle places were too expensive at the time — but it was a beautiful place in the Traprock country between Inglewood and Stanthorpe in southern Queensland. Most cattle people refer to sheep as "ground lice" or "monkeys", but we were unlikely to find a cattle place that we could afford.

Verona was 1870 hectares and had about nineteen dams and several permanent spring-fed creeks running through the property. It also had four sets of sheep yards and one substantial set of cattle yards, and of course, an excellent shearing shed and weather shed.

We were able to secure the property for $220,000, so it was only necessary to take out a stock mortgage with the stock and station agents, Primac, in order to stock the place.

I remember saying to Tim when we bought Verona: "Isn't it great — all we will need to run this place will be a horse and a pair of pliers!"

How little did I know about growing wool? Absolutely zero. I had no idea there was so much work in running sheep. You were always poking something down their throats or spraying something on their backs, when you weren't mustering them for shearing or crutching.

Verona actually comprised two soldier settlement blocks named Verona and Wylarah. The Soldier Settlement Scheme was established to assist returning discharged soldiers after the two world wars, and was administered by state governments.

The idea was an excellent one, but the implementation left much to be desired. Firstly, most of the blocks were too small to make a living from, some were very rough and needed a lot of hard work to develop, and lastly, but probably most importantly, many ex-servicemen had no knowledge of farming and grazing.

Tim had had some experience with sheep when he had jackarooed in the Riverina, and we were lucky enough to have great neighbours, Pam and Anne Reddell. These extremely capable ladies were "dyed in the wool" sheep cockies, and steered us on the right path from the beginning, helping us to buy appropriate stock for that Traprock fine wool-growing country.

Pam and Anne were two sisters who proved that you can survive on a single soldier settlement block. The property and a considerable mortgage were left to them by their father, who died when they were in their thirties. They trapped and skinned rabbits, worked in the sheds of all their neighbours, did their own shearing and crutching, and in so doing, were able to negate the mortgage and live to a reasonable old age. They loved a rum and smoked Camel cigarettes by the packet (they were a lot cheaper then!). We couldn't have wished for better neighbours.

Not long after we arrived at Verona, they had a party — a fairly lavish affair — and we had the opportunity to meet all the other sheep cockies in the district.

It was a bit of a shock to me, though, when all the women adjourned to the house to gossip and prepare food and all the men stayed on the lawn, drinking and discussing wool prices and the weather. It was a far cry from our Territory days when we all boxed on together.

Soon after buying Verona, we decided to diversify and bought 120 feral goats from an Inglewood grazier for the purpose of growing cashmere. We considered these animals very suited to the poorer country of the Traprock, and they would be good to help control regrowth and woody weeds, of which there were plenty.

These animals are hardy and easy to handle, and many of them became our pets. We were, however, looked down upon by some of the locals, as they considered goats rather inferior to Merinos at that time. Now goats have become very fashionable and a lucrative investment.

The only thing that upset me about growing cashmere was the fact that the animals had to be shorn at the end of autumn, as they would shed their fleeces before the end of winter and all the cashmere would be lost. Even though we built substantial shelter sheds in two of their paddocks, for some reason they never ventured into them, and I was very conscious of their suffering from exposure.

Tim did the shearing and I classed the fleeces, and we became active members of the Australian Cashmere Growers' Association, Region 41, of which I became secretary.

We eventually got out of the goats, but they had been a successful diversification and a pleasure to deal with.

The previous owner of Verona had been blinded by a chip flying up from an axe, and we were amazed that he had been able to carry on to a ripe old age when he sold to us. I think owing to his blindness he was unable to see the number of rabbits that were overrunning the property, so one of our first jobs was to lay poison baits over the entire place.

This is done in collaboration with the Department of Primary Industries (as it was then), which supplied a mincing machine and laid a trail of carrots over the entire property. This process is repeated over two nights, then on the third night the carrots are laced with 1080 poison.

The result was spectacular — the smell was overwhelming and there were dead rabbits everywhere, though most of them had gone into their burrows to die. A sad but necessary act to help to rid the country of these unfortunate pests.

Verona had a fairly primitive but liveable homestead, so the next job we set about doing was to build a set of stables, a tack room and a fowl run. The property had loads of good ironbark timber, so all the posts and rails for this job we were able to harvest on the place. Eventually, Tim built a verandah on two sides of the house, also using timber cut on the place, so we considered we had a veritable mansion,.

Most of the fences needed straining, and regrowth and woody weeds kept us busy on the Tordon axe and the brush cutter most days. One of the hazards of clearing was the presence of wasps. There were three types, the first two of which would dart out and sting you as soon as you touched the bush that their nest was attached to. If you dislodged the nest, they were no longer predatory and would be harmless, but you were usually stung before you discovered the nest.

The third type, however, was a different matter. They were big, red creatures that were known locally as king wasps. Fortunately, Tim and I only encountered these horrors once and never wanted to repeat the experience. As soon as we touched the tree they were nesting in, they attacked, but when we fled the scene, they continued to follow us and attack, which is something the smaller wasps would not do. So we had to shed our Tordonning gear and take off as fast as we could go, only returning next day to retrieve our utensils. They inflicted a large and painful sting that lasted for weeks.

Owing to the previous owner's blindness, we would sometimes find wires connected wrongly, that is, the fourth wire would be connected to the third wire and so on.

It wasn't all work and no play. We had arrived in a very social district, so dinners, parties and tennis days were a welcome break from hard work.

OUR FIRST SHEARING

This we did in January, and it was an exciting time. My sister Mollie came to do the shearers' cooking, and her two daughters, Sonie and Trixie, helped on the wool table doing the skirting, along with neighbours Pam and Anne, and also Barry. The experienced wool people must have had a laugh at four people doing the skirting, as this is usually done by two people, but three of us were greenhorns.

Our neighbour Barry did the wool classing, Anne did the picking up and sweeping, while Tim did the pressing. Amazingly, we got a good price for our wool and earnt in that first year, 1984, more than we had ever seen.

I decided to do a wool classing course so we wouldn't have to pay a classer, and took myself to Brisbane to a technical college to obtain my wool classing stencil. I think I must have attracted a few smirks when I asked the instructor what the "M" stood for when wool bales are branded. The obvious answer was Merino, but I was totally inexperienced in the wool industry — this must have seemed elementary to the other people in the class.

Anyhow, during our next shearing, we obviously were doing all right as our wool topped the sale for twenty-one micron wool. I give this credit to Pam and Anne, as they had helped us to buy excellent wethers (castrated male sheep) producing beautiful wool.

As we became more experienced, we were able to reduce the number of employees at shearing time, and ended up with two people doing the skirting. For the next eight years while we were at Verona, we had tremendous help from all our neighbours, which made it all so much easier for us.

In 1987, we had a lovely line of wool for which we received the grand sum of $88,000! This was an amazing amount of money for a couple of battlers, so we started to look for an off-farm investment.

STRADBROKE ISLAND

Eventually we found the perfect place — a two-storey beach house at Stradbroke Island, which we bought with our Territory friends, Ralph and Thea Hayes, for the grand sum of $125,000. Many wonderful holidays ensued on this spectacular island, whose attractions could rival anything in southern Queensland, visitor numbers being limited by the fact that it is only accessible via barge and ferry.

Conveniently located with easy access to three main beaches, our house was in a prime location. It consisted of two flats, one of which was permanently rented and the other on a holiday basis, so it gave us a reasonable off-farm income and a delightful place to spend any time we were able to have away from the property. We eventually sold our share to Ralph and Thea. Ralph has since died and Thea has only recently parted company with this great little holiday opportunity. So it is finally goodbye Straddie.

During the wool boom, many woolgrowers invested in further grazing properties, and a lot of them suffered financial stress when wool eventually crashed. We were pleased that we had diversified our investment. Properties that had been well maintained started to show signs of neglect as cash ran short — it was the end of an era.

LIFE GOES ON AT VERONA

During the winter, it was normal to feed corn to sheep every three days. It is amazing how a tiny ration of corn can sustain them with little grass supplement. When feeding them, we would toot the horn and sheep would come running from all directions, bleating their little heads off. All this for a few mouthfuls of grain, but that was all it took to sustain them through the hard winter months.

We grew our own fruit and vegetables, broke in horses, and did our own crutching using a portable crutching plant. We also cut and sold firewood and split posts, and later set about building a hay shed. We had no tractor so all this work had to be done by hand, cutting logs, barking them, loading them on to our truck using the principles Tim had learnt in the Kimberley.

The posts for the hay shed were about twelve feet long and I am still amazed that we were able to lodge them into the holes that we had dug using a crowbar and shovel. (It's no wonder that Tim needed a hip replacement a couple of years later!)

Sid joined our dog team, a great little red kelpie, faithful and obedient. We had trained the dogs to stay when told. One day we were out mustering, but needed to leave the dogs under a tree while we drafted out some sheep. Job finished, we headed home, only to find that we had forgotten the dogs! We returned to find them still camped under the tree, obedient little critters that they were.

Soph would give us a hand when able to come home on holidays. She also learnt to shoe her own horses after she joined the Gatton polocrosse team. She became proficient at roping from the bronco horse during branding time when working for Rob and Graham on their station, Ooratippra, in the Territory.

Andy went jackarooing on a few more places in the Kimberley, and eventually went bull catching on Tipperary and Douglas Stations. He became a confident bull rider, and rode in various rodeos in the north. Brave fellow, I reckon, daunting looking creatures with their sharp horns, great strength, unpredictability and wild-looking eyes.

He finally made his packet barramundi fishing out of Borroloola in the Gulf, and could tell us some harrowing stories about this episode in his life. He was able to save enough money to get his chopper licence, a course which he sailed through — he had finally found his forte.

THE WOOL CRASH

We had been lucky to have purchased Verona during good years in the wool industry. The Australian Wool Reserve Price Scheme had been set up by the Australian Wool Commission in 1970 in order to smooth out fluctuations in wool prices. The objective was for the AWC to buy wool when its price was below the floor price, and the scheme was funded by a levy on wool sold by growers.

The scheme worked well until the mid-eighties when the floor price was set too high. This encouraged over-production and the market eventually collapsed, but the AWC (then the Australian Wool Corporation) kept buying the wool. A massive stockpile of 4.7 million bales was reached, incurring around $3 million a day in storage and interest costs.

By 1991, the AWC had built up a stockpile that would crash the industry. The reserve price was cut to 700 cents a kilogram, but there were still no buyers. When free market auctions resumed, wool sold for 430 cents a kilogram.

The last of the stockpile was finally sold in 2001, but this dramatically depressed the market price and many farmers and wool-related businesses went broke.

Because of over-production of wool, there were also too many sheep, so the awful business of shooting sheep occurred. We were caught up in this horrible ordeal too, but after shooting only a small number of wethers we just couldn't keep doing it, it seemed to be so wrong. The sheep would be run up the race, and as each one reached the head of the race it was killed with one shot from a .22, then dragged to the side ready for the next one. Then, of course, the bodies had to be disposed of, stacked in a big pile and burnt. If my memory serves me correctly, we were even supplied with the bullets, but I am not sure about this.

TIM HAVING HIP PROBLEMS

Tim was starting to have pain in his right hip. He soldiered on for months, agonising with himself whether or not he should have an operation until eventually the pain got the better of him, so plans were made to have a replacement.

He arranged with Dr Robert Ivers in Toowoomba to have this done late in 1990. Tim took a long time to recover back to normal operations and required a lot of nursing after he had returned home. He seemed to suffer an abnormal amount of pain. He was laid up for about three weeks, but was unable to return to normal duties for several months. Fortunately, Soph was able to give a hand during this time.

The operation, however, was a great success and a credit to Dr Ivers, who told Tim he could expect to have a good hip for at least ten years if he didn't work it too hard. Famous last words! He continued to work hard and the hip lasted for much longer than ten years — it never gave him any more trouble.

We continued on at Verona as before, interspersed with fabulous Straddie holidays, but Tim had never become a focused sheep man and was becoming less and less keen on the hard work, so we decided to put the place on the market.

In 1992, a buyer was found and we nearly doubled our money, so we could have a good holiday before starting on our next venture. Verona had been very kind to us, giving us a good income, off-farm investment and a handy capital gain. We had made a lot of improvements, which had become a recipe for our lifestyle.

FAREWELL VERONA

This was a very sad time for me as I loved Verona and could have stayed there, but I knew it was the sensible thing to do. We had been working hard basically since 1966 when we were married, and a good spell had plenty of appeal.

We leased a house on a cropping property at Bongeen on the Darling Downs, so we were free to travel to our hearts' content, but I think I cried every night for the first month or so, I missed our beloved Verona so much.

We went to Brisbane to look for a suitable 4WD station wagon to rig up for our ventures into the bush. We were extremely lucky to obtain a 1986 HJ Toyota Land Cruiser wagon that had done about 186,000 kilometres. This amazing vehicle clocked up just on 500,000 kilometres before it was sold in 2016.

We would pull up at service stations to refuel and people would comment to us: "You want to hang on to that vehicle, they don't make them like that anymore."

How true it was. It still had the original engine and we only had to renew the gearbox in all that time.

We purchased a large fly (canvas square), a car fridge, camp ovens and suitable camping equipment and, with our swags, we were ready to see Australia. Our only concession to comfort was a double mattress, which sat atop all our gear in the back and provided a good vantage point for our two dogs, Sally and Lulu, who accompanied us on our trips.

With our powerful, sturdy 4WD, this method of camping gave us much flexibility to camp in isolated, out of the way places, always keeping out of sight of roads or habitation. It also gave us that luxury of camping under the stars, a pleasure we hadn't experienced since the Territory days.

ON THE WALLABY

On our first trip, we caught up with an old friend from the cashmere days, David Armstrong, who was on the road near Surat with four thousand head of sheep during the drought. It was a fun experience. We stayed with him for four days, but we weren't sorry that we didn't have to stay until the end. He was on the road for months with his eleven loyal, hardworking dogs and several horses.

We then went to Ooratippra Station, 350 kilometres north-east of Alice Springs on the Sandover Highway. This station was owned by our friends Rob and Graham Fulcher who were going on holidays, and we were caretaking for them for six weeks.

Not long after they departed, on Christmas Eve, the station bore broke down and needed pulling. It was equipped with a tripod, which needed to be climbed to attach the tackle for pulling the bore rods. Since his hip replacement, Tim was in no fit state to climb this erection, which I assessed needed nothing less than a monkey to perform this feat. I gave it a few attempts but could get no further than about the first six rungs, and being Christmas Day, we could not call the assistance of a bore mechanic.

The neighbour from Argadargada Station came to our rescue and attached the necessary equipment, and together we were able to pull the bore. Water emergency saved — all remedied in a few hours.

After Rob and Graham returned, we went on to Oodnadatta, but it is not recommended to travel in this country in the summer months. Our camping arrangements involved laying the fly out on the ground, then our double mattress, and on top of this we would roll out our swag. It was so hot that we had to keep putting wet towels on our bodies to get a modicum of sleep, and to top it off, the flies and ants were all in a biting mood!

We then went on to William Creek Roadhouse, Lake Eyre South, Leigh Creek, Maree and the beautiful Flinders Ranges. It was then on through South Australia until we reached Morgan on the Murray, where we camped by the river. We did carry a primitive tent for emergencies, and we encountered one this night. By nine o'clock, we found ourselves changing our sleeping mode — we had to rig up the tent in great haste to avoid being carried away by mosquitoes.

Then on to Victoria for a stay with Tim's family and to visit the Supreme Court, where Tim's brother-in-law was conducting a murder trial — fascinating. On to New South Wales and Mount Kosciusko, Thredbo, Perisher and Canberra, including a visit to the new Parliament House. A visit to Burragorang Valley brought back memories, before we went to Sydney to catch up with my family, then back to Bongeen after eleven glorious weeks on the road.

As we had no ties, we then went to Straddie for a few days with Ralph and Thea.

Our next trip was to north Queensland, Karumba, Doomadgee and on to Borroloola, where we stayed with an old Territory friend, Ross Robertson, commonly known as "Can't Tear 'em Ross". He used to come to the Renner Springs Rodeo every year and ride in, and just as often win, the buckjump. He used to stay in our camp so we got to know him pretty well.

He took us for a flight in his Cessna 210 to inspect his tourist venture on the edge of the MacArthur River. He demonstrated steep turns, low flying — thirty metres and less, buzzing campers and following the river, then he dropped a message in a bottle to some fishermen below us. Talk about exciting!

My presence on the aircraft nearly tipped the scales at being overweight, but that didn't worry Ross. Sadly, he was later killed in an aircraft accident in New Guinea.

Then it was on to Katherine where we spent a few days with Shorty and Ralph Hayes. When we told Shorty about my sister Mollie, who was no longer living with her husband, he said to us: "Tell her to get on a bus and leave her knickers and her dog behind!"

Typical Shorty humour!

Next stop was Kununurra, Mount Hart (where we did a bit of caretaking for a few days), Beverley Springs, Ord River Station, Liveringa Station visiting Andy, Bungle Bungles, Broome, Windjanna Gorge, Tanami Track, Alice Springs, Ooratippra, Lucy Creek Station,

Renner Springs, Glenormiston, Middleton, Longreach (where we inspected properties for sale), then on to Jundah.

While at Jundah we received a call from Soph to say that she and Spencer Morgan had announced their engagement! Such excitement – we were now keen to get home and help with celebrations. We went on to Blackall, Roma and finally to Bongeen, where we once again slept in a bed in a house after just over three months on the road. That was the end of our travelling for a while.

WE PURCHASE ANOTHER PROPERTY

If you think this was to be our last move, hang on to your seats, we were to make two more moves AFTER THIS ONE! It's not that we were gypsies, we just liked the challenge of renovating properties and experiencing different country.

After looking round a lot of south-east Queensland hoping to find our dream — a viable cattle property — we settled on a place called Morna Lea in the Kaimkillenbun area north-east of Dalby. This place was only 324 hectares of farming and grazing land, with good improvements but very run down.

It was a most attractive property, with creek flats, gentle slopes and tree-studded hills. The Myall Creek, which also runs through Dalby, completed the picture.

We were joined by Andy, who had recently suffered a serious helicopter accident and been lucky to survive. He had been helicopter mustering on Meda Station while working for Fitzroy Helicopters, based at Liveringa Station on the Gibb River Road in Western Australia. The common fear among chopper pilots is their tendency to burst into flames in the event of a crash, but Andy was lucky this wasn't his fate.

At the time of the incident, he had descended to the ground to drop off the stock inspector in order to open a gate to put the cattle through. When he resumed flight, he found he had little or no control due to failure of the cyclic (or stick) and crashed into the ground, using his last bit of control to dodge the stock inspector, who could easily have been killed.

The machine was a write-off and a shocking mess. Viewing photos of it later it was hard to believe that anyone could have survived. Andy, however, was lucky and suffered comparatively minor injuries. He was happy to have a break from flying so joined us on our next venture. We welcomed his expertise and excellent approach to hard work.

Before we took possession, the previous owner had allowed us to camp in the hayshed for a couple of weeks and commence the major job of restoring the property to a workable proposition. This was no mean task. The piggery was in a terrible mess, tanks were leaking, watering points needed restoring, the second cottage on the place needed renovating, fences needed renewing or repairing, a suitable cattle yard needed building, the tennis court needed restoring, and last but not least, the entire property was over-run with African boxthorn, a terrible invasive weed mainly spread by birds.

While camped in the hayshed, we repaired the piggery and started looking round for suitable cows and sows, a tractor and combine. We then moved into the house, which needed painting, and we commissioned my sister Mollie to undertake this task, a job which she performed with great expertise.

With Andy living with us and with all of us being reasonably big drinkers, I reckoned I would be spending most of my time making home brew. The solution? Make it a bit stronger so we didn't drink as much. The result? We drank just as much but we all became alcoholics!

We employed a bore-drilling contractor to look for an irrigation bore site as we had a good flat suitable for growing lucerne, but despite several attempts, this was not successful. Looking back, I don't know why we didn't employ a water diviner as I know people who have had great success using this method.

However, we planted dry land lucerne and this turned out to be a very lucrative crop, though stacking it in the hayshed tested our energies. Fortunately, we were often helped in this venture by Sophie and her HUSBAND! Which brings me to the next major event in our lives.

SOPHIE GETS MARRIED

Since going to Gatton Agricultural College and playing polocrosse, Sophie had been going out with the tall, dark and handsome Spencer Morgan, whose company established The Grove Shorthorn Stud at Myall Grove, Condamine. Soph worked at The Grove during bull preparation time, but when this job ran out, she moved to Arubial on the other side of the river, owned by Spencer's cousin's family.

Amazingly, the entire time Soph was working on Arubial, the Condamine River was up forcing Spencer to make a thirty-kilometre road trip to continue his courting rather than the three or four kilometres via the river crossing.

The wedding was held at St Luke's Anglican Church in Toowoomba, followed by a reception at Lord's Function Centre. This wonderfully happy event was attended by friends from every state in Australia, after which we farewelled them for their honeymoon. Firstly, they went to Lindeman Island in the Whitsundays, then they headed down to Wagga Wagga for a Shorthorn sale. Soph says they must have broken the drought as it rained the whole time!

Sophie's cousin Sonia was married soon afterwards. Sonie had met her future husband, Laird Morgan, at Soph and Spen's engagement party. I still picture them dancing on the tennis court at Myall Grove. I would like to include here a poem that Mollie wrote at Laird and Sonie's wedding:

THE MORGAN MAZE

Sonia marries Laird
Who is the cousin of Spencer
Who is the son of Mary
Who is the cousin of Margaretta
Who is the wife of Uen
Who is the brother of Goff

Who is the father of Spencer
Who is the husband of Sophie
Who is the cousin of Sonia

Work that one out!!!

After Soph and Spen's wedding, we entertained twenty-five guests at Morna Lea, so we must have had the place reasonably presentable by then.

Soph had married into a family of horse riders, and they were able to muster enough polocrosse players to form their own team. The Grove was set up to hold carnivals on the property until Workplace Health and Safety brought that event to an end, sadly.

After the wedding, we got stuck into the hard work again – purchasing pigs and cattle, planting barley and oats and removing the boxthorn, which adorned every fence. Tim would cut off the bushes with a brush cutter and I would follow with the poison, which had to be applied immediately. Then we would push it all into big heaps for burning. Where it was away from the fences, we were able to stack it using our tractor, which resulted in some pretty big fires. Wasps once again became an occupational hazard.

Cementing leaky galvanised iron tanks required a team of four– I would mix the cement (we actually had an electric mixer), then another person would pass it by the bucketful to the next person, who would pass it to Tim, who was stationed inside the tank. Interestingly, the cement had to be applied from the top, going round the tank in about thirty centimetre widths. The following day, another layer was applied, and on the third day, it was coated with a slurry, a mixture of cement and water.

The result was effective and permanent – none of the tanks ever leaked again.

We had bought an old combine to plant our crops. This was a job I hated as I would have to sit on the combine going round and round in endless circles, keeping an eye on the seed and fertiliser to make sure everything was flowing freely. There are much more modern methods of planting now, but we were obliged to be fairly primitive.

Making hay involved a fair bit of physical labour, but we did well out of the lucerne as it was planted on a very rich creek flat. Tim and Andy set about converting the old dairy into a suitable cattle yard, and we repaired the tennis court to a playable standard, enabling us to have a bit of leisure time. Many tennis/barbecue days were held under the athel pines that had been planted on the side.

I decided to compete in an endurance ride that was coming up near Nanango. I trained up Tim's horse, Cisco, for this event, giving myself a bit of relaxation. At the event, Cisco was the fastest horse, but not being an experienced endurance rider, I was eventually vetted out as I had taken the horse too fast down the hills. Where I had been training was all flat country, so Cisco's muscles weren't accustomed to this type of exercise.

The vets took a long time to come to this decision, stroking their beards and pondering among themselves. Cisco completely recovered, but I didn't go endurance riding again, though I really enjoyed the experience.

Contrastingly, when I rode The Count in an endurance event near Katherine in 1969, he won the prize for the fittest horse.

We had built up quite a nice herd of breeding cattle. One day, we found a couple of dead ones, then more and more until eventually we had ten altogether. Totally puzzled — as there seemed to be no reason for these deaths — we called the vet for an autopsy.

He diagnosed mother-of-millions poisoning, which was a surprise to us as we had no idea we even had this toxic plant. On investigation, we found a few scattered plants in the gullies. Cattle will rarely eat this attractive garden succulent, only tempted when green grass is unavailable and its bright red flower attracts their attention.

A small amount can cause poisoning, leading eventually to heart failure. It was very sad to see the cattle die from this noxious plant, which is widespread in Queensland, mainly along roadsides. This was a fairly substantial loss to us as it represented about ten per cent of our breeding herd, but as the saying goes: "Stockowners must expect losses."

MORNA LEA SOLD AND WASHPOOL PURCHASED

In June 1996, once we had the boxthorn under control, it was time to put the place on the market and hopefully make enough profit to reach our dream –a viable cattle property.

We had quite a few lookers, but it didn't sell immediately. Eventually, some nearby graziers made us an offer, below what we had hoped for, but we were keen to get out. We received $430,000 for the property. This represented a small profit, but not enough, we considered, to compensate for the huge amount of work that had gone into its restoration.

Andy had previously left us to augment his cash supply and got a job on a drilling rig in the Eromanga Basin, before later resuming his helicopter mustering career in the Kimberley.

All over southern Queensland we traipsed until we eventually found our dream — 1686 hectares of cattle country in the Durong district, approximately ninety kilometres west of Kingaroy in the South Burnett.

As we came over a rise and had our first glimpse of The Washpool house and surrounds, we knew we had found the perfect place. We didn't even inspect all the boundaries before signing a contract, it just felt right. At $440,000 the price was right too, and we could buy the place without going into debt.

Lovely cattle country and fronting the Boyne River, it had a carrying capacity of about 220 cows, just sufficient to make a living.

From the beautifully restored colonial homestead, we had views over the entire countryside to the west from the spacious verandah. It was mainly forest country, but we did have a few hundred hectares of the really good red, scrub soil, so called because of the type of vegetation growing on it. The Boyne River finished it off, but we still had work to do — there were trees to thin and woody weeds to be controlled. It seemed as though we were destined to have this chore forever.

One of our first jobs was to build a set of stables, a tack room and a fowl run. As we had plenty of ironbark on the property and cypress pine for rails, this we were able to do fairly cheaply. We also established a vegetable garden and orchard.

Meantime, Mollie and daughter Trixie had bought the Durong convenience store, and I would help over weekends so one of them could have a break. They became immensely popular in the district, but the work was hard and constant and eventually they decided to move on.

Our Dad helped us in all our ventures, and gave Mollie a hand to make improvements at the shop. We celebrated his and Mum's ninetieth birthdays at Washpool, and family came from Melbourne, Brisbane and Sydney as well as local. The grandchildren had christened Mum and Dad "Gang Gang" and "Kikang", and this is what they were always called from then on.

Our old Territory friends, the Wixes, had a Limousin stud, and we decided to go into partnership so he could run more breeders. One day, Tim and I were working in the yard matching calves with their mothers and recording numbers. One cow took exception to my hunting her up the race away from her calf and charged me (being a very protective mother).

Normally, it is easy to get up on to the top rail in order to escape a charging beast and the animal will usually back off, but this yard had been built with a top rail the diameter of a substantial tree trunk and I was unable to get up. The cow got me down on the ground and started getting stuck into me in a fairly determined manner.

Tim was immediately on the job — he was able to fend her off with his hat and help me to my feet, shocked and bruised but with no serious injuries. That was the end of my cattle work for a few days, and we developed a different method of matching cows and calves.

For three weeks I had to sleep in a reclining chair till my bruises subsided.

We were mustering with Soph one day and I was riding my faithful mare Sasha. She had always been paranoid about wire. She somehow got tangled up in a roll of barbed wire and I had no recollection of what happened next. I woke up on our bed at home. Evidently I kept on asking Soph and Tim, "What happened, where am I?", until I just about drove them mad. I recovered with no ill effects.

One of the jobs that made me very nervous but was essential to running the place was burning the long grass. This cane grass was useless when long, but after burning, the resultant sweet green pick was as good as lucerne. We tried to burn going into the evening, and there were some nerve-racking times when it looked as though a fire was going to get away on us.

One day it did. We didn't have a hope of controlling it, so we just went home. Amazingly, that night there was a small storm, and when we went to check it during the night the country was aglow with little fires sparkling everywhere like Christmas trees. It had been a close shave.

One of the local graziers who had substantial properties in the district asked us to give him a hand mustering and branding. We happily accepted, and it was great to be paid for something we loved doing. We were eventually contract mustering for nine other families in the district.

Tim had become very proficient at butchering a beast on the ground as this was a weekly occupation while living in the Territory, and he continued to do this for our own meat supply. We had also learnt how to make sausages and our first attempt was memorable — they were inedible! We hadn't realised that you needed to include substantial quantities of fat or they are just too dry — we minced a shoulder, which is almost totally fatless. We had no idea how to twist them until a butcher friend showed us the technique.

There wasn't much Tim couldn't do, but for some reason he never mastered this art — or maybe I should say, he didn't want to, so this job fell to me. Over the years, I would have twisted hundreds of kilograms of sausages, but it was something I quite enjoyed as it was very rewarding.

HORSES AND DOGS

Skylark

Throughout this narrative, I haven't mentioned much about our animals as there would be just too much to say. Suffice to record that we always had about six horses, mainly progeny of our Helen Springs mares, and two or three dogs, who were our loyal and loved friends as well as our helpers.

We bred a horse that I called Skylark, which we had broken in by a professional horse breaker. I was aware of the fact that young horses needed plenty of exercise and education and, having ridden out with large numbers of freshly broken horses on the stations, I was aware of what they were capable of, being energetic and unpredictable. I set out to try to ride Skylark every day, but found I was becoming increasingly nervous even though he hadn't misbehaved.

I had to go to Sydney for a couple of weeks, and while there, Tim rang me one day and said, "Skylark got tetanus and I had to put him down. There was nothing I could do and Rob Somerset helped me."

I had always been suspicious that Tim was concerned for my safety and that Skylark didn't have tetanus at all, but there was no way I could find out until recently. I rang Rob and asked him if he remembered the tetanus/Skylark affair.

My suspicions were confirmed — he had no recollection of the incident. In a way, I am grateful to Tim that I was no longer obliged to ride the horse. Horses are very sensitive to their rider's emotions, and I figured that one day he would pick up on my nervousness and get rid of me.

Lulu

Tim suffered from a bad back from time to time, and on one particular day, he was laid up and I was out hoeing weeds on a contour bank with our precious golden kelpie bitch, Lulu. When I went to return home, there was no sign of her. After searching for a while, I went home to get Tim and we resumed the search, Tim in the Toyota and me on Sasha.

We were devastated to find her mangled little body — she had been killed by the dingoes, which were fairly plentiful on Washpool and could be heard howling most nights. She would have put up a valiant fight, brave little dog that she was. She had been like another child to us, and her death affected us badly, so much so that we went to stay with Soph and Spen for a few days to help us recover.

We had never had a dog like her — before or since. Not only was she super intelligent, she was also a thinking dog, a trait we had never encountered in any other dog. When out mustering I would say to Lulu, "Go to Dad", and off she would go and find Tim, who might have been far enough away to be out of sight. He could do the same thing, say to her, "Go and find Mum", and the process would be repeated.

When travelling in the bush Toyota, she would sit on the seat between us, regally surveying the countryside. When near home we would say, "Do you want to run?" If she considered it was too far, she would just sit there and completely ignore us. So we would go a bit further and ask her again. When she considered it was about the right distance, off she would go.

During a thunderstorm, however, she would be inconsolable. Though she always took refuge under our bed in the house, she would still pant and tremble and get a wild look in her eyes.

When we got the boot polish out, she would get a worried look on her face and be extra clingy, as she knew we were going to town. However, we took her with us whenever possible and she did many miles in the back of the station wagon, perched up on her (our) mattress.

Sophie had Lulu's brother, Nuggett, and he was of the same ilk, but he was luckier as he lived to a ripe old age. Nugget would impress visitors with a trick Soph had taught him. We would all be sitting on the verandah and Soph would say to Nuggett, "Perimeter check! Perimeter check!" Off Nuggett would go in full flight to check the boundary fence.

Their father, a New Zealand Huntaway, had been owned by our neighbour at Verona.

A HOLIDAY

In June 1997, we went to the Whitsundays to holiday with June and her husband Max, who had sailed their yacht up there for the winter months. We left the property in the care of Les and Lurline McLachlin, a wonderful couple from Dalby who did numerous caretaking jobs for us, and so gave us the freedom we needed from working.

Sailing all round the Whitsundays was a most enjoyable experience, passing Shaw Island, Lindeman, Pentecost, through Solway Pass, then past Whitehaven Beach where we went snorkelling — magic. Further on to Tongue Bay, Cid Harbour, through Hook Passage and into Nara inlet for breakfast. We passed *Morning Glory*, Rupert Murdoch's yacht, more like an ocean liner it was so grand.

Then we sailed across Whitsunday Passage and through Unsafe Pass where, to be in the correct position, two lights had to be in vertical alignment. Finally on to Airlie Beach where we boarded a bus and returned to our car. Altogether, a most memorable week on the water.

We had wonderful neighbours on both sides at Washpool, and regularly shared social events with each at times. Rob and Georgie Somerset were our neighbours over the river, and we had many enjoyable dinners and barbecues with them, as well as helping them with cattle work.

One night we had them over for a barbecue on Sunset Hill. We had cooked potato and pumpkin wrapped in alfoil on the coals. As I was serving the vegetables one of their sons started to cry. I asked him what was wrong and he replied: "Please don't put pumpkin on my plate because if it is on my plate I will have to eat it!" Such discipline is not very often encountered these days and naturally I removed the pumpkin.

Georgie became the president of the Durong branch of the recently formed AgForce. I, once again, became the secretary, a job which I enjoyed, and which also introduced me to the wonderful world of computers at the encouragement of Georgie. Georgie is now the general president and a very able mover and shaker is that lady. Well done, Georgie!

On the other side we had friends, Tony and Maureen. Every Friday night, we would swap places for a dinner party. Tony and Maureen were great helpers when we decided to build a tennis court. We used local timber and had a professional level the site, and a working bee assisted in the placing of the wire. So once again we were able to have tennis/barbecues on Sundays, and these were very popular with friends and neighbours.

ONE LIFE ENDS, ANOTHER BEGINS

Dad had been suffering health issues, so he moved in with us in March 1997. He had previously been doing lathe work for his neighbour and, unbeknown to him at the time, fine steel dust particles had been filtering into his lungs, obviously similar to mesothelioma. This had the effect of robbing him of his energy. He reached the stage where he could not collect the eggs without having a rest on the way.

At that stage, we had no idea what was causing the problem. It was only after his death that the diagnosis of cryptogenic fibrosing alveolitis enabled us to figure out what had been causing this debilitating condition. Sadly, Dad went to his grave without ever knowing what had been ailing him for the last few years of his otherwise healthy life.

Six days before he died on 14 May 1997, Mum, all his children and some of his grandchildren were able to gather round his bedside at Washpool for a wonderful night of reminiscing and a slide show of his remarkable life. It was a memorable evening and I was so glad that we were able to farewell him in this way.

June had come to stay with us to help me with his nursing during the last weeks, and I am forever grateful that she was able to do this. We would take it in turns to be on night shift. Every night I would say to Dad, "Are you comfortable Dad?"

He would reply, "Yes."

I would ask him if he was in any pain, and always the reply would be,

"No."

So it was amazing that, right till the end, he had all his marbles and didn't suffer at all.

I was on shift the night he died. I checked him at half past two in the morning to find that he had left us, and all I could do was scream. Nobody heard me. Eventually, I had to wake Tim and June, and the awful business of dealing with the sadness, doctors, undertakers and everything else involved in the aftermath of a death in the family started. It was the end of a wonderful and productive life. Goodbye, Kike.

Soph and Spen's first son and our first grandchild, Ashley, was born on 16 February 1998 in St Vincent's Hospital in Toowoomba. Both were in good fettle and it was celebrations all round. Welcome Ash!

WE BUILD A CATTLE YARD

The only yard on the property was down by the river on the far side of the run, so we decided that it would be advantageous to have one more central to the paddocks and closer to the house.

With Andy's help, we cut and barked trees for posts and carted probably 150 flitches, sleeper offcuts that had been left over from the days when railway sleepers were harvested off the place. Andy stayed long enough to plant the gateway posts and cap them, then Tim and I were on our own. Our only concession to modern technology was that we now had a posthole digger attached to our tractor.

It was a mammoth task. Posts were put in, and the big job of installing rails began, as well as a calf cradle, calf crush, head bail and gates. While Tim was doing the technical work, he showed me how to make the gates, which was relatively straightforward once he set me up with tools and knowhow.

The job took months, but it was very satisfying at the end to view our handiwork, and it made cattle work so much easier — but I thought installing the rails would never come to an end.

ANDY TIES THE KNOT

Andy was now helicopter mustering for Heliwork based in Kununurra, and during this time he met the most attractive Katrina Heath, who was the governess at Meda Station. Katrina fitted in with the family very easily, and we were pleased Andy had found such a delightful girl.

The wedding was to be on 20 March 1999 at Eco Beach Resort south of Broome in Western Australia. Andy had hired a fishing boat to take all the guests out the following day, supplying copious quantities of alcohol, seafood and all sorts of goodies.

To get to the boat, we had to climb on board a zodiac that held about six people but — the best laid plans of mice and men! The weather turned awful and the trip in the zodiac was not for the faint-hearted. Eventually, it had to be abandoned after it overturned and tipped its occupants into the water.

For those who made it to the fishing boat, things didn't improve. The boat was rocking so much that hardly anyone had a drink. Prawns and lobsters went to waste, and over the side or into buckets went the contents of many stomachs. Hardly anyone threw in a fishing line, and the fairly substantial amount of money Andy had spent on this venture basically went overboard along with previously mentioned items.

Our second grandchild, James Andrew, was born towards the end of the year in Kununurra. Andy later went to work for Helimuster based at Victoria River Downs in the Kimberley, and he and Katrina made their new home on this vast station.

A CHANGE OF DIRECTION

We went for a visit to Sydney to stay with my brother Roger and his wife Elizabeth in their home on the banks of the Nepean River in Wallacia, at the foot of the Blue Mountains west of Sydney. They took us to a meeting of The Investors Club. We had always been wary about borrowing money, but we came away from this meeting with a whole new outlook on financials.

At the meeting, we were taught the value of borrowing against existing equity to buy investment properties.

Filled with excitement and enthusiasm and armed with the deeds to our property, we set off to find our first house.

We headed for Chinchilla, approximately three hundred kilometres west of Brisbane, to look for our first purchase. We weren't disappointed; it didn't take us long to settle on a lovely little three-bedroom weatherboard colonial for the huge sum of $60,000, and a three-bedroom near new brick house for $92,000. These were incredibly cheap, and we were lucky to find these places before Chinchilla went into boom mode.

Next stop was a trip to Suncorp Bank in Kingaroy for an appointment with the loans officer, who readily agreed to lend us the money with Washpool as security.

Encouraged, we then went to Gympie, where we were able to snap up a lovely three-bedroom brick in a very good location for $95,000, and a three-bedroom hardiplank for $85,000.

Finally, it was off to Kingaroy and our luck was holding — we found another three-bedroom brick in a cul-de-sac for $125,000, so we considered our portfolio was full and the bank man was happy. He even said to us, "I wish I could do what you are doing," so we thought that was fair encouragement.

The income from these houses covered the mortgage and gave us some extra as well, so we were well pleased with our investments. I saved thousands of dollars by doing the conveyancing on all our purchases and sales since the purchase of Verona, the only help being from a conveyancing kit for which I paid about $25 back then, money well spent.

Pretty cheeky really, as I had no legal knowledge, but somehow I got away with it until I did one for Soph and Spen and made a minor mistake on the transfer form. As stamp duty had already been paid, it was a bit of a mess and took some correcting, but thanks to “It’s not what you know it’s who you know,” they were able to get out of the tangle.

SOME FAMILY MEMBERS LEAVE US

Later that year, Tim's father departed this earth after battling with emphysema, which developed into lung cancer. He had been a wonderful doctor and ended his career before retirement in charge of the Repatriation Hospital in Heidelberg, Victoria. When in private practice, he was very generous, and if people were unable to pay their bills he would just throw them away (the bills that is!).

He used to take our family to Noosa every Christmas after we moved down south, but despite this, Tim never established a good relationship with James. I think it stemmed back to when Tim was sent to boarding school at a very young age.

The following year, 2000, at the age of just ninety-four, my mum died. She had been in good health apart from mild dementia, and had been looked after in the later years by Roger and Elizabeth. Like Dad, she had gone to sleep and not woken up, a wonderful way for them both to end their long lives.

One day before she passed away, we had decided to take Mum to Olympic Park, which was still under construction for the Sydney Olympics . Rushing to get a train as we arrived at Penrith Station, we didn't get tickets thinking we could get them at the other end. Then I got off at the wrong station to change for Olympic Park, and we had to wait for ages for the correct train.

When we finally arrived at Olympic Park, as we had no tickets, we were unable to leave the station. There was no one in attendance and with nowhere to sit Mum was getting a bit knocked up. So we left her in a disabled toilet while we found an attendant, but she kept on coming out!

Finally, we were able to reach the park, but it was a long walk. With no seats or shade and a very hot day, Mum was nearly expiring in her woollen underwear. Then luckily I was able to locate a wheelchair, we found a bus and had a nice tour of Olympic Park (this was just before the Games). On the return journey, when we arrived at Penrith Station, Mum refused to leave the train. Fortunately, a young fellow who had witnessed our plight swept her up and on to the platform before she could object.

The car, parked in the sun all day, was stinking hot, and once again she nearly expired. When we arrived home, the incontinence pad she had been wearing was nowhere to be seen, so I guess it came off in one of the trains.

That night Mum said to me, "I don't want you here anymore, you bully me too much!" Little did she understand the dramas we had encountered. On another occasion, we visited a gentleman in the Blue Mountains who had written a book about Yerranderie. Jim gave us smoko and Mum ate half a cake and stuffed the biscuits into Jim's book! Despite these little incidents, we had enjoyed the days out.

One day she was getting dressed and proceeded to put one dress over the top of another. She commented to me, "This dress reminds me of my husband, he was a wonderful man."

There was obviously underlying admiration all the time.

A TRAGEDY IN THE FAMILY

1 March 2001

Soph had asked me to go to Meribah to babysit Ash while they did the branding on their breeding property south of Meandarra.

Ash developed a slight fever, so Soph decided we should return home to Myall Grove. At half past eight that night, a car pulled up and Spencer's mother Mary stood on the back step.

"GOFF'S DEAD!"

She was in terrible shock and said no more. Soph took control of the situation and said, "Mum, you ring the police and ambulance. Mary, you come with me and we will check him."

So they departed for the accident scene. I could see the emergency lights and many car lights at the mailbox from my vantage point on the back verandah. Spencer and his brother Godfrey were notified, and they too joined the throng at the mailbox.

The news was devastating. Goff had left his house at about half past seven to check a pump not far away. When he hadn't returned, Mary went looking for him and the scene that confronted her will never be forgotten.

He had obviously had a medical condition (suspected stroke or aneurism) that must have locked his foot on the accelerator. It is estimated that he hit the tree at a hundred kilometres per hour. The impact was so intense that the bonnet of the car was entwined round the boot.

This event was devastating to a close-knit family. The following day, it was like being in a morgue — everyone was absolutely dumbstruck. We couldn't believe that this could happen to such an enterprising, energetic, charismatic, loving family man, who had steered the course of his property from clearing it with an axe to making it the showplace that it is today.

Later on people were heard to say, "The wheels would fall off the cart, now that Goff is gone," but in fact, the reverse is true. The Grove continues to go from strength to strength.

Angus Lane said on the ABC that it was one of the biggest funerals he had ever seen in Toowoomba, and there was standing room only in the church.

Mary was understandably shell-shocked, but she is made of stern stuff and has soldiered on, thankfully with the support of her loving family of three sons and three daughters-in-law, plus their children. Sadly, the retirement she and Goff had planned was snatched cruelly from her at the age of fifty-six.

BACK AT THE RANCH

We eventually settled back into some sort of normalcy at Washpool. We hired two bulldozers and a chain to clear the few hundred hectares of good country we had. This then had to be stick-picked — an arduous task in anyone's language.

We had bought a bulldozer, so ploughed and planted the block to improved pasture. This was very successful, but required continual maintenance as trees have an uncanny knack of replacing themselves, something which scientists don't take into account when forming the vegetation management laws.

We were forever using the brush cutter and poison trying to keep the regrowth under control. The easiest way to do this is to plant annual crops for a few years till the trees give up, then plant your perennials, but we didn't have the time. So along with the weeds, wild cotton, African lovegrass and tree regrowth that continued to plague us, we were kept pretty busy.

One of our horses, Jack, was found in the paddock one day with his Achilles tendon snapped clean in two. If you have seen the size of an Achilles tendon on a horse, we considered this was something pretty unusual. There was no apparent reason for this as there was nothing in the horse paddock that could have caused such an injury, but with no remedy, Jack had to be put down.

The next horse drama was when Cisco got colic. Once again, no reason for this, as Cisco had only been grazing grass and had not been hard fed at all. Sand colic is another possibility, but as we had no sand we ruled this out. Things were looking pretty grim and we were about to call the vet when Cisco gave an enormous fart, bounded to his feet and took off! A satisfactory end to what was shaping up to be another sad loss.

Tim had been having more pain in the abdomen, and on diagnosis, it was found that he had a hernia so it was off to hospital once again. While laid up, he was able to further his passion — woodwork.

Over the years, he must have made at least a hundred pieces of furniture, and they are in every state from South Australia, Victoria, New South Wales to Queensland. He mainly used ironbark, which was plentiful on all our properties, and at Washpool, he also used the versatile sleeper offcuts.

In fact, Tim was always very industrious. Ever since I had met him he was always making something or doing something useful. He would make saddlery, counterline saddles, splice ropes and furniture, and was always observing and recording birdlife and vegetation. When he wasn't doing these things, he was making and maintaining gardens or doing general repair work round the property.

Shannie Morgan came into the world in December 2001, followed by Emily Doran fourteen months later. We now had four delightful grandchildren, but owing to geographical circumstances, we didn't see Andrew and Katrina's children very much.

To remedy this situation, we set off on a tour in our trusty 4WD of South Australia, Northern Territory, Western Australia and Queensland, lasting just over two months. We visited Andrew and Katrina at VRD, where we stayed for a few days and were able to accompany Andy on his helicopter mustering work.

Dawn at Helimuster was an exciting time. At least a dozen helicopters would be starting up, warming up, then taking off into the morning sunrise before disappearing over the horizon in the directions of their various stations for the day's mustering.

I accompanied Andy one day, and I thought it was one of the most exhilarating experiences I had ever had, swooping and climbing, darting and descending, sharp turns and suspension from an imaginary skyhook. Strangely enough, this latter made me feel uncomfortable. There were four choppers involved in this muster, and when Andy had to wait for the other choppers at any stage, he would just hover at a fairly high altitude, and strangely this gave me an unnerving feeling. I was pleased when the action started again.

At one stage, he put me down in the scrub as he wanted less weight for a difficult manoeuvre getting an errant bull to move. It was a most peculiar feeling being all alone in that vast country — I was pleased that he was equipped with GPS or he might never have been able to find me again (also pleased that he had remembered to set it when he disgorged me from the chopper!).

He always carried fishing rods strapped to the struts, and when he spotted barramundi on the way home, he would land in a rocky part of the river and throw out a line. This he did four times while I was with him and he caught a couple of beauties.

I never ceased to admire the fact that he could roll a smoke while flying — after all, a chopper has very sensitive controls, and I don't know how he managed to still have one hand on the stick.

Tim had the pleasure of a flight the next day, then it was goodbye to Andy and Treenie and we continued our tour, spending four days going through the unique Gregory National Park, named after the very successful explorer, Augustus Charles Gregory (later Sir).

This very isolated but spectacular part of the world was one of our most memorable trips. Very rough, it was definitely 4WD stuff. We encountered no one until the day we decided to pull up in the middle of the road on a creek crossing to set out our lunch. Unbelievably, just when we had everything ready to eat, another vehicle came along! Talk about Murphy's law.

We arrived home in June 2002 to find everything in good order in the care of our great caretakers, Les and Lurline.

I GET ITCHY FEET

This time it was my turn. We both loved Washpool and the cattle and horse work, but I was getting sick of droughts and government red tape, brush cutting scrub, pulling weeds, Tordonning regrowth and constant leaks in our water system, which really needed total renewal that would have involved great expense. Besides, we both wanted to be closer to Soph and her family, so we started out on the search for a suitable retirement property.

At first, Tim wasn't terribly keen to sell, but then he too could see the sense in putting the place on the market, so we went ahead and listed it. In hindsight, this was very fortuitous, as the outcome would have been totally different had we not sold at this time.

We started off our search in Chinchilla, as this was only seventy-five kilometres from Myall Grove, and it was a town we both liked. While driving around the district with Soph one day, we spotted a very likely looking property only three kilometres from town. It was a beautiful looking property with its old colonial house nestled among established gardens, complete with palm trees and what appeared to be creek frontage. Soph said, "There, Mum and Dad, that looks like a good place for you. Why don't you go in and see if it is on the market?"

Tim replied, "No, we can't do that, we'll go to a real estate agent in town and make enquiries."

So we went to an agent in Chinchilla to make enquiries about Sweetwood in Gormleys Road. He told us that it wasn't on the market, but he made a note of our enquiry.

We had planned a trip to Sydney and Melbourne a few weeks later to have a bit of a holiday and catch up with all the southern rellies. While in Sydney, we had a phone call from Jim McGahan, the agent from Chinchilla Real Estate, to tell us that Sweetwood had come on the market.

We cancelled all our plans and drove back to Chinchilla the following day. The day after that, we sat under a tree in the garden with Jim and signed a contract to buy Sweetwood, 286 Gormleys Road, Chinchilla.

We couldn't believe our luck. The property was 130 hectares in two portions, with two kilometres of Gormleys Lagoon in front of the house and three kilometres of the permanent Charleys Creek forming the boundary. The gardens were extensive and beautiful, the house was old but liveable, an old colonial with bull-nosed verandahs, and there were reasonable improvements on the run.

ALL THIS FOR $240,000!

We were lucky to find a buyer for Washpool at the grand sum of $925,000, which represented a profit of more than 100 per cent in eight years, so we were pretty chuffed. This enabled us to pay out the mortgages on the investment properties, thus we had a good retirement income.

THE SWEETWOOD STORY

The original owner of Sweetwood was Mrs Gormley, who owned a nursery in town and after whom the lagoon and road were named. She was very well known and liked, and established what was to become the beautiful gardens that we inherited.

When Mrs Gormley moved on, she left the place to her only daughter, Yvonne, who had leased the property to tenants when she and her husband moved to the Sunshine Coast.

This is where the Sweetwood story becomes interesting. Yvonne leased the property to a middle aged couple and their eighteen-year-old daughter. Actually, they were horror tenants, but they did spend a lot of money on the place, extending the gardens, edging them with thousands of rocks, building a decorative fishpond complete with rock borders and lights for night effect, and building numerous post and rail fences in the homestead area.

Their friends built a second house on the property, and decorated that building also with attractive gardens. They excavated a swimming hole in the lagoon and had commenced to build a deck over the water. They even had a flying fox over the lagoon, which gave us and our guests endless pleasure over the years.

They had applied for a grant from the government in order to set up a fish farm, and were reported in a newspaper article as "Charley's Angels" (referring to Charleys Creek.) They were paid some money towards this venture and used it to install many new four-wire cattle fences, of which we were the beneficiaries.

Now the mystery part of this story. Where were they getting all the money from? The husband would go away for a fortnight at a time, supposedly going to Russia to work in the mines, so the locals were led to believe. What he was actually doing was going interstate and dealing in drugs. This all came to a head when the family travelled to Roma, robbed a pub at gunpoint and were caught by the police with the loot and firearms in the car on the way back to Chinchilla.

Evidently, they owed money to an interstate bikie gang and had become desperate enough to commit armed robbery. After we moved into the property, we would find drug-dealing equipment buried in various places in the garden, and when we put insulation in the roof, we found manuals on growing marihuana etc.

They were tried and sent to gaol, including the eighteen-year-old daughter, for whom we felt very sorry, as it seemed "criminal" for her to be caught up in her parent's misdemeanours.

We were always concerned that, when they were released from gaol, they might threaten us, but we never encountered any problems.

Yvonne was so horrified at what was going on at Sweetwood that she put the place on the market way below its real value, and we were lucky enough to be in the right place at the right time. We kept in contact with Yvonne and Keith and gained much knowledge of the history of the property, along with numerous photos of the old days.

Yvonne had had town water connected at great expense so the property was virtually drought-proof with town water, lagoon water and water from Charleys Creek in emergencies.

With the assistance of Soph and Spen, we moved in on 30 January 2004. At last we could go into semi-retirement. I say "semi", as there was still a lot of work to do. Some of the boundary fences were in a bad way and there were regrowth and weeds to deal with. We needed a modern house, a new cattle yard, a machinery shed and stables. But living in such an idyllic location made everything a pleasure, not a chore.

We employed a local builder to construct our dream home — large open plan living/dining room, two bedrooms, fans and air conditioning, polished floors, a large verandah overlooking the lagoon, and a walkway to the old cottage, giving us plenty of visitor space.

We got a contractor to build a substantial machinery shed, on the back of which we built stables, a tack room and a day yard.

We bought portable panels to make a reasonable cattle yard, and spent mornings out in the bush Toyota taking our smoko and renovating the boundary fence. Every morning, we spent a couple of hours digging out sand burr. This terrible weed, which we called bastard burr for obvious reasons, had numerous sticky prickles that would attach themselves to anyone and anything, and it was widespread on the entire place. Visitors would also give us a hand with this awful task, and eventually we were able to bring it under control.

Another chore was to cut and poison the wattle regrowth that had erupted on what we called "the potato patch", owing to the fact that a previous farmer had grown watermelons on this sixteen-hectare patch. This took us months, but the result was worthwhile as we later planted improved pasture in this paddock.

We bought a few breeders and were able to keep our primary producer status.

We bought a couple of canoes for our afternoon excursion in the lagoon, and later bought a tinnie with a motor for towing people behind on a tyre.

One time, I was paddling away in a canoe when I noticed a snake under my thigh! Panicking, I threw the dog off the front and plunged into the water as fast as I could. The snake was brown in colour and had really put the wind up me, but as I wasn't bitten I concluded it was a Macleay's water snake — poisonous but non-aggressive, so I had been lucky. In future, I always checked behind the back rest we had installed with the seat.

Swimming was a regular pastime in the summer, also gliding into the lagoon via the flying fox.

With no pressure, it was an idyllic existence.

One day I answered an ad in the local paper: "Wanted, people to form a trail riding club. Phone Jo on ..."

I answered the ad and met Jo. There was only one other reply, but we started to ride round the local district together.

After a few Sundays riding, I asked Jo if she would like to come in for a cuppa. Then we met her husband Troy and started to have dinner parties at each other's places. Then we met their friends, so started a friendship with four other couples in the district. This group we loosely called "The Racecourse Road Riding Club", and we joined up for many social events including Melbourne Cup Day and the Chinchilla Races.

One day at the races, I complimented Jo on her dress and quick as a flash her husband piped up with, "Yes, but it looks better on the bedroom floor!" Good on you Troy!

Most Sundays, we girls would ride down to the Chinchilla Weir, a distance of about ten kilometres. The men would come down with barbecues and alcoholic beverages, and amazingly we managed to stagger home on our horses, a bit the worse for wear! No falls were recorded though.

Tim and I had always been paranoid about keeping our properties wire-free as wire and horses don't mix. Equally paranoid about wire was my special horse, Sasha, another of our Helen Springs descendants. She must have known it would be her undoing in the end, for we had only been at Sweetwood for fourteen months when she turned up in the paddock with a bad wire injury on her back fetlock.

No amount of vet treatment would heal this awful wound. We decided the best thing to do would be to get her in foal, but the injury continued to plague her, so on 25 May 2005, Tim shot her.

I was devastated. She had been my faithful mustering horse for thirteen years, always willing, never needing to be shod and as tough as they come. I never found another horse that suited me so well, so it was a great loss and sad to see such a beautiful animal having her life cut short like that.

Five years later Tim's horse, Cisco, suffered a similar injury in the same place as Sasha, and he, too, had to be shot. I wouldn't swap a life on the land for anything, but it certainly has some sad moments.

The only thing missing at Sweetwood to make life perfect was a tennis court — the solution? Build one! This we did with Andy's help, and it wasn't long before we were having tennis, barbecue, swimming/canoeing Sundays on Sweetwood with our Racecourse Road Riding Club friends and relatives.

The hardest part in constructing the court was installing the plastic lines. These were purchased along with 2500 six-inch nails, which had to be nailed in every three inches. The result was effective and permanent.

Sweetwood was a very popular place with family to have special birthday celebrations, 21sts, 50ths, 60ths and 70ths, and relatives came from all the eastern states. These were very memorable and happy occasions. The lagoon, tennis court, spacious verandah and horse riding and cattle work made this very appealing to mainly city relatives.

In 2007, we invested in a couple of quad bikes. I didn't think we would ever revert to this form of transport, but they were such fun — they didn't buck, bolt or shy and you could carry your water, your dog and your lunch! Not to say that we gave up the horses for mustering, but these were a great way to get around, and the visitors loved them — very important!

BUSH HERITAGE

To satisfy our urge to experience wide open spaces again, we applied for a volunteering job with Bush Heritage, a not-for-profit organisation set up to conserve landscapes and irreplaceable native species. At the time of writing, Bush Heritage had thirty-six reserves covering 11,330,000 hectares.

We applied to do a month on Ethabuka Reserve, a 214,000 hectare former cattle station 640 kilometres south of Mt Isa, in the north of the Simpson Desert. A haven for wildlife, it still had numerous feral camels and a few leftover cattle.

We travelled on the Strezlecki Track via, Innamincka, The Dig Tree, Moomba (gas field), Mount Hopeless and Lyndhurst.

Charles Sturt had set off to explore Central Australia in August 1844 with fifteen men, thirty bullocks, six dogs, one boat and carriage, one spring cart, two hundred sheep and eleven horses. He had been hoping to find the mythical inland sea but was held up for six months by drought, finally returning to Adelaide in January 1946 after the loss of only one man. He described this region as: "A desperate region having no parallel on earth's surface," a sentiment probably shared by Burke and Wills after their disaster at the Dig Tree sixteen years later.

At Lyndhurst, we joined the Birdsville track for Marree and Birdsville, where there were already thousands of people gathered for the famous races which were due to start in four days' time.

We were pleased to escape this noisy throng of humanity to head for Bedourie, the kick-off point, before heading off on the final 150-odd kilometres of dirt road to the Ethabuka boundary, situated at the end of the public road.

The isolation, the desert and the sand hills all had great appeal to Tim and me. We joined up with other volunteers for the work ahead, which involved pulling the station bore, building a fuel bund, digging out buffel grass (not liked by conservationists but loved by cattle people), odd jobs round the homestead area and touring round the scenic places on the property.

After the other volunteers had departed, we helped the managers, Al and Karen, construct a shade verandah on their "homestead". Evenings were spent with a glass of wine or a bottle of Dorex sitting atop the sand hill to the west of the buildings, watching the marvellous sunsets that never disappointed. Trips to the Pulchera Waterhole on the Mulligan River were also a highlight, and to the Ethabuka Spring, where there is a sad little grave of a two-year-old child with the inscription:

In loving memory of John Edward Corkhill,
inserted by his loving mother, 1st October, 1919.

How did young families ever survive out there so far from civilisation, with no amenities to make life a little bearable in that terrible climate, and far from help, both medical and social?

There had been good rain before we arrived at Ethabuka, and the sand hills and swales were alive with wildflowers and the beautiful purple parakeelya, and thousands of birds that had flocked to the waterhole to breed. This phenomenon would only occur in exceptional years and we were lucky to experience it.

Negotiating the hundreds of sand hills was great fun, and required the driver to select third gear high range in order to get up enough speed to get over the top. At one sand hill, Tim had three attempts, but eventually had to hand over to Al, the manager. It was called "Len's Landing" owing to the fact that it had a tricky turn right at the top, and Len had tipped over a Toyota earlier on. As it also had a corner at the bottom, it was difficult to get up enough speed to reach the top.

We formed a strong friendship with Al and Karen, the managers, and have since visited them in their family home in Tasmania. Before we left Ethabuka, we butchered a camel, and I was surprised how tasty the meat was — actually not unlike beef.

Other Bush Heritage properties on which we worked were Craven's Peak in the desert country off the Donohue Highway between Boulia and Alice Springs, Boolcoomatta in the desert country of South Australia, and Carnarvon Station near Carnarvon Gorge, Queensland.

A TERRIBLE SHOCK

Soph had been having pain in her right shoulder for many years and the diagnosis had eluded the medicos. In fact, Soph recently told me that the pain had started when she was sent away to St Margaret's in Brisbane. She considered that the shock of going from five thousand square kilometres to the brick and tiles of the city, as well as leaving her parents and wonderful lifestyle, caused her terrible stress and unhappiness.

This unhappiness was expressed in all of her letters, but I don't think Tim and I realised the full extent of it. After all, people living in those isolated areas had no choice but to send their kids thousands of kilometres away to school.

She continued to get this niggling pain, continually worsening, and a visit to Chinchilla hospital in 2008 failed to reveal anything.

One day, Soph accompanied Spencer and his brother Godfrey to have a consultation with Dr Toby Ford in Brisbane. They all had a stress test and Soph passed with flying colours, but the doctor was concerned about her shoulder pain and gave her a referral for a CT scan. This stands for computed tomography scan, and gives computer-processed combinations of many x-ray measurements taken from different angles.

The results were read straight away and a mass was found in Soph's chest. This was a terrible and unexpected shock to us all. Dr Ford recommended an oncologist in Brisbane, Dr Paul Vasey, who was purported to be the best. By the end of May, Soph was booked in for surgery with a very special person — Dr Peter Wragg, a thoracic/vascular surgeon. This was scheduled for 18 June 2009.

What should have been reasonably simple keyhole surgery to remove an encapsulated thymic tumour turned into a marathon seven-hour thoracotomy to remove an invasive tumour, which resulted in the removal of part of the right lung, replacement of ten centimetres of the superior vena cava with Dacron, removal of part of the left brachial vein, the right phrenic nerve and some of the pericardium surrounding the heart.

It was a terribly nerve-racking time for Spencer and Mary, who waited outside the operating theatre throughout the ordeal. Every time a nurse came out they were expecting to hear that the operation was over, but the time went on interminably until finally they were told — it was over.

(Tim and I had stayed at Myall Grove to look after Ash and Shan, as well as the gardens, dogs and horses.)

The surgeon, one of only three doctors in Australia who could have performed the operation, was confident that he had got everything, but referred Soph for more scans in Brisbane in a couple of months.

Then followed approximately seven weeks in Brisbane undergoing radiation therapy five days a week, and chemotherapy one day a week.

The thymus gland is located in the chest cavity and is part of the immune system. It usually decreases in size and activity during the teens. Being a very rare cancer, there had not been a lot of study done into this life-threatening ailment.

Shortly after Soph's operation, Dr Wragg retired, so she was very lucky to have him perform his miracle. Other specialists were either thoracic or vascular surgeons, but no others in Queensland at that time did both.

Tim and I took it in turns to care for Soph after she returned home to Myall Grove, and help generally with the domestic side of things. After such an ordeal, her recovery was long and arduous.

"WINNIE"

It was while we were in a waiting room with Soph, keeping her company while she had treatment, that Tim happened to pick up a magazine about motorhomes and caravans (I can't remember the title). Inside was a photo of a motorhome that would fit all our desire for future travel — a 4WD Isuzu truck fitted with a fully self-contained motorhome on the back. The company that made them was SLR Caravans at Nerang on the Gold Coast.

As soon as possible, we contacted SLR, and so started a long association with Stewart Bozcrome, one of the sons in the family partnership.

We went for an interview and ordered a motorhome custom built to our specifications. The cost would be about $215,000 with all the extras such as winch and bull bar, but what the heck, it was just what we needed after years of swagging it.

In June 2010, we took delivery of this life-changing vehicle and commenced our first trip up to the Gulf with my great nephew, Jake, and his delightful wife, Maree.

After that, our desire to travel took us to the Channel Country and Lake Eyre, New South Wales and Victoria, the Great Central Road and Nullarbor, the Convoy of No Confidence in Canberra, a paddlewheel boat up the Murray, the Snowy River Festival at Corryong, Tasmania and the Kimberley.

It was while we were in Fitzroy Crossing in Western Australia in May 2012 that we received a devastating phone call from Spencer telling us that Soph had more lesions and that a further operation was planned.

Tim and I immediately returned home to be with Soph for her second operation. This was to be keyhole surgery, but this time with a different specialist. The operation lasted for two hours, but owing to the amount of scarring from the first operation, nothing was achieved and Soph returned home.

Meanwhile Soph had sought alternative forms of treatment, as she didn't want to pursue the traditional chemotherapy/radiotherapy path. This involved visits to numerous integrated doctors on the Gold Coast and in Ballina, New South Wales. Her home life was constantly disrupted, but she never complained.

After two of her oncology doctors told her that, because she was terminal, she couldn't have a port-a-cath, Soph left these doctors and never went back. Being a very positive person, she eventually overcame this setback and soldiered on in her determination to be rid of this life-threatening disease.

THE FLOODS

In December 2009, we decided to put one of the Sweetwood blocks on the market for a huge price, one and a half times what we had paid for the entire place in 2004. With a lagoon and two-kilometre frontage to Charley's Creek, we soon had a buyer.

They inspected the block with us and even worked out where they would build their homestead and dog runs, as their son was into working dog competitions.

Then I got cold feet. I suddenly couldn't part with this beautiful piece of country. After all, we loved the entire place, so we reneged on the deal. How lucky for those potential buyers — twelve months later, we were hit with the 2010–2011 floods and almost the entire property went under water. The spot they had selected to build their establishment was inundated.

Our lagoon came up and up and up until it was level with our paddock fence in front of the house and nearly up to the flying fox. The cattle must have had a sixth sense, as they put themselves in the only paddock that didn't go under.

Our little tinnie came in very handy — we had it tied up to the back fence and every day we would go exploring. It was like travelling in the Everglades. In places, the current was fairly strong, and negotiating a gateway, whose post tops were just visible above the water line, was skilful navigation on Tim's part, while I sat on the bow opening the gate.

Our house was never in danger of going under, but our neighbours, Brian and Fran, also members of our RRR Club, weren't so lucky. They had a metre of water throughout their entire house. Although we went down to help them put as much furniture as possible up out of the water's way, they lost many vehicles and motorbikes, and their freezer was found floating in the kitchen.

Being Christmas time, they had many visitors who were starting to panic as their access road was becoming anything but, so Brian had to ferry them out one by one, and just in time, too.

During this flood, the entire town of Condamine was evacuated, some by helicopter and others by boat.

One of our horses was missing — we had left some of the gates open prior to the floods, so it was becoming imperative to search for her. On the third day, we found her sheltering on a tiny piece of land that had not been submerged.

She was so terrified that when we found her she refused to move, as she was frightened of getting bogged. One of us had to get behind to coax her out to the road. We borrowed Brian's horse float to bring her home, and she recovered with no ill effects except for very soft, sore feet.

The aftermath of the floods was terrible — most of our grass was dead, but trees were springing up everywhere! Since we had spent most of our time on our properties controlling tree regrowth, this was an added blow. The cattle were sent away on agistment with kind friends, Keith and Nancy Dolbel, who wouldn't take any payment, and our other RRR Club friends, Jo and Troy, came every weekend to help us clear the debris off all the fences and repair them, a mammoth task. There is no doubt about it, when the chips are down, Australians rally to the cause.

Eventually, we put the other block on the market again. Our lovely neighbours, Brian and Fran, came to us one day and said, "We'll buy it so we don't have dubious neighbours living next door to us."

So the deal was done and we both had good neighbours.

In December 2011, Katrina's father, Ross, died after a long battle with cancer, and the following day, June's husband, Max, died virtually of old age.

SOPH HAS FURTHER TREATMENT

In January 2012, a next-door neighbour and close friend of Soph and Spen's from Shorthorn days was re-diagnosed with cancer at around the same time as Soph. Instead of the usual treatment, Jack did some research as he had heard of some good things happening in Germany — treatments not available in Australia.

Soph attended the Gawler clinic with her sister-in law Amanda, and so began a new chapter in her quest for the cure. Another cancer survivor, Ian Gawler taught dietary principles, relaxation, meditation, imagery and pain management skills. Soph returned from this clinic with no physical improvement, but mentally prepared for the stages ahead.

After much research into German clinics, Soph chose to attend the St George Klinik in Bad Aibling, a picturesque town in Bavaria. This is a spa town featuring luxury health resorts, about sixty kilometres south east of Munich.

Fortunately, Tim and I were in a position to accompany Soph on this hopefully life-changing excursion. On 23 August 2012, we flew to Singapore via Qantas and arrived at Munich the following day. Unbeknownst to us, it would be our first and last overseas trip together.

We weren't going to travel to the other side of the world without doing a bit of sightseeing, so we took a trip on a hop-on hop-off bus around this fascinating and historic town, of which forty per cent was destroyed during the war. We then travelled to the Nymphenburg Palace, the summer residence of King Ludwig II, and we had never seen such opulence.

The next day, we went to the horrible Dachau concentration camp, which was much worse than we could have imagined.

Dachau was a Nazi concentration camp opened in March 1933. It originally housed political prisoners, but Heinrich Himmler enlarged its purpose to include forced labour and eventually the imprisonment of Jews, Poles, homosexuals, Jehovah's Witnesses, Catholic priests and communists. Over 41,000 people were killed until the camp was liberated by the United States army in 1945.

Then it was off to Zugspitze, the highest mountain in Germany at approximately 3000 metres. We caught a cable car, which featured the longest single span in the world, to the top where it was snowing!

We then caught a rack train to the bottom of the mountain through a tunnel 4.8 kilometres long, before returning to our hotel. German trains are fast, smooth, quiet, regular, punctual, cheap and spotless, but the people are reserved and unfriendly. You can take your dog for no extra charge, but a second dog has to have a ticket!

Then it was off to Bad Aibling to begin Soph's treatment. The taxi that took us to the Klinik via the Autobahn travelled at speeds up to 160 kilometres an hour. There is no speed limit on this road, and the driver told us that he had been up to 260 kilometres an hour, but that it was pretty scary. In areas where there is a speed limit, there are big fines for exceeding, and your licence is lost after a second offence. Trucks have to pull up at designated spots on Sundays so as not to interfere with the traffic flow of leisure seekers.

It was now time to begin Soph's treatment. The accommodation supplied by the Klinik was clean and comfortable, and a room was supplied for Tim and me too. Every day, fresh spring water would be delivered in two-litre glass bottles left in a milk crate outside our door. No plastic bottles there. Meals were healthy and varied, although meat was not on the menu. Other patients came from all over the world, but mainly from America, and they were all there for cancer treatment.

While Soph was having treatment, Tim and I occupied our days by exploring this quaint and picturesque town, sometimes walking so far that we got lost. One day, we all visited Auntie Lisa's daughter and granddaughters; it was such a pleasure to meet up with her delightful family.

We didn't find anything made in China either. In fact, everything was made in Germany except one item we found — a haircutter made in the US of A.

While we were there, we also had a visit from Spencer's Aunt Rosi, who had married Francesco, an Italian from Barigiano in Italy. This was a lovely interlude for Soph and us after she had had trouble with a reaction to a PICC line in her arm, which resulted in the line being removed and a stiff course of antibiotics, then steroids, to bring down the swelling.

Soph's very comprehensive treatment involved hyperthermia, ozone and magnetic therapy, vitamin C infusion, heavy metals remover, insulin-potentiated chemotherapy and Reiki therapy.

On Sunday, she had a day off, so we all caught a bus to Konigssee Lake, then a boat to Bartholomew Fjord Lake, where there is permanent ice on the mountain tops. We could just glimpse Hitler's Eagle's Nest Retreat perched on top of the highest mountain. Soph was very tired when we returned, but she had had a nice change from the relentless pain and treatment.

While we were in Germany, Tim complained of a bad back, but as we had an adjustable bed in our room, he was able to gain some comfort by sleeping in that. He had often complained of a sore back, so we thought this was nothing out of the ordinary.

Finally, it was time to return to Australia, this time via Hong Kong. We had an enjoyable stopover with a delightful relative, Heather, who showed us some of the sights of Hong Kong and how the expats lived in resort-style communities.

It was a joyous husband, Spencer, who met us at Brisbane International Airport after twenty-six long days away.

The trip to Germany had been very beneficial, and gave Soph some breathing room for about twelve to eighteen months before she was forced back to researching more treatment options. Fortunately, while very tough to crack, her cancer was a relatively slow-growing one, giving her time to look into available options at the time.

In 2015, my brother Roger, Health Director for the Natural Health Society, referred Soph to Katrina Ellis, the brilliant naturopath on the Gold Coast, who had beaten her own cancer using alternative methods. Katrina's fascinating story is told in her enterprising book, *Shattering the Cancer Myth*.

On their first visit to Katrina, Soph and Spen were immediately made to feel like family by this sparkling, attractive, highly intelligent lady.

Since then, Soph has continued to see Katrina on a regular basis, and every time she has new information or treatments that she has learnt about from her incredible network of experts and specialists in the cancer field. Because of her own journey and her lively scientific mind, Katrina not only talked the talk but walked the walk, her only problem being that she is too busy as more and more people try to get on her books.

Soph has been very lucky to have been supported so well by both friends and family, who have all taken turns accompanying her on various treatment regimes, both here in Australia and overseas. Soph and Spen have very good mates Chubb and Hen Attwooll, whose parents both owned units at the Gold Coast and generously offered Soph the use of them while she had treatment every second week over a two-year period. With Hen's parents being in situ at the time, Soph will be forever grateful for their generosity.

Soph also often commented how supportive the Condamine community had been during her battle with this awful disease. Another Condamine family who generously contributed their riverfront accommodation on the Brisbane River while she had chemotherapy and radiation was the Campbell family. Fortunately, this enabled Tim and me to accompany Soph as her support crew during this period.

Soph had another trip to the Klinik six weeks afterwards with cousin Sonia, followed later by two trips to Japan and one to Thailand to further her treatment.

After our trip to Germany, Tim and I were pleased to return to Sweetwood and find that our caretakers, Jan and Len, had everything in pristine condition. However, Tim's back condition was showing no sign of easing. We started on a program of blood tests, x-rays, bone scans, visits to various doctors from Chinchilla to Toowoomba and Brisbane, chiropractors and acupuncture, but nothing came to light.

In early October, Tim had an MRI that also came up clear, and I remember commenting, "Oh well, at least it's nothing sinister."

Meantime, we had planned a trip in our beautiful "Winnie", or "Dorabago", as our new motorhome had been christened. So we set off for the Flinders Ranges in December 2012, where we enjoyed three glorious weeks in one of the most spectacular places in Australia. Tim continued to complain of back pain, which we kept under control with endless doses of Panadol, but it did put a damper on his enjoyment of the holiday.

THE BIG "C" STRIKES AGAIN

On 7 January 2013, we went to Noosa for a week at No 2 Hastings Street, where we had previously booked an apartment. Tim had been given a prescription for painkillers, but I had mislaid the document, so we made an appointment with Noosa's Dr Mason Stephenson to get a second prescription. He asked Tim what the problem was and decided to order a CAT scan, which we were able to have performed in Noosa. Then the condition that Dr Stephenson had suspected was confirmed – PANCREATIC CANCER.

This was a terrible shock to us, and to Soph, who was with us at the time. I had always been confident that it "wouldn't be anything sinister". Soph was more cognisant than me that this was a death sentence, as she was more up to date with the various cancers.

Dazed and confused, we made our way home. Tim and I visited the oncologist, Dr Andrew Pascoe, at the Wesley in Brisbane, where he gave me the devastating news that Tim had four to six months to live after an ultrasound revealed the position of the cancer.

I remember walking up and down the corridor of the hospital trying to come to terms with this dreadful, shocking, awful information – how could it be? We had always concentrated on having a good diet, growing our own fruit and vegetables as much as possible. This only happened to unfit people didn't it? Why Tim? He was such a good man who didn't do a bad turn to anyone. Why did he have to contract one of the worst cancers?

I became more and more shell-shocked, but gradually gained a bit of respite from the pain by suddenly deciding that we were going to beat this thing using alternative methods. Tim had previously stated that he would not have chemotherapy and radiotherapy after seeing what Soph had been through, so I gained some courage and we set off for home once again, Tim to recuperate and me to research alternatives.

We started Tim on a special diet and I ordered Protocel, which had been promoted as an effective therapy for cancer treatment. He was conscious of trying to keep fit, so every day we would go for a walk along the lagoon, then a swim. To start with, the pain wasn't too bad, but this situation soon changed. Two days later, we were forced to admit him to Chinchilla hospital for pain stabilisation.

After one night, he was able to return home, but he was very weak and had no appetite. He had lots of visitors, and Soph even arrived by chopper one day when flooding prevented her from driving — it landed just outside the verandah where Tim had been settled! Andy and Spen came to visit, and June arrived to stay for a while. The pain was starting to subside and his appetite was returning.

The next few months were filled with extreme pain, nausea, vomiting, diarrhoea, constipation, lots of visitors from every state in Australia, and occasionally a good day when we could go for a walk along the lagoon.

We were lucky to find a great Chinese doctor in Chinchilla, Doctor Christy Yang, who was prepared to visit Tim at any time of the day or night, and this was a great comfort to him.

Blue Nurses also visited him every few days, and a special bed was delivered to the verandah so he could find a bit of comfort during the long days. From there he could see the trees and watch for his precious birds, which had always been a special part of his life.

His cocktail of painkillers included Amitriptyline, Panadol Forte, Nurofen, Endone, Lyrica, OxyContin and Fentanyl patches — these all interspersed with the other drugs for the accompanying bodily malfunctions. Most days were pain days. There was occasional relief when we could go for a short walk, but even this eventually became a walk round the garden with Tim in a wheelchair.

Soph's almost daily visits were a great comfort to Tim, and Andy visited as much as geography and work commitments would permit. I had to take Tim off the Protocel as it seemed to make him feel sick, and obviously wasn't being the panacea that we had hoped.

Bedsores were also becoming a problem, especially as the cancer pain only allowed him to feel comfortable lying on his right side.

His right hip became a source of major discomfort despite all the efforts of the Blue Nurses to alleviate this.

The pain of seeing this special man suffering so much was unbearable, but I had to keep strong for him. I was still using alternative methods, but it was becoming more and more hopeless.

At the end of April, he was visited by a Doctor Soosa, who advised Tim that it would be best for him to go to hospital. He was taken by ambulance, a most uncomfortable experience, he later revealed.

Fortunately, I was able to stay in the hospital too, as they had a very good palliative care ward set up there to accommodate relatives. He stayed there for six days while they set up a syringe driver, but the hydromorph they were administering through this caused him even more pain and nausea.

On his return home, a palliative care team came out to Sweetwood to set up a special bed at home, and the shower was modified for his use.

On 15 May 2013, as it was not possible to control the pain at home, he was admitted to hospital for the last time. I was so grateful that I was able to stay in the room with him and have my meals there too, even continue to have a Dorex at night, which helped me to get through this nightmare.

Relatives and friends continued to visit, and June stayed with him during days when I had to go to Sweetwood to attend to things there. June was a great help, and I couldn't have coped during this time without her.

Tim was becoming skeletal, comatose and disorientated. He hadn't eaten for thirty-six days, and was only able to drink small amounts of water.

At three o'clock on Friday, 7 June 2013, Tim took his last breath.

THE AFTERMATH

This cruel disease had claimed another victim. Tim's suffering was now ended, but for those of us left behind, our suffering was just beginning. He had been deprived of the future we had planned of endless travel in our go-anywhere-in-comfort Winnie, and lazy days languishing at our beautiful Sweetwood.

Throughout his terrible ordeal, neither of us had ever made any reference to the fact that he was dying. This I still ponder today – did he not want to admit the fact, or did he not want to discuss the possibility of my life without him? Sadly, I will never know.

I now faced life without him, a prospect I found unbearable. For two years, I could not mention his name without crying. He had been the wind beneath my wings. Andy and Sophie were also bereft, he had been their special friend and confidant.

For forty-seven years, we had worked side by side, renovating rundown properties, interspersed with wandering at leisure around the land we loved. We had rarely been apart – people said we were "joined at the hip". We had lived in ten different locations since we had been married, and rejoiced in every one of them. We started our wanderings using a swag, an esky, a camp oven, a frying pan and a billy, and finished with a 4WD motorhome with all mod cons. We had been blessed.

I can't remember us ever having an argument – we were on the same wave length, and amicably worked out all our moves and adventures together.

One couple we had worked for while volunteering with Bush Heritage summed Tim up with these words:

We think you are a great bloke which we could both relate to in so many ways. With your wealth of knowledge, experience and skills you would still pleasantly smile at a useless volunteer with an impractical solution to a simple problem. Your no fuss demeanour suited the wide brown land you worked. And know that you have made an impression and a difference to both the people and the country you have been in contact with.

A poem written by Damian Morgan, Spencer's brother, summed up our life together:

Life is like a highway to a destiny unknown
And maps to find that destiny are drawn up on our own
The twists and turns are easy, but a fork upon the track
Is where we shape our future, and there is no looking back.
And those who trust their heart at times when push can turn to shove
Are those who know that freedom comes from doing what you love
So let me tell this story — it's of one who felt the push
And started up a romance with the Great Australian Bush.
This story starts in India in 1939
And quickly moves to Melbourne, where the way of life was "fine"
Fine schooling and fine clothing and the finest airs and graces
A proper education and the proper social places
He knew he should feel lucky and was grateful for his start
But something was still missing in the bottom of his heart
So after school, despite advice that always meant the best
The boy was drawn from Melbourne to experience the West
The land so raw and rugged seemed so beautiful to him
And so the romance started with the outback life for Tim
But speaking of true romance and his love of station life
Some say he only loved it 'coz it brought him to his wife
A glamorous young hostie who went west to see a friend
And so she joins this story — and will be there till the end
The legend tells that Tim and Joce found love in their first sight
One thing we know for certain is that Tim put up no fight
And so they wed in Sydney back in 1966
Their honeymoon ... a one way trip to "way out in the sticks"

And side by side the princess worked beside her handsome prince
They made an awesome couple and they have done ever since
They worked with mother nature — in far more ways than one
By breeding station cattle ... and a daughter and a son
A daughter they could spoil and a son 'coz he'd be handy
And so the world was introduced to Sophie and to Andy
The 'Dorans of the Territory' loved all that nature brings
They lived the vision splendid on the plains of Helen Springs
Tim's life was an adventure but one promise he did keep
He said he'd take on anything but "NO MORE BLOODY SHEEP!"
From Washpool to Verona and the rough bush tracks between
There's nowhere Dorabago goes the Dorans haven't seen
And those who've shared a Dorex and a laugh with Joce and Tim
From Sweetwood to the Kimberleys — you share our love for him
A gentleman and caring soul whose word was one to trust
He'd always find a bright side through flooding rains or dust
His bushman skills are legend — but of all the skills he had
His finest skills of all were as a husband and a dad
His love lives on in those left here who've had that love from him
And that's a life well lived my friends — a life well lived by Tim.

SARAH AND JENNY AND TIM'S MOTHER

Tim's sister was two years older than him. They were very close, in fact, people said that they were like twins. She attained a law degree after leaving school at Clyde in Victoria, but her marriage to Bill and the production of three boys put an end to her career in that profession. Her husband, however, continued in a very successful career, eventually becoming an Appeals Court Judge in Victoria.

In 1995, Sarah contracted breast cancer, which she battled for twenty years. It eventually metastasised to other organs, leading to her untimely death on 16 May 2013 , just twenty-two days before Tim died. Her only reprieve was that she was able to die at home where she could still view her beloved garden.

Owing to the circumstances, Soph was the only member of the Queensland family who was able to attend her funeral.

My beautiful friend Jenny, with whom I had attended both primary and secondary school, contracted a brain tumour, and after a two-year battle, died just three days before Tim. The loss of such a dear friend was devastating, and of course, I was sadly unable to attend her funeral.

Jane had made our lives difficult since I stole her beloved Tim in 1966, but after she suffered dementia while living in a home for the aged in Chinchilla, she forgot to hate me and we finally developed a good relationship, albeit a bit too late. Fortunately, she was unaware that both her children had predeceased her. She lived to be just shy of 101 and received her telegram from the Queen, the Premier of Queensland and the local member.

ADJUSTING

Two weeks after Tim's death, I was able to accompany Soph, Spen and grandson Ash on a cricket tour of the UK to represent his school, Toowoomba Grammar. We were also able to visit the place of Tim's mother's childhood, Taunton, Somerset, as well as my nephew and his wife in Paris and Mary Morgan's sister in Italy, south of Rome.

I was grateful to be able to get away from places full of memories, but I didn't really enjoy the travel. In fact, the whole trip was a bit of a blur and even now I don't have much memory of it. I was able to travel business class, which made the flight bearable, and the hostess very kindly let me share my bed with Soph — we had half the night each in it as they were travelling premium economy.

On returning home, I set up Winnie at Soph and Spen's property Myall Grove, and lived there for six months, going home to Sweetwood at weekends to tend to stock etc. Our wonderful caretakers, Keith and Nancy Dolbel, kindly stayed at Sweetwood during the week, and the company of my family at Myall Grove helped to ease the pain.

Keith and Nancy had to put three animals down during this period. We had a bull with a broken pizzle and, though they tried hard to care for him, the pain became too much and they had to shoot him.

Then our beautiful Jersey dairy cow, Polly, had a prolapse while calving. It wasn't only the uterus that was ejected, but her intestines as well, so she also had to be shot.

My ever-faithful, intelligent kelpie–blue heeler cross Red Dog (named previously by Tim because he was blue) then developed paralysis in the hind legs, probably due to an enlarged prostate pressing on a nerve, and he too met the same fate.

All these sad events fortunately took place while I was away, as I don't think I could have taken any more pain at that stage.

To help overcome my loss, I had to be forever on the move and our motorhome enabled me to fulfil this need which persists with me till this day.

DROVING

In 2014, I joined Mike and Annie Rayner and their daughter Maria with their 1120 head of cattle on the road as their St George property was in drought. This was a most memorable experience for me, starting at Wandoan and leaving them between Surat and St George. The day I arrived at the camp, I spent the entire time catching up with their washing, as their washing machine had broken down and my motorhome contained a front loader.

The entourage comprised: horse truck with showers, freezers, lighting plant, bulk items like bags of potatoes and beds for the two backpackers. The truck towed a caravan for Mike and Annie and their daughter, who was having School of the Air lessons. A Land Cruiser utility towed a horse float with saddles, quad bike, electric fence equipment for the break at night-time, and dogs when not needed on the drove. Their Land Cruiser station wagon towed a trailer, which was set up as a very practical chuck wagon where all meals were prepared. Annie made bread every day, and I was happy to be able to relieve her of this chore now and then.

Then there was a ten-tonne International truck with a water tank holding 22,000 litres of the precious liquid, and this towed a water trough, so the whole outfit was very self-contained. All this gear had to be moved every night, and when I came along there was my motorhome as well! Five vehicles in all required a bit of to-ing and fro-ing to get set up every night — the electric fence had to be rigged and cattle contained.

Not to forget "the money makers", as Tim used to call horses in the north. There were fifteen fat horses and eleven dogs. The Rayners believed in looking after their horses, and they were ridden only in halters to enable them to graze as they drove, and also to prevent inexperienced riders from hurting their mouths. There was no such thing as a skinny horse in the Rayner camp.

As we came into Surat on the Carnarvon Highway, we had to put the cattle over a two-lane bridge crossing the Balonne River. This was a considerable challenge with 1120 head of cattle and fifteen horses, but the Rayners were experienced stockmen and were not fazed by the challenge.

The highway was blocked on each side by police, then I crossed first with the horse plant. Cattle are usually inclined to follow horses, and this is what they did, with a bit of encouragement from Mike, Annie, Maria, and with the two backpackers and dogs bringing up the rear and controlling the wings. We all felt like film stars as the tourists camped on the river and most of the town turned up with cameras to witness the spectacle.

At Surat, there is a four hundred hectare common, so we were able to let the cattle go for two days and have a bit of "R & R". It was a treat to be able to sit round the campfire every night, downing a Dorex and telling yarns after a pleasant day with horses and cattle.

A TOUR OF THE KIMBERLEY

In 2015, I was lucky enough to be able to do a tour of the Territory and our beloved Kimberley with Graeme and Val Wicks. One night, we set up camp somewhere on Inverway Station, and in the morning I went for my usual walk. I became quite overcome with emotion when I stumbled on the airstrip where Tim and I had made our fateful meeting fifty years ago.

I battled on at our beloved Sweetwood for three and a half years, but then I decided it was all getting a bit too much without Tim, so with much angst, I put Sweetwood on the market.

For a long time, I had battled night-time nerves. If the dogs barked at three o'clock in the morning, I would be up with my torch, peering all round the extensive gardens to see if there was an intruder. Chinchilla had been a delightful country town of about three thousand people when Tim and I bought our first investment properties there, but it was a different proposition now, with the advent of the mining industry and resultant increased crime rate.

I slept with a hammer under my pillow and a .22 under the bed. A policeman once told me that if you have to shoot in self-defence, kill the offender first, then shoot him in the knees as proof that you had given a warning, or you could be charged with manslaughter. Amazing, but glad that I was never confronted with that dilemma.

The other feature of Sweetwood that became increasingly negative for me was the constant battle with tree regrowth, poisonous mother-of-millions, African lovegrass, and eventually the dreaded Pimelea, a potentially fatal weed for cattle. Pimelea poisoning is also known as St George disease. Seasonal variations had caused this weed to infest Sweetwood, and it was just another problem that I didn't feel like tackling. Maintaining a huge garden was also taking its toll.

It surprised me that it took some time to sell. I had to lower the price to an unacceptable level, but finally a couple, one of whom had been one of Tim's Blue Nurses, made an offer.

Not long before I moved out of Sweetwood, I had to live through three violent electrical storms — not one after the other, but three storms converging on Sweetwood at the same time from different directions. I normally quite like storms as I find them rather fascinating, but this was a different matter altogether, with the storms increasing in violence as they came together. The dogs and I huddled on the verandah comforting each other while the tempest raged around us, but fortunately, when they abated, we had all survived without any mishap.

A NEW LIFE

In the meantime, I sold Winnie for $135,000, which was well below what we had paid for it and it was still in very good condition. I then set about finding a replacement motorhome that was more suited to my situation in life. Rhonda and I had been travelling after Tim died, and her brother rang me one day and said, "There is a motorhome advertised in the *Caravan and Motorhome Club* magazine that is just what you are looking for. It was in the Queensland town of Childers."

I replied, "Okay, that sounds good, but I won't be able to go to Childers for another week yet as I have commitments."

Bill replied, "You had better get up there sooner than that as it is very cheap and won't last that long."

So I made the momentous decision to purchase it, sight unseen, as I had every faith in Bill's judgement.

I made the arrangement to deposit the $42,000 in the seller's bank account, then a week later Soph accompanied me to Childers, where we took possession of a 2005 Mercedes Sprinter with 140,000 kilometres on the clock. It was perfect. It had a larger than usual fridge, for which the table and chairs were sacrificed, but this suited me as I like to take a lot of pre-prepared food on trips. TV trays made up for the lack of a table.

Toilet and shower, cruise control, two-way radio, GPS, three-burner gas stove and two single beds — with enough storage to carry six cartons of Dorex — completed the picture. I soon equipped it with sufficient solar panels to enable us to travel without having to charge our batteries, and I installed a 1000 watt inverter so I had 240 volts as well.

The only drawback was the gearbox — it was manual, and a very difficult manual at that. I stalled it many times, and still do occasionally.

This type of vehicle is eminently suited to women travelling alone, as if disturbed during the night, one can hop into the driver's seat without having to go outside the vehicle.

Rhonda and I have made many trips together, including twice to Tasmania. She also has a Mercedes Sprinter — I call mine a Standard model and hers a De Luxe model, as she many more comforts, including a griller and oven. As we take it in turns to cook the evening meal, I am the beneficiary with delicious meals such as racks of lamb, but Rhonda has to put up with my pre-cooked casseroles.

On one of our trips to the Territory, we visited Muckaty Station, next door to Helen Springs. It had been handed over to the Traditional Owners, and the government had built quite a community there. Four four-bedroom air conditioned houses, complete with all mod cons, a lighting plant and a phone box, were all present, but not a soul was to be seen. The houses were all empty, and you could call anywhere in Australia from the phone box without having to pay.

We were to witness this terrible waste of taxpayers' money in many places in the north, where communities were constructed for the Aboriginals, but they had no desire to live in them. Mostly they didn't want to be too far from a township and a pub.

In June 2018, we attended the Outback Film Festival in Winton. This was a most successful event, staging only Australian films in the outdoor theatre in that great outback town. As Rhonda lives in Mount Isa and I was living in Toowoomba at the time, it was necessary for each of us to travel alone to Winton for the event. I went via Cunnamulla, Quilpie, Windorah, Jundah, Stonehenge and Longreach. The country was severely in drought, and I encountered some very lonely stretches, with no traffic or grass between Quilpie and Windorah. Fortunately, I had no flat tyres or breakdowns as I am no mechanic.

After Winton, we went to the ABC Races at Brunette Downs Station. This refers to Alexandria, Brunette and Cresswell, well known Barkly Tableland stations, which formed the race club over a hundred years ago.

While travelling up the Tablelands Highway, we passed two men in a ute travelling in the opposite direction. One was driving and one was standing on the back, obviously searching the side of the road for something. Shortly afterwards, I had a flat tyre in the motorhome. Luckily these fellows were able to give us a hand on their return journey, so they told us their story.

They had travelled over from Kalgoorlie in Western Australia on motorbikes to attend the races, and one of them had lost his wallet. That was what they were searching for, unsuccessfully. So he proceeded to cancel all his credit cards etc. and tried to enjoy the races. They were camped with the Road Trains of Australia boss, so they had fairly good connections.

Later, we met them at the bar and heard the conclusion of this humorous or unfortunate story, depending on your point of view! It turns out that the wallet was in one of the numerous pockets that bikers have in their trousers, and he had failed to search every pocket. He took it all in good heart and proceeded to thoroughly enjoy the races.

BLAZEAID

BlazeAid is a volunteer organisation set up by Kevin and Rhonda Butler in 2009 after the Black Saturday bushfires in Victoria. It helps families and individuals in Australia after natural disasters such as fires, floods and droughts. Many cash donations are received, and these are distributed as seen fit to people in distress for the purchase of fencing materials etc., though the money must be spent locally.

I decided this was something I could do, so my first foray in this direction was to Barraba, New South Wales, to a property that was in drought. The family was putting their cattle on the road every day. I was able to take over this task, and the motorhome was handy for being able to see both the front and the rear of the mob, and to go from one end to the other to turn them back.

Next I went to Richmond in north Queensland, where massive floods had killed over 600,000 head of cattle from either drowning or exposure, or both. The poor animals had to endure temperatures of forty degrees one day, down to nineteen degrees the next day, and stand in water for as long as they could cope. This is just more than most cattle can tolerate, but for the heat-adjusted Brahmans, it was a very destructive combination. Hundreds of kilometres of fencing were also destroyed, and it was for this job that I volunteered.

I was awfully lucky that I was able to hook up with a great crew. John, or JL as he was known, was our very talented and charismatic coordinator. In the team on the fence line were Darlene, Tracie, Shelley and Lexie, and holding the fort at the camp was Robert. They were a great bunch, and we had endless fun and lots of socialising at the pub after a hard day's work (or should I say they went to the pub and I was the chauffeur as I wasn't into that sort of drinking.)

I then went to Tenterfield to restore fences after the fires, and once again caught up with John and Darlene.

I was hoping to join up again after the drastic bushfires of 2019, but after COVID-19 hit, BlazeAid wouldn't take anyone over seventy, so it looks as though my days with that organisation are, sadly, over.

SOPHIE AND ANDY

Soph still battles on valiantly with her cancer, and has suffered many terrible pain days. Recently she was referred to a specialist in Perth who performed targeted radiation, and she has returned from this trip almost pain free. Anyone wanting to gain further knowledge about this treatment could Google Cyberknife.

This has been a tremendous breakthrough, and she has plans to return to Perth for further treatment once the borders open. Whenever the opportunity arises, she competes in campdrafts, but is still waiting to win the big one!

She is a very active worker at The Grove Shorthorn Stud at Condamine alongside husband Spen, his brother Godfrey and Godfrey's wife Megan.

Andy is no longer with his former wife, Katrina. He now lives happily with Anna Brown on their picturesque seven acres just outside Bathurst. Andy and Anna met on Newcastle Waters Station after Anna's husband died at a very early age when she was pregnant with their third child. Anna has been a tremendous battler and a survivor, successfully rearing three delightful children, now adults.

Andy flew helicopters for fifteen years, after which he decided he had better get out while he was still alive.

He is very good at building things "that don't move", and at this stage has constructed about seventy cattle/sheep yards, including the huge cattle-selling complex at Barnawatha, Albury–Wodonga. For this mammoth task, he had a partner, but did not install the roof, which was done by a separate contractor. His partner, Anna, runs a very successful rural employment agency.

PROLOGUE

I finally decided the sensible thing to do would be to move to a retirement place, so I found a second-hand villa at Palm Lake Resort in Toowoomba.

I had always felt sorry for people off the land who moved to the city in retirement, but now I realise sometimes it becomes necessary. An aged care facility has just been completed here, so I shouldn't have to be a burden on either of my children should the occasion arise. I couldn't have picked a better place to retire — facilities are first-class, the people are lovely, and every possible entertainment is available to residents.

Life without Tim has been made easier by being able to still "go bush" in the motorhome, and spend time at Myall Grove with Soph and the family, but not a day goes by that I don't grieve for him.

COVID-19 is now upon us, so I have had ample time to complete this epistle. It has brought moments of great happiness and intense sadness. In fact, when I typed the moment of Tim's departure from this earth, my word processor behaved as though it had a virus and I couldn't get any sense out of it, so had to start a new section — "The Aftermath". Someone was looking down on me as I typed that sentence.

oooOOOooo

I'll walk beside you through the world today,
While dreams and songs and flowers bless your way,
I'll look into your eyes and hold your hand,
I'll walk beside your through the golden land.

I'll walk beside you through the world tonight,
Beneath the starry skies ablaze with light,
And in your heart love's tender words I'll hide,
I'll walk beside you through the eventide.

I'll walk beside you through the passing years,
Through days of cloud and sunshine, joy and tears,
And when the great call comes, the sunset gleams,
I'll walk beside you to the land of dreams.
Edward Lockton

END

Mustering horse plant Helen Springs

Tim drafting broodmares at Helen Springs

Stockcamp at Milla Milla muster

Bundy, the camp cook with her stockcamp buggy

36 decks loaded for Mt Isa at Helen Springs

Helen Springs gorge, the scene of weekend r & r

Bert the Eagle and Honky Tonk at Helen Springs

Tim the bush butcher

Soph and Andy off to boarding school in Brisbane

Leaving Helen for Allora, Wixes and Doran

Kurande, Allora 1981

The verandah Tim built at Verona, Stanthorpe

Tim and Soph breaking in Remington (a Helen Springs descedant) at Verona

The stables we built at Verona

Our precious Lulu

The troops on Tojo, ready for mustering sheep at Verona

Tim, self, Ralph and Thea Hayes, Graham and Rob Fulcher at Verona

My mother and father, Spen and Soph, Andy, Tim and self at St Lukes, Toowoomba

Spen and Soph on their wedding day

Andy and Katrina tie the knot at Eco Beach, Broome, W.A.

Andy's narrow escape from his chopper disaster

Tim and Andrew at Liveringa Sation, W.A.

The Washpool homestead, Durong Qld

The yards we built from scratch at Washpool

A close up of our yards at Washpool

Mum and Dad's 90th birthday celebration at Washpool

Sweetwood, our beautiful retirement block outside Chinchilla

The lagoon at our back door at Sweetwood

My surprise 70th lunch organised by Tim and Soph at Sweetwood

Our first style of camping, on the road outside Urandangie

We graduate to a 4WD and a double mattress!

Luxury – our 4WD SLR custom built motorhome beside Newcastle Creek, N.T.

Andy and Anna at home in Bathurst, N.S.W.

Tim and self at a birthday celebration in Sydney, circa 2009

Doran family at Andy's wedding

Tim and his sister Sarah, gone but not forgotten

POSTSCRIPT

During the publication of this book, popular and well known Territory identity, Jack Wheeler, passed away after a short illness. He will be sadly missed.

DEDICATION

This book is dedicated to my daughter, Sophie, whose determination, perseverance and positivity in her battle against seemingly insurmountable odds has been an inspiration to all who have come into contact with her.

And to my grandchildren, Ash and Shan, without whose encouragement this book would not have been written.